Fear of Contamination

Cognitive behaviour therapy: science and practice series

Edited by

David Clark, *Institute of Psychiatry, London, UK*
Christopher Fairburn, *University of Oxford, UK*
Steven Hollon, *Vanderbilt University, Nashville, USA*

Other titles in the series:

Edited by

James Bennett-Levy, Gillian Butler,
Melanie Fennell, Ann Hackmann,
Martina Mueller, and David Westbrook

Fear of Contamination:
Assessment and Treatment

S. Rachman
Department of Psychology
University of British Columbia
Vancouver
Canada

OXFORD
UNIVERSITY PRESS

OXFORD
UNIVERSITY PRESS

Great Clarendon Street, Oxford OX2 6DP

Oxford University Press is a department of the University of Oxford.
It furthers the University's objective of excellence in research, scholarship,
and education by publishing worldwide in

Oxford New York

Auckland Cape Town Dar es Salaam Hong Kong Karachi
Kuala Lumpur Madrid Melbourne Mexico City Nairobi
New Delhi Shanghai Taipei Toronto

With offices in

Argentina Austria Brazil Chile Czech Republic France Greece
Guatemala Hungary Italy Japan Poland Portugal Singapore
South Korea Switzerland Thailand Turkey Ukraine Vietnam

Oxford is a registered trade mark of Oxford University Press
in the UK and in certain other countries

Published in the United States
by Oxford University Press Inc., New York

A catalogue record for this title is available from the British Library

Library of Congress Cataloging in Publication Data

Rachman, Stanley.
    Fear of contamination : assessment and treatment / S. Rachman.
    Includes bibliographical references and index.
    ISBN–13: 978–0–19–929693–4 (Pbk., alk. paper)
    ISBN–10: 0–19–929693–6 (Pbk., alk. paper)
    ISBN–13: 978–0–19–929247–9 (Hbk., alk. paper)
    ISBN–10: 0–19–929247–7 (Hbk., alk. paper)
    1. Fear of contamination.   I. Title.
    [DNLM: 1. Fear—psychology.   2. Environmental Pollution.
3. Hygiene. 4. Morals. 5. Obsessive–Compulsive Disorder—therapy.
6. Phobic Disorders—therapy.   WM 178 R119fa 2006]
RC552. F38R33   2006
616. 85′225—dc22

Typeset by SPI Publisher Services, Pondicherry, India
Printed in Great Britain
on acid-free paper by Biddles Ltd., King's Lynn

10 9 8 7 6 5 4 3 2 1

Acknowledgements

It is with pleasure that I acknowledge the assistance and advice of many colleagues. Doctors C. Philips, R. Shafran, and A. Radomsky have been close collaborators throughout. Several of the earliest and most intriguing cases were treated in collaboration with Dr M. Whittal of the Anxiety Disorders Clinic at the University Hospital in Vancouver. Her contribution to the evolving ideas about contamination has been paramount. Other colleagues at the Clinic who made helpful contributions were Drs P. McLean and S. Woody. I am particularly grateful to the three research colleagues who made important contributions to the experimental analyses of the concept of mental pollution, Drs N. Fairbrother and S. Newth, and Ms J. Herba. The work of P. de Silva and Melanie Marks on OCD and trauma, and Paul Rozin's writings on the topic of disgust were important influences in the development of the concept of mental pollution. I also wish to express my thanks to Bethan Lee of OUP, and Emily Rachman, for their invaluable assistance in producing the book.

Contents

Introduction

The fear of contamination is among the most fascinating of all human fears. It is complex, powerful, probably universal, easily provoked, intense, difficult to control, extraordinarily persistent, variable in content, evident in all societies, often culturally accepted, and even prescribed, tinged with magical thinking and full of psychological twists and turns. Usually the fear is caused by physical contact with a contaminant and spreads rapidly and widely. When a person feels contaminated it drives a strong urge to remove the contamination, usually by washing. The fear and subsequent urges over-ride other behaviour. Surprisingly, a fear of contamination can also be established mentally and without physical contact. The fear can arise after exposure to violation, physical or non-physical, humiliation, repugnant thoughts or images, or even from self-contamination. Fears of contamination are more complex, extensive, and subtle than they appear to be at first sight, and the concept of mental contamination opens wide the door. It is my hope that the ideas expressed in this book will expand our ability to recognise the full range of fears of contamination, make certain untreatable cases treatable, and reduce the number of incompletely treated patients.

From a clinical perspective, fears of contamination are important because they feature so prominently in obsessive-compulsive disorder (OCD), and are associated with cleaning compulsions that are out of control, bizarre, and unadaptive. Over time, the cleaning turns robotic and stereotyped. It is not uncommon for patients to complain that they have forgotten how to wash normally, and even ask for demonstrations to remind them. Compulsive cleaning is so obviously abnormal that it has became almost definitional of OCD.

People who have an abnormally elevated fear of contamination over-estimate the probability and the potential seriousness of becoming contaminated. They believe that they are more susceptible than other people to contamination. People who labour under the illusion that they are particularly vulnerable to contamination are persistently anxious, excessively vigilant and highly avoidant.

The compulsive behaviour is driven by fears of contamination. It is an attempt to clean away a perceived contaminant in order to reduce or remove a significant threat posed by the contaminant. Contamination can threaten harm to one's physical health, mental health, social life. The contaminants fall into four broad classes: disease, dirt/pollution, harmful substances, mental contaminants.

Of all the manifestations of OCD the dread of contamination is the most obviously phobic in nature (Rachman and Hodgson 1980). The associated cleaning compulsions are the second commonest form of OCD compulsion, exceeded only by compulsive checking. In a sample of 560 people with OCD, Rasmussen and Eisen (1992) found that 50 per cent had fears of contamination, very similar to an earlier figure of 55 per cent compiled from a series of 82 patients seen at the Maudsley and Bethlem Hospitals in London by Rachman and Hodgson (1980). Comparable figures on the incidence of compulsive cleaning have reported in a number of studies (Antony et al. 1998).

As with virtually all human fears, there is a continuum of fears of contamination, ranging from the mild and circumscribed to moderate fears and ultimately to those which are abnormally intense, abnormally extensive, and abnormally sustained by belief and conduct. Abnormally strong fears of contamination are unyielding, expansive, persistent, commanding, contagious, and resistant to ordinary cleaning.

The present analysis goes beyond the conventional boundaries of contamination to include the concept of mental contamination (Rachman 1994), a phenomenon that like psychology itself can be said to have a long past but a short history. Centuries ago John Bunyan introduced the term 'pollution *of the mind*' to describe his horrifying blasphemous obsessions—'tumultuous thoughts'... 'masterless hellhounds (that) roar and bellow and make a hideous noise within me', (Bunyan 1947 edn, p.136). Mental contamination, a sense of internal dirtiness, can be provoked by direct physical contact with a contaminant or by indirect contacts such as violations, insults, moral criticisms, ill-treatment, objectionable intrusive thoughts, memories, symbolic associations. During the behavioural period of psychology, the concept of mental contamination was noted but not developed because at that time it was too mentalistic for comfort. 'If one construes obsessional-compulsive cleaning disorders as having their basis in a fear of contamination, liberally defined to include "mental contamination", the removal of the offending fear stimulus by washing it away is the natural, fitting escape behaviour' (Rachman and Hodgson 1980, p.113). It is timely now to explore the liberal definition.

These feelings of internal dirtiness, mental contamination/pollution, are imperfectly connected to observable, identifiable sources of pollution. Even touching items that look clean can evoke feelings of dirtiness. Moreover, the feelings of dirtiness are not properly responsive to cleaning. Mental pollution falls into the wider category of 'mental contamination'. Feelings of mental contamination can be induced with or without direct contact with a contaminant; the primary source of the contamination is human rather than contact with harmful substances. In 'ordinary' familiar contact contamination, the origin, source, and site of the (tangible) contaminant are known, but in mental contamination they tend to be obscure and the contamination is unique to the affected person. It can be evoked or re-evoked by mental acts such as memories or images of people/places associated with the contamination, and remarkably, can result from one's own thoughts, by self-contamination. The complexities of contamination have given rise to a classificatory scheme in which a broad division is made between contact contamination and mental contamination. Within the two divisions, 8 subtypes are set out (see p. 12). Interestingly, in the course of elaborating the concept of mental contamination it became necessary to re-analyse the nature of the familiar, contact form of contamination.

Historical examples of the fear of contamination and OCD (Rachman and Hodgson, 1980), include Martin Luther and the fastidious humanist philosopher Erasmus, who worked hard to keep physically clean and mentally clean. He avoided a wide range of people and places, protecting himself from the 'danger of infection in the foul air of crowded inns... common cups... smelly substances' and anything associated with 'venereal diseases or other illnesses' (Huizinga 1957, p.117–120). In recent times, the severe fears of contamination that tormented Howard Hughes have brought the problem to the attention of the public. 'In order to avoid infection he constructed... a sterile, isolated environment in which his contact with potentially contaminating people (and items) was kept to a minimum. For the most part he successfully avoided touching any person or object directly... he withdrew into a small, sealed germ-free environment serviced by a group of carefully selected attendants. His wealth enabled him to pay these people to carry out compulsive rituals on his behalf... (when a bottle broke on the steps of his home) he marked out a grid of one-inch squares on each step' and had his employees clean each square meticulously as he watched progress from his window (Rachman and Hodgson, 1980, pp. 25–26). In principle, his fear of contamination was treatable.

The time for a re-appraisal

The earliest successes of the behaviour therapists were achieved in the treatment of phobias, social anxiety, and agoraphobia, during the period 1950 to 1970. OCD proved to be a far more difficult proposition, and despite the accumulation of promising experimental results on animals, the isolated reports of successfully treated patients were easily outnumbered by the failures. The novel treatment of two cases described by Victor Meyer in 1966 provided a starting point for the widely adopted method now known as exposure and response prevention. The need for a psychological treatment was pressing because the prevailing methods—electro-convulsive therapy (ECT, shock therapy), drugs, psychosurgery—were of dubious value

Working in the Middlesex Hospital, London, Meyer took on the treatment of two severely ill women, one of whom was being considered for a leucotomy and the other for her second leucotomy. The first patient was incapacitated by intense fears of disease and dirt and spent most of her day cleaning and washing compulsively. Despite three admissions to hospital and a great deal of treatment which included ECT, drugs, and supportive therapy, she remained seriously ill and therefore psychosurgery had been recommended.

Dr. Meyer was a dedicated, energetic, extraverted therapist who arranged a unique, intense period of hospital treatment for the patient and devoted long hours to its implementation. The plan was to change her expectations about the consequences of touching contaminants by exposing her to a full range of the objects and places that induced her fear of contamination and to prevent her from carrying out any compulsive cleaning. The patient was placed under continuous supervision, her cleaning agents were severely limited, and he even had the taps in her room turned off. After 4 weeks of this intensive treatment the restrictions were gradually eased and in the remaining 8 weeks the effects of therapy were consolidated. At times the patient was distressed and uncooperative but progress was achieved despite some setbacks. Her fear and compulsive cleaning declined to manageable levels, although still excessive. She continued reasonably well during the follow-up even though she avoided some contaminated items and places. The frequency of her cleaning decreased, but the duration and thoroughness of her cleaning increased. Nevertheless, her life had improved significantly and she was able to resume a number of social activities.

The second patient had a lengthy history of distressing blasphemous and unacceptable sexual obsessions (e.g. having sex with the Holy Ghost) that evoked a wide range of demanding and endlessly repetitive neutralizing compulsions; for example, she took hours to dress herself. She had received a wide variety of treatments over many years but with little benefit—drugs, ECT, 11 years of psychoanalysis and psychosurgery. A second operation was being considered. Using the same treatment strategy Meyer provided exposure sessions to the innumerable items, imaginal scenes, and places that evoked the obsessions, while ensuring that no compulsive behaviour followed. The patient found the intensive 9-week hospital treatment difficult and distressing but persisted and finally made progress. The obsessions and compulsive behaviour declined to manageable levels, and despite some fluctuations in the follow-up period, her life was significantly improved.

For several reasons Meyer's cases attracted considerable interest. He was the first therapist to attempt such an intensive test of the effects of exposure and response prevention on OCD. Experimental findings on animals (Baum 1970; Eysenck and Rachman 1965; Wolpe 1958) had shown that fear-induced 'fixated' behaviour can be reduced by prolonged exposures to the fear stimuli but therapists were understandably hesitant to test the method on patients. Meyer showed that it is possible to implement the method, and that it produced an encouraging degree of change in two severely ill patients. It was recognised that the method was too demanding and impractical for general use, but the possibilities had been demonstrated.

There was another important reason to pay attention to the reports. At that time no psychological methods of treatment, not even the new behaviour therapy, had proven useful in the treatment of OCD (Eysenck, 1960). As this comment by the pioneer of behaviour therapy, Dr. Joseph Wolpe, illustrates, little could be offered to sufferers. '…The patient who had always been "nervous and faddy" began to be plagued by unwelcome thoughts. He had had psychoanalysis and then ECT, but instead of improving he had become steadily worse, so that when I saw him he could not perform simple movements such as sitting down unless "favourable thoughts" were in his mind. There was no response to the measures I used (avoidance conditioning) and I did not persist, feeling sure I could not help him' (Wolpe 1958, p.214).

At that time the behaviour therapists, whose rationale and methods were confined to observable behaviour, were confronted by an insuperable problem in attempting to deal with disorders that are wholly or largely cognitive, such as obsessions. It was outside their realm and they were reduced to *ad hoc* techniques that did not fit in with the prevailing methods, and in the event proved to have little value. They included thought-stopping, avoidance conditioning, and stinging oneself with a rubber-band attached to the wrist. This was not a high point in the history of clinical psychology. The method then in use for many anxiety disorders, systematic desensitization of fear, was too laborious for treating OCD, and made no progress. As late as 1983 it was stated bluntly that 'the main obstacle to the successful treatment of obsessions is the absence of effective techniques' (Rachman 1983, p.35).

The major advance in the psychological therapy of OCD, much influenced by Meyer's (1966) inspiring work, was accomplished in the treatment of the observable aspects of OCD, primarily in the reduction of compulsive behaviour driven by a fear of contamination. Later, the evolution of behaviour therapy into cognitive-behaviour therapy led to an expansion of psychological methods for treating other manifestations of OCD and other disorders (Rachman 1997). Encouraged by Meyer's results, psychologists at the Maudsley and

Bethlem Royal Hospitals in London, extended their clinical research on the effectiveness of exposure therapy to include patients with OCD. Influenced by the writings of Bandura (1969), Hodgson and Rachman had been experimenting with the addition of a modelling component to the standard exposure method and quickly found that modelling and exposure exercises were indeed helpful in treating OCD patients who had fears of contamination (Rachman and Hodgson 1980). Over three years a simplified and less restrictive, less demanding form of treatment than Meyer's original method was fashioned. This treatment generally required 15, hourly sessions, and was provided mainly on an out-patient basis. Assisted by Marzillier and Roper, Hodgson and Rachman published a series of case studies and later embarked with a group of colleagues on a randomized control study of the effects of behaviour therapy for OCD. The results were positive (Rachman *et al.* 1979) and replicated in other centres (e.g. Abramovitz 1997; Abramovitz *et al.* 2003; Clark 2004; Foa *et al.* 2005). The main outcome of the research was that fear of contamination and the consequent compulsive cleaning can be reduced by a programme of graded exposure to the perceived contaminants and the prevention of undoing, neutralizing behaviour, mainly cleaning. The provision of modelling before and during the exposures facilitates the process. It has also been shown that the method, now abbreviated as ERP (exposure and response prevention), is also effective in the treatment of some other manifestations of OCD such as compulsive checking, but is of little use in treating compulsive hoarding, obsessional slowness, or obsessions. In addition, the Maudsley group carried out experimental analyses of compulsive behaviour and developed a scale for measuring OCD, the Maudsley Obsessional Compulsive Inventory (MOCI, Hodgson and Rachman 1977).

The progressive development of the treatment was a mixture of behaviour theory, general clinical experience and knowledge gained earlier in treating phobias, plus a good deal of trial and error. The research team worked closely together and repeatedly analysed and discussed the difficulties encountered, in between celebrating some successes at the nearest obliging pub willing to serve scruffy, garrulous psychologists. There was a feeling of restrained excitement at the growing evidence of positive therapeutic effects, and much was learnt, not least from the patients. The fact that most of these people, who were in hospital because of their intense and uncontrollable fears, were willing to endure a demanding treatment, during part of which they experienced the very fears that had disabled them, was impressive. We were impressed.

The paradox that intensely frightened people were able to behave so bravely during treatment, led to a reconsideration of the concept of courage. It became more appropriate to speak of courageous acts rather than courageous actors

(Rachman 1990). In specifiable circumstances virtually everyone, including patients suffering from anxiety disorders, can behave courageously.

The team was happily surprised by the resilience of the patients, almost all of whom recovered their composure very soon after the conclusion of each treatment session during which they were exposed to the items and places that evoked their greatest fears. Within minutes of the end of the session they were able to talk comfortably about other topics in a composed manner, fortified by the inevitable cups of industrial-strength tea.

There were moments of amusement such as the patient who confessed, with a mixture of embarrassment and pride, that she had outwitted the programme by secretly burying bars of soap in the hospital gardens, and washing her hands in the visitors' waiting area. In another instance, the team arrived at the hospital ward on Monday morning as usual only to find it festooned with posters emphasizing the need for cleanliness and exhorting everyone to wash their hands thoroughly and carefully. This adventure in public health education was the work of a new nurse who was unaware of the the nature of the treatment that was being tested, and had no idea what response prevention meant. Compulsive handwashers really need no encouragement to continue washing. Fortunately, the patients found it amusing and this eased the team's dismay and irritation.

The idea that fears of contamination can be reduced, and that behaviour therapy is the means to do so, was confirmed and many patients benefited from the treatment. In recent years however, it has become evident that the therapy needs to be improved. The overall success rates are less than satisfactory. Significant numbers of patients are unable/unwilling to undertake this demanding treatment. Other patients begin treatment but find that they cannot tolerate it and drop out. Yet others are able to carry out the necessary exposure exercises with the therapist at the clinic or hospital but are unable to do so at home, and/or unassisted. In too many cases the fear returns after a period of weeks or years, and worse, the returning fear can exceed the intensity and span of the original fear. It is intriguing that when the fear returns after *a dormant period* it often arrives with fresh elaborations. That is, the fear apparently acquires some new characteristics during the dormancy. This fascinating phenomenon remains to be investigated.

Fears of *contamination* are challenging because the current treatment for OCD in general, exposure and response prevention, reduces the fear but is demanding and many patients find it exhausting. According to some reports (Foa *et al.* 1983), as many as 30 per cent decline the treatment. The long-term effects of behavioural treatment of OCD can be disappointing. 'The average patient...continues to experience mild to moderate OC symptoms upon termination' (Eddy *et al.* 2004, p.1025), and O'Sullivan and Marks (1991) reported that even after relatively successful treatment, 40 per cent of the initial symptoms were still evident at long-term follow-up. What started out as the easiest type of OCD fear to treat, no longer warrants that position. Jacobi *et al.* (2005) recently reported that of the 122 patients who participated in two successive randomized control trials, only 16.2 per cent of those with a fear of contamination showed clinically significant improvements. Across the two trials, 51 (43.2 per cent) out of a total of 118 patients with OCD met the criteria for improved clinical status. Only 2 out of 20 of the patients with a fear of contamination who received group CBT (cognitive behaviour therapy) were clinically improved, and of the 17 who received ERP treatment, just 4 attained the status of significant clinical improvement. In other randomized trials the number of clinically improved patients tends to be higher, but the overall success rate for OCD patients hovers around 50–60 per cent.

This is a troubling aspect of the psychological treatment of OCD in general, and contamination fears in particular. It is disappointing that the current treatment is no better than it was at the start (Rachman *et al.* 1979). The results of a recent trial (Foa *et al.* 2005) are not appreciably different from the success rates achieved in the first randomized control study, reported 26 years ago. It is troubling that *the improvement rates are not improving*. Evidently we need to do much better, and hopefully a fresh analysis of the fear of contamination will stimulate progress.

There is an additional, positive reason for carrying out a reappraisal of our explanations of the fear of contamination. Psychology, including clinical psychology, has undergone a massive expansion of scope and methodology during the past 20 years, the so-called cognitive revolution (Clark and Fairburn 1997). Cognitive theories have been advanced to account for most of the anxiety disorders, and specific theories have been set out to account for important manifestations of OCD (obsessions, compulsive checking). The time is ripe for a cognitive-behavioural analysis of the fear of contamination. Many intriguing questions about contamination are introduced and will, I hope, arouse the curiosity of clinicians and research workers.

Chapter 1

Contamination defined and classified

Contamination is an intense and persisting feeling of having been polluted, dirtied, or infected, or endangered as a result of contact, direct or indirect, with an item/place/person perceived to be soiled, impure, dirty, infectious, or harmful. The feeling of contamination is accompanied by negative emotions among which fear, disgust, dirtiness, moral impurity, and shame are prominent. Typical examples of pollutants are fecal matter, putrefying flesh, urine, and decaying vegetable matter. Infectious/dirty contaminants include contact with items or people carrying germs, public washrooms, doorhandles, contact with bodily products such as blood/saliva/semen, contact with people or places believed to be infected (e.g. blood, hospitals, places/people thought to be associated with sudden acute respiratory syndrome, AIDS). Potentially harmful substances such as chemicals, pesticides, and certain foods can be sources of contamination. Mental contamination can be caused by associations with impurity, dirtiness (rupophobia), immorality, accusations, nasty memories, direct or remote contacts with people who are regarded as enemies or as untouchables (culturally or personally defined), and by violations such as a sexual assault, betrayal, manipulation. It can also be self-generated.

Contact with any of these four sources of contamination—soiled, infectious, harmful substances, mental pollutants—produces a feeling of dirtiness or danger, and instigates vigorous attempts promptly to remove the contaminant, most frequently by cleaning. 'My hands feel aflame with contamination'. The feeling of contamination also triggers avoidance behaviour and attempts at prevention by removing potential sources of contamination. The idea can be summed up in this way: 'Avoid if you can, but escape if you can't'. In cases of contamination it is a matter of 'Avoiding if you can, but washing if you can't'.

Affected people attempt to prevent the spread of the contamination by 'isolating' their hands, for example by using their feet or elbows to open doors. If this is not practical they will resort to protecting themselves by wearing gloves or holding tissues. A simple demonstration of this feeling and its consequences can be carried out by asking people to insert their fingers into a jar containing sticky jam. It makes them feel dirty, and so they isolate their hands, avoid touching their clothing or face and hair, and have a strong urge to wash away the offending jam. Patients who suffer from OCD in which contamination is a major component have a daily struggle trying to overcome intense, pervasive, and frightening feelings of this character.

In clinically significant fears of contamination it is believed that the infectious/polluted/dangerous substances will cause serious harm to the person's physical and/or mental health or present a social threat. It is also believed that the contamination will persist until adequate cleaning has been completed, but it is difficult for patients to achieve certainty about the sufficiency of their cleaning. It is believed that unconstrained contamination will spread to other parts of one's body, clothing, possessions. It is almost always believed that the contamination is transmissable to other people, places or objects. Among those many patients with OCD who labour under the burden of an exaggerated sense of responsibility, the fear of contaminating others is a second layer of the fear and brings with it additional distress and leaden guilt. It comes as no surprise that people despair over their of lack of control of the waves of contamination. Compulsive cleaning which over-rides the person's rational appraisals is behaviour that is largely out of control; abnormal and recognized as abnormal.

It is understandable that that the person thinks it is abnormal because their thoughts and behaviour are out of control, irrational, and perplexing. Some of their thoughts and beliefs are bizarre, for example those about the weird properties of 'active germs'. Their friends and relatives obviously regard their behaviour as abnormal, even deluded. Small wonder that so many of them fear they are heading for a mental breakdown.

A note on terminology

As the fear of being harmed by contamination and the fear of being polluted share some important characteristics, it can be difficult to disentangle them. However, there are instances in which the differences between them are evident and significant, especially in the assessment of cases of OCD. The instances in which they are easily disentangled—e.g. the fear of being harmed by touching infected material is contact contamination; feeling dirty and distressed by an incestuous image is mental contamination—present little difficulty, and the terms contamination, or pollution, are appropriate.

Although the concept of mental pollution is now in common use, for present purposes, the term *mental contamination* (Rachman and Hodgson 1980, p.113) is preferred on the grounds of simplicity. Much of this exposition involves analyses and comparisons of 'ordinary' familiar *contact contamination*, in which physical contact with a tangible contaminant takes place, and *mental contamination* in which the primary source of the contamination is human and may or may not involve physical contact. As far as possible the term 'contamination' is used when referring to instances of contamination arising from physical contacts with identifiable and localizable contaminants, and the term 'mental contamination' is used for those instances of contamination which have a human source, can arise without physical contact with a contaminant, and the person feels uniquely vulnerable.

In almost all instances the terms mental contamination and mental pollution are interchangeable, but when the dominant feeling is one of of mental/ moral impurity, the term *mental pollution*, is preferred.

There has been a tendency to use the terms fear of contamination and compulsive cleaning interchangeably, and the confusion is particularly noticeable in the psychometric literature. Early scales, constructed during the behavioural era, focused on observable behaviour such as compulsive cleaning (e.g. the Maudsley Obessional Compulsive Inventory, Hodgson and Rachman 1977). Patients' scores on the cleaning factor were implicitly interpreted as signifying a fear of contamination. Given the high correlations between psychometric scores on subscales of compulsive cleaning and of contamination (many of the items on the subscales are similar) the confusion was understandable. An analysis of the psychometric data is provided in Chapter 8. For the sake of conceptual clarity it is well to distinguish between the fear of contamination and compulsive cleaning wherever possible.

Classification of fears of contamination

There are different types of the fear of contamination, and in order to provide clarification they have been classified into two groups (see Figs 1.1 and 1.2). A division is made between the obvious, common, familiar form of contamination that arises from physical contact with a tangible, harmful substance—*contact contamination*—and the contamination that usually arises without physical contact and derives from people not tangible substances—*mental contamination*. As indicated in the figures, the two categories sometimes overlap.

Within the two divisions, contact contamination and mental contamination, there are sub-types. Contact contamination comprises contamination from germs or other sources of threat to one's health, or contact with dirt such as decaying material, animal/human bodily waste, or contact with substances that are believed to endanger one's health, such as pesticides. These three forms of contact contamination are distinguishable but sometimes are entangled (e.g. mixtures of dirt and disease).

Unlike contact contamination, the second division, mental contamination, is difficult to observe and has perplexing features. The five sub-types set out in this classification, all associated with people, are contamination that is associated with physical or mental violation, mental pollution, morphing, and self-contamination. The five forms are distinguishable but overlaps are common, especially after a physical violation such as rape. In these cases, elements of both contact contamination and mental pollution can be present. The overlaps are phenomenologically interesting and will also entertain psychometricians, but the therapeutic consequences are the most challenging. It will be especially interesting to study the summation, and the subtractions, of the two overlapping fears. At present our knowledge of fear summation rests largely on laboratory tests of the connections between the fear of spiders and the fear of snakes (Rachman and Lopatka 1986). In brief it has been found that summation occurs when a strong fear is added to a moderate fear. In the reverse case, the addition of a moderate fear to a strong one leaves the overall level of fear unaltered—no summation. It remains to be seen whether the same pattern occurs in overlapping fears of *contamination*. From a practical therapeutic point of view it is well to keep in mind that discrepancies between verbal

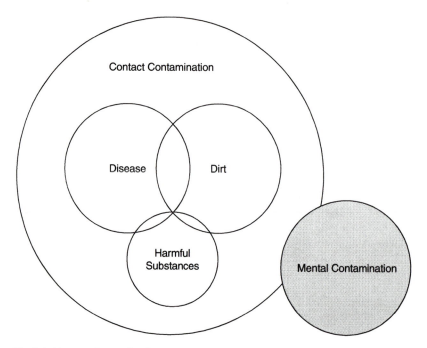

Fig. 1.1 Contact Contamination

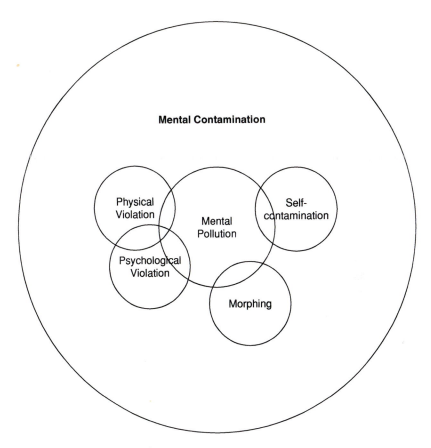

Fig. 1.2 Mental Contamination

reports and behavioural observations are often encountered, hence it is to be expected that a patient's assessments of the degree of connectedness between their fears of contamination will not necessarily be matched by behavioural evidence of connectedness. Fears of contamination provide an excellent testing board for investigating the summation and connectedness of fears.

Detailed accounts and analyses of the two divisions and the eight sub-types of contamination are given throughout this text, and the classification is set out as an atlas. (Two phenomena, socially accepted or prescribed ideas and practices pertaining to contamination, and feelings of contamination that arise from personal guilt about one's actions, fall outside the scope of this work.)

The broad division into contact and mental contamination, with overlaps, is illustrated in Figs 1.1 and 1.2.

The co-occurrence of contact and mental contamination

Contact and mental contamination commonly co-occur. However the association is largely one-sided. In cases of mental contamination it is common to observe accompanying contact contamination, but there are many cases of contact contamination without a trace of mental contamination or pollution. Presumably this difference arises from the source of the feelings of contamination. In instances of contact contamination the source is known, tangible, and can be localized. Mental contamination is more complex. The sources are less tangible or even obscured, the actual contaminants are not always identifiable and can be inconsistent and perplexing. Hence there are more opportunities for confusing the nature, localization, and sources of the contamination. In attempting to make sense of their intrusive and disturbing feelings of uncleanliness and pollution, people affected by mental contamination focus on the familiar, common construal of dirtiness. 'When dirty, clean it away, and avoid further contact with the perceived contaminant.'

Mixed cases

In some cases there is a mixture of contact contamination and mental contamination because the fear of becoming contaminated by dirt or disease is associated with people who are felt to be dirty/diseased/immoral. When other people are regarded as potential carriers of the threat of disease/dirt, some confusion can arise because in cases of mental contamination the source is invariably human. Mixtures of mental and contact contamination are common after sexual assaults. Feelings of moral degradation are accompanied by feelings of dirtiness and often by a fear of disease.

If a patient is well able to identify and localize the disease/dirt threat from the person, it falls into the class of contact contamination, but if they are unable to identify the nature and the localization of the human threat it is likely to be a manifestation of mental contamination. Fine distinctions are of theoretical interest but in most clinical circumstances the mixed cases can be treated by a combination of the methods deployed for treating contact and mental contamination.

Chapter 2

Contact contamination

Feelings of discomfort and/or dread are easily evoked by physical contact with items, places, or people perceived to constitute a threat to one's mental or physical health or social life. The primary sources of contamination are contact with dirty, infected, dangerous substances. In addition to these primary sources of contamination, identical feelings of dread and discomfort are evoked by contact with stimuli that are associated with the primary contaminants, the 'secondary contaminants'. The feelings of contact contamination are focused mainly on the skin (especially the hands), spread rapidly and are slow to degrade. Everyone attempts to avoid contact with perceived contaminants, and if they fail to do so, experience strong urges to remove the contamination, usually by cleaning. The unpleasant feelings provoked by contact with contaminants are universally shared, and many items and places are universally regarded as contaminated. The feelings and specific sources of contamination are normal, in the sense that they are universal, and so is the associated fear of contamination. The extreme forms of contamination, those which are too intense and too persistent, and/or too easily provoked, and/or inappropriate, are the subject of this analysis.

Cases of contact contamination

A 39-year-old academic was fearful for many years that he would become seriously ill unless he scrupulously avoided touching anything associated with germs. He recognized the source of his contamination, contact with tangible contaminants, and how widely the threat of contamination had spread. The patient handled many items with gloves or tissues, and washed all coins before re-using them. He washed himself for up to 3 hours a day and delayed cleaning his kitchen and bathroom because it took many exhausting hours to carry out the process safely and satisfactorily. Simply cleaning his clothing took a good deal of effort and his washing machine was used every day. The compulsive cleaning and avoidance are characteristic in cases of a fear of contamination. He derived a moderate amount of benefit from a course of exposure treatment.

At the age of 16 a schoolboy developed an intense fear of getting lice in his hair. In order to protect himself and avoid contaminating other people he compulsively washed his hair several times a day. He stored his clothes in a freezer for at least 2 days before wearing them, and of course avoided contact with other people. This included potential therapists as he was frightened that he would contaminate them as well. In this instance the boy's unrealistic and inflated sense of responsibility added a second dimension to his fear—fear for himself and a fear of harming others. No treatment was possible and he remained fearful. In the following case account an inflated sense of responsibility was the driving force.

As a 30-year-old father became increasingly worried about the health and safety of his three children he developed extreme measures to protect them. His fears of accidentally contaminating them with germs or harmful substances reached such an intensity that he washed his hands up to 50 times per day, spent at least 3 hours each day cleaning the bathroom and kitchen, and maintained a constant vigilance over possible dangers. He was pre-occupied with the need to protect the children at all times. As is common in cases of contact contamination, the presence of an inflated sense of reponsibility fueled compulsive checking to ensure that his family was safe from illness. After a course of exposure treatment his fear, hypervigilance, and compulsive cleaning were reduced.

A 25-year-old man who described himself as easily disgusted became frightened of chemical contamination after cleaning his barbecue with a powerful cleansing fluid. The fear was incited when the bathroom sink in which he had washed his hands became stained within days. The fear and consequent vigilance intensified until he was pre-occupied with avoiding and removing any and all possible contaminants. He improved slightly after treatment.

An architect developed feelings of disgust and fear about her bowel movements after a prolonged bout of gastric illness characterized by episodic diarrhea. She spent up to 15 minutes cleaning herself after each bowel movement and used so much toilet paper that the drains blocked repeatedly. In most instances she followed this cleaning with a lengthy hot shower. The fear of dirt contamination spread to all parts of her house, then her car, buses, shops, and of course public toilets were unapproachable. She feared that she might inadvertently disgust or contaminate others or that they might contaminate her. She responded moderately well to a full course of exposure treatment.

These cases illustrate common features of contact contamination. After perceived contact with a contaminant the person feels dirty/infected/threatened, and engages in compulsive washing and avoidance of recontamination.

The contamination spreads and is transmissible to others. Other people are regarded as being vulnerable to the contamination and its consequences. Given the presence of inflated responsibility, repetitive checking is associated with this fear. The contaminant is tangible and the site and the source are known; the contamination is accessible. It is transiently responsive to cleaning, and in many cases the fear diminishes after exposure treatment.

Table 2.1 Features of contact contamination

◆ Feelings of pollution, infection, threat provoked by perceived contact with a source of harmful, infectious, soiled substances (mainly concerned with dirt or disease)

◆ Feelings evoked instantly by contact

◆ Mainly focused on the skin, especially hands

◆ The contaminant is tangible

◆ The source of the danger/discomfort is known

◆ The site of the contaminant is identifiable

◆ Contamination spreads widely and rapidly

◆ Does not easily degrade

◆ Transmissible to others

◆ Other people are considered to be vulnerable to the contaminant

◆ Associated with compulsive checking if person is prone to inflated sense of responsibility

◆ The contamination is readily evocable by direct contact

◆ Anxiety is evocable by relevant memory/image of contamination

◆ Lacks a moral element

◆ Accompanied by revulsion, fear, nausea

◆ Transiently responsive to cleaning

◆ Treatment is moderately effective

Primary and secondary sources of contamination

Direct physical contact with items/places perceived to be dirty, diseased, or dangerous provokes feelings of contamination, usually instantly. Examples of primary contaminants include substances perceived to be infected with germs (blood-stained bandages), toxic substances (pesticides, chemicals), excrement, and people who are sullied or infected. Secondary sources are places or objects that are associated with the primary contaminant, or people who are believed to be associated with a contaminant (e.g. hospital nurses, workers in chemical plants, police who work with rough people). The expanding chain of associations can reach extraordinary levels in which the affected person comes to feel and believe that an entire city, and all of its citizens, are sources of secondary contamination. Contacts with secondary sources can induce feelings of contamination, usually instantly, but the intensity of the contamination from a secondary source is generally lower than that arising from contact with a primary source.

There are gradations of contamination, with the primary source usually heading the list as 'totally' contaminated. Secondary sources are graded in intensity along the dimensions of closeness to the primary contaminant, the expected spread of the contamination, perceived threat of a contact, and possiblity of avoiding or removing the threat. There are *degrees of contamination*, much as there are degrees of pollution, and people are expected to do penance according to the degree of pollution (Douglas 1966).

Chapter 3

Mental contamination

'This disease is beyond my practice'

The concept of a peculiar sense of pollution, mental contamination, was introduced because some patients with OCD express great frustration about their inability ever to feel fully clean (Rachman 1994). *'It looks clean but feels dirty.'* They continue to feel dirty despite strenuous attempts to clean themselves. Taking four, five, or six hot showers in succession fails to produce the desired state of cleanliness. How is it possible to wash repeatedly and yet remain dirty?

Mental contamination is a feeling of dirtiness/pollution/danger provoked by direct or indirect contact with an impure, soiled, harmful, contagious, immoral human source. The feeling of contamination is difficult to localize and is associated with a range of negative emotions that include disgust, fear, anger, shame, guilt, and revulsion. The unpleasant feelings instigate attempts to clean away the discomfort, and to avoid recontamination.

Mental pollution is a form of mental contamination, described as 'a sense of internal un-cleanness which can and usually does arise and persist regardless of the presence or absence of external, observable dirt' (Rachman, 1994, p.311). Mental contamination 'has a slight or indirect connection' with soiled material and generally emerges in 'the absence of physical contact with soiled items' (Rachman 1994). The source and the site of the dirtiness are unclear to the affected person—and no doubt this intangible quality of mental contamination is part of the explanation for the Macbethian futility of trying to clean it in the customary manner. Applying soap and water to the outer surfaces of one's body is misdirected because it fails to address the internal dirtiness that characterizes mental pollution. Moreover, the feelings of contamination persist long after any initiating contact, if any, has been removed. The distinctions between an 'ordinary' sense of dirtiness and mental pollution are set out by Fairbrother *et al.* (2005), and Rachman (1994). As mentioned, feelings of dirtiness arise after direct physical contact with soiled material, decaying matter, bodily excretions, and/or animals. The source of the feelings of dirtiness is known. Contact with the soiled material will produce feelings of dirtiness in anyone; unlike mental contamination, it is not exclusive to one person, not unique. However, if the feeling of contamination arises from a mental event, such as a memory or image, rather than a physical contact with a harmful substance, the site and source of the contamination are obscure. In the absence of a tangible site of contamination, attempts to remove the feelings are bound to be frustrating.

The concept of *pollution of the mind* was introduced in 1666 by Bunyan to describe his life-long affliction. An intensely religious man, he was flooded with blasphemous urges and malicious thoughts—'When I would do good, evil is present with me', (Bunyan, 1666, 1998 edn., p.94). He wrote '. . . darkness seized upon me, after which whole floods of blasphemies, both against God, Christ and the Scriptures were poured on my spirit . . . none but the Devil himself could equalize me for inward wickedness and pollution of mind' (Bunyan 1947 edn., p.134). He struggled to rid himself of satanic ideas and his renunciations of God and Jesus, but achieved only occasional relief and suffered from misery, despair, and 'clogged' guilt for much of his life. He was sore with 'great affliction' and held "captive" by "uncleanness, blasphemies, and despair" (ibid, p.31). He yearned to be cleansed and finally, 'the Lord . . . did discover himself unto me' and delivered Bunyan from 'the guilt . . . laid upon my conscience, but also from the very filth thereof' and he was 'put into my right mind again' (ibid, p.34). He was a religious reformer who rejected the established church and struggled to help himself in accordance with a major principle of the reform movement, namely that salvation is accomplished *sola fide*, by faith alone. The autobiographical account of his protracted battle against agonising blasphemies and mental pollution, *Grace abounding to the chief of sinners*, (1666) is a moving account of the suffering caused by his feelings of mental pollution and the frustration of being unable to achieve relief from the recurring, intrusive, painful thoughts of blasphemy.

Lady Macbeth is the supreme example of mental pollution. Incessant washing failed to give her peace or even relief. Her nurse observed Lady Macbeth persistently rubbing her hands, 'It is an accustom'd action with her, to seem thus washing her hands: I have known her continue in this a quarter of an hour' (Shakespeare 1623: *Macbeth*, Act 5, Scene 1). Lady Macbeth's repeated attempts to clean herself were futile, 'What will these hands ne'er be clean?' and later, 'Here's the smell of blood still: all the perfumes of Arabia will not sweeten this little hand. Oh,oh,oh.' Her doctor reacts, 'What a sigh is there!' and concedes that 'This disease is beyond my practice'.

In cases of OCD the feeling of being polluted goes beyond the discomfort of feeling dirty and can cause significant harm. Feelings of contamination that arise without physical contact are diffuse, have a moral element, are rarely feared as a threat to one's physical health, but can cause significant mental distress. Mental contamination is so difficult to control because it is obscure, difficult to comprehend, and not localized. Feelings of pollution are closer to feelings of disgust but can become a source of fear and distress.

Mental contamination is specific and unique to the affected person. It is not easily transmissible, and the characteristic way in which 'ordinary' familiar contamination is transmitted, by physical contact, need not be involved. 'I feel the need to wash again and again even though I know that I haven't touched anything' Mental contamination can be induced or exacerbated by 'mental events' such as accusations, insults, threats, humiliations, assaults, memories and even by unwanted and acceptable thoughts and images (e.g incestuous images, impulses to molest children etc.). The occurrence of intrusive and repugnant images/impulses/thoughts is the central feature of obsessions. Mental pollution as such is not transmissable from person to person, objects to objects, or person to objects, probably because it is uniquely personal. However, the occurrence of secondary contamination can be confusing; a person or an object that becomes associated with the primary (human) source of the contamination can be turned into a secondary source of contamination. This is obvious in cases in which the affected person avoids becoming contaminated by the primary (human) source but also avoids contact with clothing or other possessions of the primary contaminant.

After a physical violation, such as rape, there is a threat to one's health and persisting feelings of pollution and mental distress, including a risk of PTSD. The persisting feelings of pollution are intolerable and cause mental harm, including fear (e.g. 'I am irrevocably polluted and permanently damaged').

After a psychological violation the person might be left with a mixture of pollution and fear, depending on the nature of the violation. Betrayals tend to be followed by feelings of pollution, self-doubt, and anger rather than fear. Prolonged domination is usually followed by feelings of pollution, self-denigration, anger, and fear. Pollution that arises after serious manipulation is accompanied by self-criticism and anger towards the violator. The fear of becoming contaminated by touching or even coming into proximity with an 'undesirable' person is at bottom a fear of mental harm as a result contracting the undesirable qualities of that person. In extreme cases the threat extends to a fear of actually turning into the undesirable person, a fear of morphing. In caste communities, people take great care to avoid physical contact or even remote contact with members of a lower caste, such as the 'untouchables', for fear of pollution, and a possible fall into the lower caste, a degradation.

The magical practice of deliberately transmitting harm, not contamination, to an enemy by being unkind to a model of the enemy, for example by inserting pins into a wax image, is an exploitation of the law of similarity (see p.70), but is not applicable to mental contamination. Any sign that mental contamination can be conveyed by modelled similarity is bound to unsettle the futures market in the supply of wax.

In summary, contact contamination is caused by physical contact with harmful, tangible substances that transmit dirt/disease, spreads widely and is easily transmissible to others. The source is known and the site is identifiable. It lacks a moral element. Other people are vulnerable to contamination by contact with similar dirt/disease stimuli. The predominant emotions are fear and revulsion, and the main consequences are escape and avoidance. Cleaning can be transiently effective.

Mental contamination is a sense of mainly internal dirtiness of uncertain site and is traceable to a person/s not a tangible harmful substance. Some stimulus generalization occurs but the pollution is rarely transmissable to others. It has perplexing qualities and the affected person feels uniquely vulnerable. The associated emotions are anxiety, shame, anger, and moral uneasiness. Avoidance is broad and can be puzzling to the person and others. Cleaning is ineffective. Some attempts at 'mental cleansing' provide relief, if only temporarily. Broadly, *mental cleansing* is an attempt to replace a bad unacceptable thought with an acceptable, virtuous thought. It can be direct—e.g. replace thoughts of Satan with thoughts of God—or indirect and involve a variety of mental manipulations, some magical in quality (magical items, magical words, counting compulsions). Spiritual manipulations range from familiar religious rituals such as praying, confessing, repenting, renunciation, and charitable service (see Chapter 5) to virtuous thoughts and resolutions. One way or another, the person tries counter-moves in attempting to replace the unwelcome, bad intrusive thoughts with clean, pure, virtuous, good thoughts. John Bunyan's (1947 edn.) struggles to replace blasphemous thoughts with clean, pure religious ones are vividly described. Mental cleansing is also preventive; the affected person attempts to clean away repugnant thoughts and also tries to block the entry of such thoughts, mainly by distractions. Patients who are intent on prohibiting their unwanted, sinful thoughts are hypervigilant and constantly scan their thoughts for the unacceptable ones. One patient spent a great deal of his waking hours scanning and classifying his thoughts into acceptable and sinful, leaving little time and less energy for more tranquil and constructive thinking.

Case illustrations of mental contamination

A young actor complained of an intense fear of contamination. He was frightened of becoming ill as a result of touching germ-contaminated material and also dreaded becoming disgusted by contact with such material, complaining that it left him feeling dirty. His fear of becoming ill was diffuse and elusive; 'I will become very weak and ill'. The patient avoided contact with a wide range of objects, places, and most people. He avoided touching other people and was unable to hold or hug any of his relatives/friends because it made him feel uneasy; if he was unable to avoid the contact, he had to wash himself. He washed his hands up to 30 times per day, using anti-bacterial soaps and wipes. His household possessions were cleaned repeatedly, and on those rare occasions when he allowed people into his flat he watched carefully to remember what they touched. After their departure he cleaned the flat and all of the objects/items that the visitors had touched. (Incidentally, patients' recall of the contaminated items is usually accurate and not beset with doubting. The enhanced recall of contaminated items/events is a subject of considerable theoretical interest, see Chapter 5).

In the cognitive assessment of his contamination some significant facts and connections emerged. The present 3-year period of fear of contamination had been preceded by a similar 2-year period when he was a young adult. Both periods of the fear of contamination had emerged after painful disappointments in personal relationships. In both instances he had been deceived and left with a sense of betrayal. He couldn't bear the sight of the offending people, and the rare telephone calls he had with them were followed by bouts of washing. He kept away from places that he had visited with them, and avoided reminders of them. The feelings of contamination emerged shortly after the betrayals and expanded over the next few years.

In order to carry out exposure exercises at the clinic, he brought a selection of contaminated items from his home. One of the items high on the list of contaminants was a sorry-looking credit card that had belonged to his late but definitely unlamented aunt, a person who had humiliated and criticised him throughout his unhappy childhood. Although the aunt had died 15 years earlier, touching the card instantly produced strong feelings of contamination, and a need to wash his hands. Moreover when he was asked simply to form a vivid mental image of his aunt's face, a task that he was reluctant to undertake, comparable feelings of contamination were evoked. The feelings were removed by cleaning his hands with anti-bacterial wipes that he always had available.

This person's experiences of mental contamination illustrate a number of features of the phenomenon. The feelings and fear of contamination arose after a lengthy period of domination during his childhood and were revived and intensified in adulthood when he felt betrayed by his partners. The power of the contaminants did not degrade and neither did the memories of the contamination. The feelings of contamination were provoked by direct contact with the person responsible for the violation or any of her belongings, by indirect contacts, or by memories/images even without any contacts. Temporary relief from the contamination, however the contamination was induced, was achieved by compulsive cleaning. His feelings of contamination had elements of fear and disgust. Most interesting, the emergence of his fear of becoming ill as a result of contamination arose from a sense of violation rather than from any contact with potentially harmful substances. In addition to this feature of mental contamination, the feelings of pollution were easily evoked by images or memories. Physical contact with dirty contaminated material was not necessary.

Another patient tried to reduce his feelings of dirtiness by repeatedly showering in very hot water. Despite using strong soaps and stiff brushes, he felt just as dirty at the end of each shower as he had before he began. 'No matter how many showers I take, and how hard I try, I can't get clean!' His experiences are a clear illustration of the phenomenon of looking clean but feeling dirty. The feelings of dirtiness emerged after he was sharply accused of being sexually immoral. A similar description was given by a young man who had fears of contact contamination and was also tormented by self-contamination—'I shower over and over to reduce the feeling that I am a bad person'.

Yet another patient who was accused of immorality by her family became overwhelmed by such intense feelings of dirtiness that she repeatedly tried to clean herself with abrasive materials which ultimately damaged her skin. Her feelings of dirtiness could be triggered by telephone calls, by letters from 'contaminated' relatives and other remote stimuli. The feelings of pollution were not altered by the cleaning. These three patients dealt with ordinary dirt in a normal fashion, and none of them had elevated fears of disease. Their feelings of pollution were particular, personal, not originally provoked by physical contact with a contaminant, and unresponsive to straightforward cleaning. Other clinical examples are described by de Silva and Marks (1999).

A 24-year-old woman complained of uncontrollable compulsive washing that blighted her every day and was threatening her job in a busy restaurant. She had strong religious and moral beliefs and was easily upset by blasphemous or salacious remarks; her friends were careful to respect her views and chose their words accordingly. Unfortunately the voracious customers at the restaurant were less considerate and when she was exposed to rough and rude remarks it upset her and made her feel so dirty that she tried to avoid touching their used dishes and table napkins. When this was impossible she promptly went to the washroom and vigorously cleaned her hands with anti-bacterial soap. On a bad day she had to repeat the compulsive washing up to 25 times, leaving her hands cracked and sore. When she returned home from work it was necessary to change out of her work clothing immediately and take a prolonged hot shower. Exposure to salacious magazines or movies produced the same reactions of discomfort and dirtiness, and outside of work she took care to avoid the proximity of unkempt people and anyone whose behaviour was loud and 'disorderly'. In this case the primary source of the feelings of contamination was people using rough, offensive, or blasphemous language and this set off the compulsive washing; the only contact contamination came from secondary sources. The patient made progress in treatment and although her reactions to offensive language remained on the excessive side, she successfully reduced the compulsive washing to tolerable levels that no longer interfered with her work. Some four years later the feelings of contamination and compulsive washing returned but she overcame them after booster treatment.

A young lawyer was under threat of losing her excellent job because of the behaviour of a colleague With whom she had to share an office for several months. The woman invaded her space, used her work materials and space without permission, and ignored her complaints. The patient described the colleague as nasty, disrespectful, over-bearing, and unpleasant. 'Whatever her intentions, her behaviour and actions harmed me. I loathed her.' During the period of maximum stress, in which she felt that she could not continue at work, but was unable to find suitable alternative employment, the patient encountered a woman with a serious psychomotor disorder at the entrance to the building in which she was employed. The patient felt at risk of contracting the unknown, disabling illness from this woman and immediately resorted to the nearest washroom where she cleaned herself vigorously in order to wash away any dangerous germs. However the contamination was not controllable and quickly spread to her office, work clothing, then to the entire building. She was overwhelmed. Soon she was avoiding many places, anyone with an evident disability, colleagues who had themselves been in contact with contamination in the building, and so forth. The troublesome colleague was a strong source of contamination and contact was avoided. The patient developed intense, compulsive washing, at work and at home. In order to protect her family she scrupulously removed her work clothes before entering the home after work. On weekends, holidays, and evenings she avoided leaving home lest she encountered disabled people or colleagues. Her fear and avoidance diminished after treatment but she required continuing support and advice for a number of years.

A Chinese student who feared contamination from other Chinese people was untreatable. The source and focus of the fear was his hated stepfather who had emotionally abused him throughout his childhood. He regarded the dreaded stepfather as evil and the fear spread to all members of the family and finally to all Chinese people. The contamination was easily and frequently evoked by the sight of Chinese people (visual contamination) and he avoided any proximity to them. Images or memories of his stepfather were sufficient to produce feelings of contamination. The fear of contamination was so intense that he declined treatment because it would ultimately involve contact with Chinese people. He was a compulsive cleaner and his hands were abraided.

An intelligent young woman feared that she was vulnerable to 'mind germs' which emanated from a psychic whom she believed had harmed her by manipulating her mind and future. After two sessions of fortune-telling, she felt that the psychic had twisted her mind, that she had been infected with 'mind germs'. She regarded the psychic as evil and hated him and anyone else who shared the psychic's name, physical characteristics, style of dress, or accent. The psychic's forecast, she felt, had severely restricted her life, and as a result fled from the now contaminated town in which the infection had taken place and avoided it, and any reminders of it, for many years. She repeatedly engaged in vigorous and at times frantic compulsive cleaning. There was no evidence of a delusional disorder in this intelligent and highly educated young woman. Instead her difficulties are best construed as mental pollution. She felt that her mind had been polluted, the feelings of contamination were easily and daily evoked by mental events such memories, images (or physical contacts with items/places that had some association with the psychic or the town), her pollution was not transmissable to other people, had a moral component, and cleaning and intense disinfecting were at best temporarily relieving but ultimately futile.

A deeply religious Catholic man sought treatment for his feelings of contamination and compulsive washing, and for his blasphemous thoughts. The trouble began 5 years earlier after he became friendly with a man who belonged to a small, fringe religious group that promoted extreme views. The patient had been drawn into the group by the strong urging of his friend, and ceased attending church, missing mass and no longer going for confession. He was troubled by the change in his religious beliefs and practices and became preoccupied with the conflict in which he found himself, feeling guilty about turning away from Catholicism. After 6 months he decided that he had been misled, that the fringe group was a false religion and that his friend was unreliable and mentally unstable. As a result he returned to his former religious practices, but felt extremely sinful and guilty over his lapse from Catholicism, and fell into repeated self-criticism. He was angry with the friend who had manipulated him, and angry with himself for his own weakness. The patient tried to compensate for his lapse by resolving never to allow any irreligious thoughts to enter his mind, but his attempts to suppress the unacceptable thoughts failed and instead he was assailed by floods of intrusive thoughts and blasphemous images. He also began washing compulsively.

A woman who was sexually betrayed by her fiancé was initially angry but then became anxious, indecisive, and developed feelings of contamination. Her apartment, much of her clothing and other possessions, and anything associated with the former fiancé triggered the contamination (perhaps better described as pollution) and consequent washing. She also developed a compulsion to keep her possessions in fixed positions and was upset if anyone moved them even slightly. Memories, images, even conversations connected with the betrayal and its distressing consequences, were sufficient to evoke the feelings of pollution. The feelings of contamination/pollution were unique to her, evoked even without physical contact, initiated by personal events not by dangers from harmful substances, and had a strong moral element. Treatment was focused on the betrayal and its effects, supplemented later by conventional exposure exercises.

A young woman developed intense washing and cleaning compulsions, using large quantities of powerful detergents and disinfectants, when her marriage became intolerable. She had been manipulated into an arranged marriage with an older and unsuitable man whose behaviour towards her was over-bearing, distasteful, and insensitive. Initially she tried to make the marriage work but found his behaviour increasingly repulsive, and started to avoid any physical contact with him or his personal belongings. It was at this time that she began to experience feelings of dirtiness and pollution, and tried to obtain relief by intensive washing. Her compulsions became overwhelming and this, coupled with her despair, led to a termination of the marriage. After they separated, she avoided all contact with her former husband and his family. Any reminders of them or contacts with items or possessions associated with him or the family, evoked feelings of pollution and triggered her compulsions. Eventually the entire town in which they had lived before she left him became contaminated. She felt that she had been violated by the manipulations of her husband and his family, and was angry and bitter towards them. Treatment was slow and difficult but ultimately she made significant improvements (reduced pollution, much reduced washing, and she stopped using the powerful cleaning substances). Progress in treatment was slow until the emphasis shifted from 'ordinary' contact contamination to her feelings of mental pollution and their origin.

In some cases of mental contamination there is an evident moral element. A young man sought treatment because of his overwhelming feelings of contamination, most of which were stimulated by contact with dirty substances. However, equally intense feelings of contamination were triggered by proximity to shabby and disreputable-looking people, especially if he perceived them to be addicted to drugs. Even the sight of such people induced feelings of contamination, and as was usual in his case, his immediate response to these feelings was to wash his hands intensively, repeatedly. His skin, from the finger-tips to the elbows, was abraided, red, and blotchy. His reaction to the perception of disreputable people had generalized to policemen, probation officers, even social workers; anyone whom he thought might come into contact with the disreputables was polluted. He responded well to an intensive course of CBT and the fears of contact contamination and of mental contamination declined in parallel. His mental contamination occasionally produced secondary problems and in one instance a policeman told him to pull his car over to the side of the road. The patient became extremely anxious, not about a potential booking, but because the policeman was touching his car. Worse still, when the policeman returned the patient's driving licence, he was reluctant to touch it, and was forced to wrap it in a paper tissue before accepting it from the officer. There is no written record of the policeman's private cognitions.

A detailed list of the properties of *mental pollution* and how it differs from contamination by contact with dirt and contamination by contact with infectious materials was set out in Rachman (1994) and a refined table provided by Fairbrother *et al.* (2005). An up-to-date and expanded version of the table is given here. The original concept of mental pollution has been expanded to include all five subtypes of the wider category of *mental contamination*.

Table 3.1 Features of contact contamination and mental contamination

Contact contamination	Mental contamination
Feelings of discomfort/dread	Feelings discomfort, uneasiness, dread
Provoked by contact with dirt/disease	Physical contact not necessary
Not applicable	Can be generated internally
Feelings evoked instantly with contact	Occasionally, see above
Focused mainly on skin, especially the hands	No typical focus
Generated by contact with external stimuli	Can be generated internally (e.g. urges, images)
Not generated by ill-treatment	Can be generated by perceived ill-treatment
Contaminants are dirty/harmful substances	Primary source is a person not a substance
Feeling dirty/infected	Internal dirtiness/pollution predominantly
Spreads widely	Some generalization, but

Table 3.1 (*contd.*)

Contact contamination	Mental contamination
Easily transmissable to others	Rarely transmissable to others
Others considered vulnerable	Uniquely vulnerable
Source known to affected person	Source of contamination obscure to affected person
Site identifiable	Site inaccessible
Tangible contaminant	Intangible contaminant
Contamination re-evocable by contact with dirty/diseased source	Contamination re-evocable by contact with human source
Contamination evocable by secondary 'carriers'	Contamination evocable by secondary sources, 'carriers'
Common in childhood OCD	Rarely occurs in childhood
Pollution rarely re-evoked by mental events	Pollution re-evocable by relevant mental events
Anxiety evocable by relevant mental events	Anxiety evocable by relevant mental events
Lacks a moral element	Moral element common
Revulsion, disgust, nausea, fear	Anxiety, revulsion, anger, shame, guilt, disgust common
Not applicable	Level/range of contamination fluctuates in response to changes in attitude to contaminator
Generates urges to wash	Generates urges to wash
Generates urges to avoid	Generates urges to avoid
Transiently responsive to cleaning	Cleaning is ineffective
Treatment moderately effective	Treatment under development

Assessing mental contamination

In the assessment of mental contamination a number of questions are useful. Can you describe the feelings? Are they feelings of dirt/disease? What causes these feelings? Is there a particular person or persons who can cause these feelings of dirtiness? Would other people also be affected in the same way if they touched the dirty/disease source? Are you the only person who would be affected by touching the source? Are there certain things, places, or people that make *you* feel dirty but would not affect other people? Where exactly is the dirty bit? Do you have strong urges to wash it away? Can it be washed away? Is it particularly difficult to clean it away? Do you often have to wash many times over to get clean? Is the dirt mainly on the outside of your skin? Does it ever feel as if you are dirty inside as well? Do you ever feel dirty all over, inside and outside? If yes, do you have strong urges to wash it all away? Do you ever experience these dirty feelings even though you have not touched anything dirty? Do you ever have the feeling that some things look clean but actually feel dirty? If you *imagine* the source of the feelings does it make you feel dirty? Do you have the urge to wash it away? Does it make you feel anxious? If you *remember* the source of the feeling does it make you feel dirty? Do you have an urge to wash it away? Does it make you feel anxious? Do you ever feel contaminated after looking at someone who seems to be disreputable, weird, or mentally unstable? If yes, do you have an urge to wash?

In addition to the Interview Schedule provided in the Appendix, administration of the VOCI Scale, the Mental Contamination Sub-scale, Contamination—TAF Scale and Contamination Sensitivity Scales is recommended (see Appendix).

Probes

A few simple behavioural/cognitive tests, probes, can be informative. After asking the patient to report the baseline degree of contamination they are feeling, if any, request the patient to form a clear, realistic image of the person who is the primary source of the contamination (the 'violator'). The patient indicates by a hand signal when s/he has formed the image, and is asked to hold the vivid image for approximately 2 minutes and then report any feelings of contamination or dirtiness, and any urges to wash. The second test follows the same pattern—baseline, then image, then self-report—and this image should be of the 'violator' touching the patient. The third test involves an image of the patient handling a significant possession of the violator; clothing such as a shirt or blouse often is effective. A fourth test is imagining handling a garment belonging to the violator that is sweat-stained. A fifth test is imagining sharing a drinking glass with the violator. Depending on the details of the individual problem, the tests can be tailored to assess the patient's contamination sensitivity. (There is experimental evidence of the induction of feelings of dirtiness/contamination by imagery—see p.35, and during treatment patients spontaneously report that memories, images, associations, can all induce feelings of dirtiness.)

The key features to look for are feelings of contamination without a physical contact, human source/s of the contamination, re-evocation of feelings of contamination by mental events, difficult to localize, indications of inner contamination, unresponsive to washing, and the person's unique vulnerability to the contaminants. Naturally, the assessment can be conducted before, during and after treatment. The Interview Schedule (see Appendix) can provide structure and coverage.

There is one feature of mental contamination that offers therapeutic promise. It appears that if the mental roots of the contamination are reduced, the associated fears sometimes decline in tandem, in an automatic spontaneous fashion. It is not always necessary to deal with each fear separately and independently. The fears of contamination collapse without special effort and in synchrony. In cases of contact contamination each *category* of fear needs to be dealt with separately.

Secondary sources of mental contamination

The sources of mental contamination, arising without physical contact, are more complex than those that arouse contact contamination. Feelings of contamination can be elicited when the affected person thinks about, or pictures, the primary source of contamination (touching a bloody swab, a sexual violation, or the violator, etc.). An interesting report of the elicitation of anxiety by forming mental images of the primary source of contamination was described in a clinical study by Lipsedge as far back as 1974 (see Rachman and Hodgson 1980, p.183). All twelve of his patients experienced anxiety 'during real or fantasised contact with a contaminant'. Even earlier, when he was testing the effects of imaginal desensitization treatment on patients with OCD (disappointing), Wolpe (1958) had little difficulty in eliciting anxiety by getting the patients to form mental images of the contaminant. Of course the question of greater interest now is whether the patients treated by Lipsedge and Wolpe experienced feelings of contamination in addition to anxiety. It is possible that in some of these cases, even many instances, the mental images of contaminated items elicited anxiety but no feelings of contamination. We shall never know, but mental images are certainly capable of inducing feelings of contamination. Given that these feelings are usually unpleasant, the anxiety that the patients reported when asked to form images of their contaminants is not surprising; additionally, some of them may well have experienced feelings of contamination during and after forming the images.

Thoughts and/or images of *secondary* sources of contamination also can evoke feelings of contamination. Significantly, the feelings of contamination can be evoked by memories of the primary, even secondary contaminant, and especially by memories of any particularly upsetting contacts with the contaminant. (For example, primary and secondary memories of sexual violations can be powerful instigators of strong and persisting feelings of contamination.)

A third, but overlooked source of feelings of pollution, is *self-contamination*. Repugnant intrusive images/thoughts/memories/dreams can provoke feelings of contamination, and in this manner become a source of self-contamination. At first sight the concept of self-contamination seems absurd, or at least, paradoxical. Absurd and paradoxical perhaps, but it does occur, however unknowingly and inadvertently. Clashes between intrusive urges/images and one's moral values can induce feelings of contamination, with objectionable sexual thoughts, such as incestuous ones, at the top of the list. Troubling dreams of an objectionable nature can also induce contamination. Memories can evoke contamination, and just as the experimentally instructed formation of certain images can induce feelings of mental pollution (Fairbrother *et al.* 2005), images too can induce feelings of pollution/contamination Clinically, unacceptable sexual images and thoughts, especially intrusions of an incestuous kind or of molesting children, are encountered as sources of self-contamination. Moreover, the personal significance which the patient attaches to these thoughts and images is sometimes reinforced by dream fragments on these themes. Patients do not readily make a connection between their repugnant intrusive thoughts and the feelings of pollution and/or their compulsive cleaning. The guilt and secret shame caused by these obsessions ensure that they are concealed from other people. During treatment the full content of the obsessions gradually emerges in the later stages of the process, given the development of a sense of trust in the therapist (Rachman 2003). Self-contamination can also be provoked by personally unacceptable acts such as masturbation, watching pornographic movies, and internet pornography. Bursts of cleaning often follow. In her study of unwanted, unwelcome thoughts in a sub-clinical OCD sample Zucker (2004, p.47) incidentally found that 'sexual thoughts were significantly associated with cleaning compulsions'. A peculiarly troublesome aspect of self-contamination is that the potential for triggering the contamination is always present. There are no time-outs.

There is a fourth form of contamination, best regarded as a variant of self-contamination, that arises from acts that violate one's moral values. Lady Macbeth's vain attempt to wash away her guilty pollution is a dramatic example. This was symbolic cleansing not cleaning. In most instances, self-contamination is better construed as mental or moral pollution. Mental/moral pollution is subject of great and enduring interest, and is the theme of innumerable dramas, books and all self-respecting operas.

Chapter 4

Contamination after actual or perceived violation

The idea that an emotional shock can cause OCD was discussed by Janet (1903, 1925) and elaborated and illustrated in the series of cases described by de Silva and Marks (1999). All of their eight patients had developed OCD shortly after experiencing a traumatic stress; they also had concurrent PTSD. In most of the cases the OCD symptoms (compulsive cleaning, obsessions, compulsive checking, ordering) had a direct connection with the nature of the trauma, but for present purposes the two patients who developed feelings of contamination and compulsive cleaning are especially interesting because they exemplify the emergence of contamination after an 'emotional shock.'

Immediately after being sexually assaulted while away on holiday, Patient 3 felt 'dirty and spent a long time washing herself and everything she had with her at the time. After her return home she continued to feel dirty and said that she could not stop or resist the urge to wash repeatedly. She washed her person and her clothes and other things in her flat; she spent hours doing this . . . she had obsessional thoughts about being dirty and unclean ("I am dirty"; "I am filthy"; "Everything is unclean") which were linked to the washing compulsions' (de Silva and Marks 1999, pp.943–4). The patient recognized that her washing was irrational and excessive but was unable to resist the compulsion or the obsessions. In this case her initial washing was appropriate but the feelings of uncleanliness, pollution, persisted for a long period, as did the associated compulsive cleaning. The feelings of contamination showed the usual spread from the original primary source of the dirt/contamination to her clothes and possessions at home. Her feelings of uncleanliness were not confined to the affected parts of her body but were general; no doubt she experienced feelings of internal as well as external dirtiness. In addition to feeling contaminated after direct physical contact with the contaminant, she also described features of mental pollution—broad feelings of dirtiness, a moral element, unyielding feelings of pollution, and the failure of intensive washing to reduce the unclean feelings or to have any effect on the obsessional thoughts of unclean-ness and filth. After being raped, Patient 5 developed PTSD and OCD, in which the major symptoms were contamination and compulsive washing. 'She felt unclean and washed her hands, body and home repetitively and in a ritualistic way' (de Silva and Marks p.944).

Feelings of contamination and associated cleaning were not evident in those patients who had suffered assaults that had no sexual element (e.g. being robbed at knife point) or those whose OCD emerged after vehicle accidents. Their OCD symptoms included compulsive checking, ordering, and intrusive thoughts.

Some of the complex relations between traumatic experiences and feelings of contamination were dissected by Gershuny *et al.* (2003). Four patients with severe, treatment-resistant OCD and PTSD were treated in a specialized residential facility of the Massachusetts General Hospital, USA. All of them had experienced horrific trauma and despite receiving a good deal of previous treatment (psychodynamic, behavioural, pharmacological), remained seriously disturbed. The connections between their PTSD and feelings of contamination, with associated compulsive washing, are vividly described. One of the patients reported that 'trauma-related intrusive thoughts and nightmares immediately triggered obsessions related to cleanliness and a feeling of being "dirty" which then lead to her showering an excessive number of times throughout the day.' (ibid, p.1037). Another patient described feeling 'tainted', contaminated, by her thoughts about the violent and sexual trauma she had experienced, and engaged in excessive washing and avoidance. In three of the four cases 'some of their contamination fears are not actually related to germs or filth; rather, they seem to feel "dirty from within" or tainted in some way… and such perceptions appear triggered by "contaminants" even without physical contact to such "contaminants",' such as intrusive thoughts and nightmares (ibid, p.1039).

During exposure treatment of OCD, the PTSD symptoms of one patient intensified when direct thoughts regarding her traumatic experiences emerged (ibid, p.1033). Feelings of mental contamination can be evoked by memories, images of trauma, and these case accounts show how exposure sessions that stir up such images, memories, can inadvertently intensify contamination and lead to compulsive cleaning. A troubling part of their findings is that in some cases there was an inverse relationship between PTSD and OCD—'when symptoms of OCD lessen, symptoms of PTSD increase; when symptoms of OCD increase, symptoms of PTSD lessen' (ibid, p.1038). As the authors comment, a full cognitive analysis of the common and distinctive features of the two disorders might have been productive. In principle, a surge of feelings of contamination is predictable if standard exposure treatment for OCD is provided for patients who have significant mental contamination in addition to their more obvious OCD symptoms of contact contamination, obsessions etc.

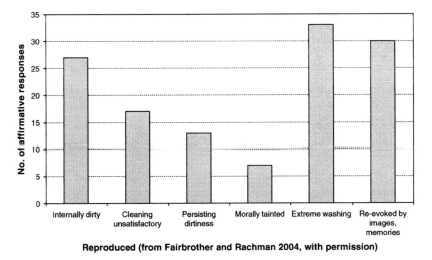

Reproduced (from Fairbrother and Rachman 2004, with permission)

Fig. 4.1 Responses reported by victims of a sexual assault

Three of the four cases described by Gershuny *et al.* (2003) had undergone traumatic sexual experiences, two were gang-raped and a third suffered repeated sexual molestation from her violent father It is hardly surprising that victims of sexual assault should feel violated and indeed polluted, and the study reported by Fairbrother and Rachman (2004) confirms that for a majority of such victims, even after excluding those who suffered particularly nasty/threatening assaults, feelings of mental pollution are a common aftermath of sexual assault. Thirty of the 50 students who participated in the study endorsed such feelings on a scale devised to assess mental pollution, and there was an association between feeling polluted and excessive washing (see Fig. 4.1). For the group as a whole, the deliberate recall of the assault evoked elevated feelings of dirtiness, distress and urges to wash. Recalling a pleasant event produced negligible feelings of dirtiness, but recall of the assault produced a mean dirtiness score of 34 per cent, a highly significant increase. Similarly, they reported a significantly high urge to wash, 24 per cent, after the recall. Nine of the women spontaneously washed their hands after the deliberate recall of the assault. Sexual assaults can produce a blend of physical and mental pollution.

Mental pollution

It has been demonstrated experimentally that feelings of dirtiness can be induced by asking female participants vividly to imagine a party scene during which they experience a non-consensual kiss (Fairbrother *et al.* 2004). After imagining a *consensual* kiss however, very few participants reported feeling dirty. A sample of 121 students were asked to imagine experiencing a non-consensual kiss at a party described on an audiotape, or a consensual kiss described on a comparable audio recording. The experimental manipulation succeeded and the participants in the non-consensual condition reported experiencing mental pollution that included feelings of internal dirtiness (5 times as strong as did the participants in the consensual group), and feelings of a non-physical type of dirtiness. The non-consensuals reported urges to wash (mean of 2.92) but the consensuals did not (mean 0.20). A balanced order method was used. The participants in the non-consensual group reported some negative emotions; sad, upset, anxious, angry. The main results are summarized in Table 4.1.

Remarkably, 8 of the participants spontaneously washed/gargled after imagining the non-consensual kiss. In a replication experiment, this time 28 out of 100 participants drank water or rinsed their mouths in order to rid themselves of the unwanted sensations they experienced after imagining the non-consensual kiss (Herba 2005). None of the participants in the consensual condition had a drink for this reason. The women who drank or rinsed had stronger feelings of dirtiness and urges to wash than did the women in the consensual condition. Interestingly, the rinser/washers had significantly higher scores on the scale to measure 'Fear of Negative Evaluation', indicating a possible social component in feelings of mental pollution and the urge to wash away such feelings. In some cases of the fear of contamination patients have a co-morbid social phobia (see Chapter 10).

Table 4.1 Mean results from an experimental induction of mental pollution by an imaginal procedure: responses to an imaginal non-consensual kiss

Mental pollution scores	Consensual kiss (n=30)	Non-consensual kiss (n=91)
Dirty/unclean	0.37	2.79
Dirty on outside	0.20	2.78
Dirty on inside	0.47	2.40
Dirty non-physical terms	0.43	2.51
General distress scores Upset	0.23	3.20
Anxious	1.00	2.92
Sad	0.03	1.99
Angry	0.10	3.46

(Reproduced from Fairbrother et al. 2005, with permission.)

Evidently feelings of mental pollution can be induced by imaginal means. The participants reported feelings of internal and external dirtiness, had urges to clean, and some did so. This demonstration of pollution induced without contact recalls Rozin and Fallon's (1987) observation that disgust too can be induced by what they describe as ideational means, such as contact with items that are clean but resemble dirty items (e.g. eating off a dish that resembles a toilet bowl).

Feelings of mental pollution can have a moral, rather immoral, element (Rachman 1994) and some of the participants in the experiment by Fairbrother *et al.* (2005) said that the images which they formed while listening to the non-consensual audiotape made them feel sleazy, cheap, ashamed. In the replication study, one of the participants in the (imaginal) consensual group reported an unusual amount of guilt and dirtiness and later explained that she was guilty because imagining kissing someone else, even as requested, made her feel unfaithful to her boyfriend (J. Herba personal communication). This is another instance of the connection between guilt for an unacceptable behaviour/feeling and a sense of internal dirtiness.

In the study of 50 women who had endured a sexual assault Fairbrother and Rachman (2004) found evidence of mental pollution in 60 per cent of them. Twenty-seven said they felt internally dirty, 17 could not clean to their full satisfaction, 13 felt dirty long after contact with a contaminant, and 7 felt morally tainted. Two-thirds of the victims reported that after the assault they had carried out extraordinary washing (51 per cent had a longer/hotter shower, 9 per cent carried out extra washing of genitals, 6 per cent used special cleaning products). Sixty per cent reported that the feelings of pollution could be re-evoked by memories, images or information. When specifically asked to recall the event the participants reported a 33.84 per cent rise in feelings of dirtiness (versus 3.49 per cent after a neutral memory) and a 24.19 per cent increase in the urge to wash (versus 4.28 per cent after a neutral memory). Eight of the women washed their hands after the deliberate, requested recall of the event.

An important feature of mental pollution is that feelings of dirtiness are easily re-evoked even without physical contact with a contaminant. Memories can evoke the feelings, as can images and thoughts, especially the intrusive and unwanted ones. The site of the dirtiness is difficult to localize, and the feelings of pollution are not properly responsive to cleaning. In cases of contact contamination, imagery/memories can produce anxiety but seldom provoke feelings of dirtiness/contamination.

These features of mental pollution were evident in the memories and reactions of a middle-aged patient who had been sexually molested by a relation during childhood. When he recalled the face and the dirty, greasy finger-nails of the perpetrator (a motor mechanic), over 30 years after the events, it evoked feelings of dirtiness. 'Whenever I remember and imagine his appearance I feel dirty inside. I have to wash myself all over.' His childhood fear had evolved into adult fear and loathing. Test probes, in which he was asked to form vivid images of the violator, produced the feelings of inner dirtiness and an urge to shower. He felt dirty all over and as he was unable to localize the site of the pollution, showered his entire body.

Contamination arising from perceived violation

Feelings of contamination can arise from physical violation, such as sexual assault, or from psychological violation, in which the person perceives that they have been seriously ill-treated. As the broad concept of psychological violation is too unwieldy, a list of violations described by patients was compiled. Psychological violations leading to feelings of contamination/pollution have been recorded after periods or instances of betrayal, degradation, humiliation, domination, or manipulation. Often the sense of violation emerges after a period in which the perpetrator, and hence the source of maximal contamination, has dominated, degraded, or ill-treated the affected person. The perpetrator/s and anything associated with them convey feelings of contamination that persist and grow even in the absence of any physical contact. For example in case of the young actor described on p.22, whenever he received a (rare) telephone call from the perpetrator of his distress, the woman who had betrayed him, he felt polluted and engaged in compulsive cleaning. Another illustration of the emergence of feelings of pollution after a betrayal is given on p.27. The betrayals involve a loss of trust, and are encountered in a range of relationships, including friendships, sexual, religious, financial, and work relationships.

The affected person develops a fear/dislike of the people responsible for the violation, and the aversion is often accompanied by anger and avoidance. In more than a few cases the avoidance extended to the city in which the violation had taken place. In addition to taking steps to avoid any direct or indirect contact with the violator, the affected person may engage in classical compulsive handwashing to remove the sense of contamination. The compulsive cleaning is dependably triggered by direct contacts, but can also be triggered by non-physical contacts such as memories, images.

In most cases the patient is extremely angry with the perpetrator and repeatedly remembers and recounts particularly upsetting remarks or hurtful events. No doubt in many instances these repetitions facilitate emotional processing, but in cases of mental contamination they have evidently failed. The resentment, anger, even hatred, are so powerful, and central, that they often provide important clues about the origin, range, and persistence of the fears of contamination. Hence, questions about people who have harmed or deeply upset the patient are included in the Standardized Interview Schedule provided in the Appendix. Information about the primary source of the mental contamination is obviously of importance in directing and facilitating treatment.

The contamination experienced by the affected person can be spread by them to other people and places, but importantly, other people are seldom believed to be vulnerable to becoming contaminated by contact with the primary source. Essentially, the patients say that the person who violated, degraded, and dominated me can contaminate me but not other people. However, if contaminated, then I need to ensure that I do not spread it to other people (family etc.). The lawyer who endured psychological abuse from a manager at work and developed intense feelings of contamination (see p.25), changed out of her work clothing before entering the family home and ensured that she refrained from touching anyone until she completed a lengthy hot shower. She was worried by the threat of secondary contamination. In some cases, it is as if the secondary source of contamination is a 'carrier'. People other than the patient are not themselves vulnerable to being harmed or contaminated by contact with the person who is the primary contaminant. However, if they come into contact with the primary source of the patient's contamination they can transmit the contamination to the patient. ('He can't contaminate you, but if you do contact him, then I don't want you to touch me.')

Most interestingly, the intensity and degree of contamination have been observed to fluctuate with changes in attitude and negativity towards the primary contaminator. If a reconciliation takes place, the contamination declines or even disappears. If the breach recurs, so does the feeling of contamination. If the primary contaminator apologises or makes amends, the contamination tends to weaken but not disappear. In one instance, after the contaminator sent an apology and a gift to the patient, the feelings of contamination set off by contact with or proximity to the clothing he had left behind in their flat, declined from 100 per cent contamination to 30 per cent. The level and range of (mental) contamination appear to fluctuate in concert with fluctuations in the patient's feelings and attitudes to the primary contaminator. The interplay between these two phenomena is worthy of close investigation for its own interest but also because it can clarify a potentially important mechanism involved in mental contamination. It is possible that the degree and persistence of the mental contamination varies as a function of the affected person's negative emotional feelings towards the primary source of the contamination—even regardless of physical contacts. This postulated functional relationship is testable.

Some confusion

For understandable reasons, a sense of mental contamination/pollution caused by psychological violation has been overlooked. The temporal relation between the violation, which often spans years, and the emergence of the feelings of contamination and washing, can be obscure. The patient may sense a connection between the violation and the current feelings of contamination, but remained puzzled by the time gap, 'Yes, but why *now*?'.

A second source of perplexity arises from the difficulty which people, and perhaps patients in particular, experience when trying to describe or recognize the sense of internal dirtiness. Our concept of dirtiness implies physical contact with a tangible and identifiable contaminating substance. Feelings of internal dirtiness resemble feelings of external dirtiness but lack the familiar characteristics of 'dirt'. It looks clean but feels dirty. Lady Macbeth's attempts to clean her hands are an example of a royal confusion between internal and external pollution. In clinical circumstances, the fact that many patients with feelings of personal pollution have at the same time feelings of 'ordinary' contamination can confuse matters. At times it is a toss-up as to whether the patient or the therapist is the more confused. Therapists naturally tend to concentrate on the observable and familiar form of 'ordinary' contamination, to the possible neglect of the mental contamination. A retrospective analysis of case data collected at the Anxiety Disorders Clinic in Vancouver, Canada suggests that patients with mental contamination did less well in treatment than did the patients with ordinary contamination (Jacobi *et al.* 2005). The hopeful expectation is that clarification of the nature and modifiability of mental contamination will ultimately facilitate treatment and reduce the unacceptable incidence of failures in these cases.

Instances of violation greatly outnumber the incidence of mental contamination. At present we do not know what makes the difference—how do most people endure violations without developing significant feelings of pollution/contamination? How do they complete the necessary emotional processing? Clinicians and psychopathologists will be more concerned about the setting or predisposing conditions that make a small minority of people vulnerable to significant mental contamination or pollution as a consequence of a personal violation. The likelihood of a pre-existing sensitivity to feelings of contamination and pollution is considered on p.83, and the likely existence of a contamination-sensitive *state* on p.85.

The main features of contamination by violation are set out in Table 4.2.

As discussed earlier, contamination by violation shares some of the features of the common form of contamination and some features of mental pollution. The difficult question of why a small minority of people who have endured violation, domination, betrayal, humiliation develop feelings of pollution and

Table 4.2 The features of contamination following ill-treatment, violation, domination, degradation, manipulation, betrayal, or humiliation

Following an incident or period of ill-treatment:

♦ The patient develops feelings of contamination *and*

♦ Feelings of dirtiness that can arise without any physical contact with a contaminant

♦ The primary source of the contamination is a person/s, not a harmful or disgusting substance

♦ Items, places, or people associated with the primary person/s can turn into secondary sources of contamination

♦ The feelings of contamination spread

♦ The feelings promote urges to clean away the perceived contamination

♦ And promote avoidance of cues of contamination

♦ And promote the avoidance of reminders of the incident/perpetrator and any cues/ memories that are associated with the incident/period/perpetrator

♦ The feelings of contamination can be induced, and revived, with or without direct physical contact with items/places/people associated with the perpetrator

♦ These feelings of contamination are often accompanied by more common forms of contact contamination (from sources such as dirt, disease), and by consquent compulsive cleaning behaviour

♦ The affected person is uniquely, specifically, vulnerable to the primary source of the contamination

♦ Fluctuations in the affected person's feelings/attitudes to the contaminator are followed by fluctuations in the level and range of contamination

♦ The transmissability of the contamination has three facets:

 ● Other people are not vulnerable to becoming contaminated by contact with the primary source

 ● But are vulnerable to secondary contamination, usually via the affected patient

 ● People who come into contact with the primary source of the contamination can become secondary sources of contamination (carriers) for the affected patient

♦ The contamination is associated with a range of negative emotions and reactions that include anger, self-criticism, guilt, damaged self-esteem, general anxiety

contamination remains to be tackled. Another difficult question is how the experience of violation comes to generate feelings of pollution and compulsive cleaning. One possibility is that the violator comes to be regarded as an enemy, and as Rozin and Fallon (1987) observed, the person and possessions of an enemy evoke feelings of aversion and disgust. In a simple illustration, people avoid wearing or even touching the clothing of an enemy. No doubt unavoidable contacts with a violator/enemy or his possessions can generate feelings of pollution and compulsive washing.

Self-contamination

A less obvious but damaging form of mental contamination can arise from one's own thoughts/images/impulses. The source of the trouble is internal. No physical contact with harmful substances is involved. In common with other forms of mental contamination, the primary source of the contamination is human not harmful substances; paradoxically, in these cases the affected person is the source of his own contamination. Escape is exceedingly difficult and the threat of re-contamination is always present. Patients are trapped in a cycle of uncontrollable, recurring, repugnant thoughts/urges and subsequent feelings of contamination.

The idea that people contaminate themselves seems absurd at first, but on reflection, there is much unused evidence to confirm that self-contamination does indeed occur. Many clinicians who have cared for people with OCD have probably encountered patients who report that at times, in specifiable conditions, they feel compelled to wash away the effects of nasty, intrusive thoughts, images, or impulses. This phenomenon is best construed as a manifestation of self-contamination. Repugnant intrusive thoughts are the common trigger for the compulsive washing, but personally unacceptable acts, such as masturbation, looking at pornography, can produce the same effect. Additionally, some patients feel self-contaminated by their bodily excretions and wash compulsively to remove the 'contaminants' and the associated sense of mental pollution.

In the religious domain, the experiences of Bunyan (1998 edn.) illustrate the occurrence of spiritual mental pollution. He interpreted his flooding blasphemous thoughts as satanically sinful and they left him feeling mentally polluted. His readers no doubt understood what he wrote but were not left in his mentally polluted state; no more are contemporary readers of these descriptions of nasty intrusive thoughts at risk of feeling mentally polluted. The mental events are unique to the person experiencing them. They can be described to other people but are not otherwise accessible, and the personal appraisals which the person makes of the significance of these mental events are unique. Lady Macbeth's thoughts about her terrible crime were unique to her and gave rise to her unique sense of pollution. Her handwashing was of course ineffective; it was misdirected.

When patients tell us that they are uniquely vulnerable to the feared contamination and its effects, those who are suffering from mental contamination, at least, are correct. The raw material (intrusive thoughts, incestuous images, memories etc.) is unique to them, their appraisals are unique to them and hence, in these cases, they are indeed uniquely vulnerable to the contamination

Self-contaminating thoughts are encountered in blasphemous ideas, incestuous images, dreams, and aggressive impulses, and some case illustrations follow. In many instances the self-contamination is best seen as a form of mental pollution in which the person feels sullied by their unacceptable, objectionable, even repugnant images/ideas/impulses because they clash with their moral standards. For this reason guilt often accompanies self-contamination. Objectionable, unacceptable sexual or aggressive dreams can be polluting, and can be misinterpreted as confirmation of a suspected moral flaw. A patient who was receiving treatment for his paedophiliac obsessions had occasional dreams in which children featured, and interpreted them as confirming that he had sexual urges towards children. After these disturbing dreams he felt polluted and took a hot shower, but with little effect. In this as in similar cases, it can be said that part of the problem is a *mis*-interpretation of dreams. The patient benefited from a 12-session course of CBT and was symptom-free at the conclusion (see pp.157–158). Given the close connection between obsessions and depression (Ricciardi and McNally 1995), it is to be expected that the feelings of self-contamination will vary with mood state, and specifically that exacerbations of contamination are probable during periods of depression. The feelings of contamination tend to be increased by criticisms, including self-criticism, but in most instances are unaffected by feelings of anger. These influences were illustrated by a patient whose feelings of internal dirtiness provoked prolonged washing. The duration of the bouts of washing increased significantly after she was criticised but were unchanged when she was angered.

The guilt and shame caused by emotionally and morally repugnant images, thoughts, impulses, and dreams, reach such high levels of distress and self-doubt that they prevent the person from ever revealing their 'dirty nasty secrets'. If and when patients overcome their prolonged concealment during therapy, it can be an extremely emotional event that leaves the patient shaken but unburdened. After the initial, difficult disclosure of the self-contaminating thoughts further distressing revelations tend to follow. The overall therapeutic value of such disclosures needs to be determined but in the short-term it appears to be an enormous relief and it certainly helps to focus the remaining sessions of therapy. Hopefully the disclosure and subsequent CBT will lead patients to an improved interpretation of the significance of their intrusive thoughts.

The expectation is that the feelings of mental pollution and contamination will diminish as a result of the patient's improved, realistic interpretation of the significance of the self-contaminating thoughts. The current CBT methods for treating obsessions can be modified for application to cases of self-contamination (Chapter 10).

A 22-year-old woman sought help in struggling against her compulsive hand-washing. Whenever she experienced strong feelings of dirt-contamination she felt driven to wash repeatedly, taking up to 60 minutes per day. She found it difficult to give a clear description of the contamination but was able to confirm that it was a type of uncomfortable, internal dirtiness, and was definitely under her skin. In some ways it resembled ordinary feelings of dirtiness, but was invisible and diffused within her body. The contamination was spontaneously evoked by thoughts, images, or memories, but could also be generated by physical contact with certain objects or with her bodily products. (Inadvertent episodes of self-contamination, mainly from bodily waste, occur but are of no particular theoretical interest. An exception was a patient who suffered from an abnormal perception that he had inadequate control of his bladder and repeatedly felt dirty and smelly, leading to compulsive washing.) The onset of the compulsions was traced to a period during which she had been distressed by intrusive, repugnant incestuous images. She was deeply ashamed, guilty, polluted, and distressed by the images and had concealed them for years prior to starting treatment. She strongly resisted the images, but without success, and her self-esteem had been damaged by the obsessions. The images were interpreted as a sign of some latent and disgusting element in her character, and as she was incapable of controlling the images, feared that some day she might lose control of her behaviour as well. By trial and error she had found that some relief was attainable by repeatedly washing her hands, but the abhorrent images and their damaging effects on her self-appraisal persisted until she received treatment.

In this case of self-contamination, the feelings of pollution were a combination of internal dirtiness and moral repugnance, evocable by mental events, and with minimal contact with a visible contaminant. The feelings of dirt-contamination were not properly responsive to her repeated cleaning. During treatment she learnt how to regard and deal with the intrusive images and thoughts, and as their frequency and intensity declined, her fears and compulsive washing diminished significantly.

Table 4.3 Particular features of self-contamination

- The person himself herself is the source of the contamination
- Hence the opportunities for contamination and recontamination are constantly present
- Unwanted, intrusive, repugnant thoughts, urges are a major source of the feelings of contamination
- Many of the intrusive and repugnant thoughts involve unwanted sexual/religious thoughts
- Intrusive, repugnant thoughts that cause feelings of self-contamination are concealed
- Feelings of self-contamination are influenced by mood states, especially depression
- There usually is an (im)moral element
- Unmanageable contact with one's own bodily products is a common source of feelings of pollution/contamination
- Repugnant habits (e.g. watching pornography) can cause feelings of contamination/ pollution
- Commonly associated emotions are shame, guilt, self-distrust
- The contamination is relevant to the patient but not to any else; uniqueness
- The appraisals of the contaminants, and their threat, are unique

Another patient obtained temporary relief from anxiety by compulsive washing after he experienced unwanted, repugnant thoughts of a sexual and aggressive nature that left him feeling polluted and 'mentally dirty'. He also used repeated hot showers to reduce his general sense of mental pollution; 'When I feel that I am a bad, dirty person, having a good shower makes me feel a bit better'. The obsessions were greatly reduced during CBT, and the compulsive washing faded out.

Certain aspects of self-contamination resemble the feelings of pollution that afflict some people after they have behaved immorally, as in the Lady Macbeth phenomenon. That very large subject requires a book of its own, and the similarities between immoral pollution and self-contamination may well provide the bridge that connects the two phenomena.

The remarkable fear of morphing

A remarkable type of contamination arises from a fear that one might be tainted or changed by proximity to particular 'undesirable' people or classes of people. The 'undesirable people' are unusual in their appearance or behaviour and generally living on the fringes of the community. They are regarded as weird or mentally unstable or dirty, and of low status. The fear can be provoked with or without physical contact, and affected patients take care to avoid these people. No one, seemingly, is troubled by the prospect of morphing into a person of elevated status.

In extreme instances the fear can go beyond a dread of being tainted or changed by the characteristics of the 'undesirable' person. The affected person fears that he might be transformed into the undesirable person, *morphed*. 'I fear that if he touches me I will morph into him', 'I fear that if I continue to look at him I might morph into him', 'I will become like him', 'I will become as weird as him', 'If he repeatedly approaches me, I will become as useless, ineffective, incapable as him'. In such cases it is not unknown for the affected person to check his appearance in a mirror.

The mere sight of the person or persons is aversive and can raise the threat of being altered by their characteristics—perhaps best described as *visual contamination*. It can be expressed in this way—'If I keep looking at him then I might become like him or turn into him; I must avoid staring'. In most cases of the fear of morphing, the aversive reaction to the 'undesirable person' includes an element of distaste or even disgust. It is embarrassing to admit to being put off or disgusted by other people or classes of people, and sufferers from a fear of morphing tend to be so ashamed of their problem that they attempt to conceal it. Expressing an aversion to classes of people is regarded as unfair and prejudicial, and hence shameful.

The fear of being contaminated by the sight of the undesirable/unacceptable/weird people probably increases with the duration of the exposure, and inevitably the affected person is paradoxically drawn to stare at the threat. The fear can also be provoked, less commonly, by 'auditory contamination', such as an unwanted telephone call from a primary source of the fear.

The fearful thoughts about morphing can be intrusive and disruptive, and impair the person's ability to concentrate. At their worst these unwelcome intrusions displace the patient's other thoughts and interfere with their work and social behaviour. Attempts to block or suppress the thoughts rarely succeed in overcoming the problem. After a close encounter, powerful urges to wash or neutralize arise and dominate any competing behaviour.

In a calm state the patients recognize the hopeless irrationality of the fear that they will somehow be morphed, and all resist the idea. These patients are not delusional and generally function tolerably well at work and socially, while struggling to cope with their psychological problem. In most cases there is a clear dread of becoming tainted or of frank contamination, but in others the possibility of a damaging transformation causes fear, avoidance, and attempts at neutralization, but lacks other features of contamination. The almost certain link between a fear of morphing and a fear of contamination is supported by the observation that most (all?) of the patients who report fears of morphing also have typical fears of contamination, past or present. For example, the patient who feared that if he stared at weird people, their weirdness would be transferred to him, also suffered from a fear of being contaminated by harmful chemicals.

The belief and fear is that proximity, or visual, or physical contact with the disliked/despised persons will change me in particular. I will be unwillingly changed for the worse and may even morph into one of them. 'If I come close to, or merely see a weird person or someone who is evidently mentally ill, against my will I might be damagingly changed by them, and come to resemble them.' In some cases the patients try to make sense of their fears by drawing an analogy with the transmission of infections. Just as flu is contracted by proximity to an infected person—the virus is airborne—so they feel that germs of mental instability might be airborne and transmit mental instability or mental illness. It is a curious belief in the contagiousness of mental illnesses. They feel compelled to avoid coming close to obviously unstable people, and if they do come too close, it commonly triggers decontaminating compulsive cleaning or mental cleansing.

Numbers of affected people attempt to make some sense of their strange feelings of contamination by thinking of them as an airborne transfer of 'mind germs'. Other terms introduced to explain the threat of a mental contagion are 'goof germs' and 'thought germs'. It should be emphasized that these people are neither ignorant nor delusional, and most of them function reasonably well despite their fears.

The fact that fears of contact contamination are almost always associated with the fear of morphing confirms that this remarkable phenomenon is indeed a manifestation of contamination, and not merely an unconnected oddity. They are members of the same family.

The fear of morphing is a fear that contamination will be produced by proximity to undesirable *people* and cause unwanted and even damaging mental changes; mental to mental. With the exception of fictional accounts such as Kafka's (1912) masterpiece, *The Metamorphosis*, in which Gregor Samsa awakens to find himself transformed into gigantic insect, the psychological fear of morphing is confined to other *people* or their undesirable characteristics.

Case illustrations

A bright and ambitious student experienced repeated, intensive fears that she might somehow 'morph' into one of the failing students in her group, and went to lengths to avoid touching or sitting near any of them. If her attempts at avoidance failed, she became distressed and compulsively washed her hands. She spent long hours trying to neutralize the fearful thoughts by internal debates and suppression, but without success. She responded moderately well to a course of CBT.

A financial analyst reported religious obsessions, fears of 'ordinary' contamination and mental pollution. In addition she described visual contamination, in which she felt contaminated by observing or being in close proximity to people whom she believed were 'unlucky' (e.g. a coworker whom she knew was going to be fired) or had a 'self-destructive personality' (e.g. homeless people). She felt so contaminated by picking up their undesirable qualities or bad luck that she was compelled to 'purify' herself by washing her hands, touching a pure object (e.g. white table), retracing her steps while looking away from the person, or singing a 'good' song.

Another patient, with a long history of contamination fears and compulsive washing, responded well to CBT but experienced an odd recurrence several years later. The feelings of contamination and associated washing had returned but at lower intensity. However, he had developed checking compulsions and also a pervasive fear of being changed for the worse—he had become fearful of encountering people who appeared to be mentally unstable or addicted to drugs, and was even afraid that if he looked at them for too long they might hypnotize him and change him into one of them. 'If they come close to me it is a very uncomfortable feeling, maybe I'll turn into somebody like them. If they touch me I have to go and wash immediately. That usually helps, but not always. If they touch me or I touch their clothing, it is scary; similar to the feelings I get if I touch garbage or chemicals, and I have to make sure that I don't spread it to the rest of my body or possessions.' His fearful beliefs about contamination, and the danger of harm being transferred to him from unstable or unfortunate people, were not part of a delusional system and he continued to work and socialize in his customarily selective manner. He recognised that the beliefs were irrational but was unable to control them. On re-treatment the fears of morphing responded favourably to cognitive methods combined with exposure exercises, but his attendance, from a distance, was erratic and the re-treatment of the familiar contact contamination fears could not be completed.

An adolescent patient developed a fear of becoming contaminated by physical contact with dirt that gradually expanded into feelings of contamination even when observing at a distance anyone whom he perceived to be dirty. Finally he began to fear that the sight of a dirty person would transform him into a similarly dirty person, and compulsively rubbed his eyes to neutralize the threat. He had no delusions.

A young patient washed compulsively to suppress her extensive fears of contamination and later developed an associated fear of the sight of dirty people and of people addicted to drugs. She worried that the sight of such people might unwillingly convert her into an addict and was forced to avoid widely and engage in complex attempts to neutralize the threat. Her typical fears of contamination responded well to CBT but she never fully overcame the fear of being unwillingly influenced into addiction by visual contamination.

A 35-year-old woman sought treatment for a range of OCD problems, some of which dated back to her adolescence. Raised as a Catholic, she became an agnostic in early adulthood and left the church, but was troubled by religious doubts and obsessions. Her feelings of contamination were provoked by contact with any items, places, or people that were associated with germs or pollution, and led to compulsive cleaning. In addition to ordinary contamin-ation, she endured mental contamination that arose without physical contacts. She felt contaminated when she encountered people who were unfortunate, unlucky, or self-destructive (mentally ill, homeless, drug addicted). Proximity, or even the sight of these people produced feelings of contamination that were virtually identical to those evoked by actual contact with disease/pollution contaminants. The fear that she would acquire their unfortunate/undesirable characteristics, and end up in their despairing state, was so intense that she even 'avoided their airsteam'. If she touched them or any of their belongings she was contaminated by what she called their 'goof-germs', that is germs which would harm her mentally. Observing that she was particularly prone to fears of morphing when she was tired, this patient used sleep as a counter tactic—'Sleep is my antibiotic for the mind germs'.

This patient's account is another example of the belief in the contagiousness of germs of mental instability. She was sure that she was uniquely vulnerable to contamination from the unfortunate strangers, and fully aware of the absurd-ity of the notion The patient was gainfully employed and had a successful marriage. She recognized the irrationality of her fears and feelings but was overwhelmed by their power. Her attempts to control the fear were predom-inantly mental, with an occasional resort to ineffective washing.

In cases of morphing there is a blend of the fear of being contaminated and the fear of being harmed. The contamination is acquired by a process of mental assimilation with little or no physical contact, and the feelings of contamination are perceived to be a threat to one's mental stability. As described, some patients ascribe the contamination to the effects of contagious 'mind germs', 'goof germs' or 'thought germs'. The underlying fear is that they are susceptible to a perplexing form of contamination, in which strange germs can transmit their harmful effects remotely and cause mental damage.

The interpretation of this threat as a form of contamination by germs is bolstered by the fact that when they do come into physical contact with the 'undesirable' person, of low status, they experience feelings of contamination and need to wash themselves. Physical contact with the 'undesirable' person produces a stronger reaction than does remote contact, which is generally visual contact. The fact that remote contact produces less strong feelings of contamination suggests that direct physical contact is the basic threat, and the remote contacts are an extension or generalization of this basic threat. It follows that if the threat of contamination by direct physical contact with the 'undesirable' person is extinguished, the (secondary?) remote/visual threats should automatically decline.

Clinically significant fears of contracting a mental illness, or mental instability, by contact are uncommon but not unimportant. (However, a mild belief in the possible contagiousness of mental illness might be more common than is recognized. Somewhat similar beliefs have also been encountered in various cultures.) For people who are seriously affected, the fear is also a source of embarrassment because they know that the belief is absurd and expressing it can lead to teasing. The fear can be manifested openly or indirectly. In clinical interviews patients who complain of the threat from 'mind germs' or 'goof germs' are candid, and their consequent behaviour, mainly avoidance of anyone who appears to be mentally unstable, is consistent. Less obvious manifestations are the seemingly inexplicable avoidances, such as people who travel long distances to avoid coming within sight of mental hospitals, or who avoid touching anyone associated with mental illness, or who avoid all mention of mental illnesses. A highly motivated trainee nurse changed his career when he was informed that his next clinical rotation included two days work a week at a mental clinic. The fear of picking up a contagious mental disease is unsupported but not as absurd perhaps as many other unsupported, false beliefs about health, illness and treatment. For present purposes it is significant because of its connection with a fear of morphing.

However, not everyone who has a morphing fear thinks of the threat as coming from contagious 'mental germs'. They are at a loss to explain the nature and causes of their strange fear. For those who have also experienced one of the more common forms of contamination fears in the past, or at the same time as the morphing fear, they find it easiest to construe the morphing as one more, rather exotic, manifestation of contamination. So do we.

When an affected person fails to avoid contact with contaminating people, they try washing or a variety of neutralizing tactics—prayers, magical words or songs, touching a lucky talisman, undoing the damage by retracing their steps. Some patients construe their corrective tactics as a mental cleansing.

Table 4.4 The main features of a fear of morphing

◆ The person fears that she might unwillingly pick up undesirable characteristics from people whom she regards as weird, mentally unstable, marginal, shabby, drug-addicted, low status

◆ And/or that she will be adversely changed by contact, physical or not, with such people

◆ This assimilation of the unacceptable characteristics can occur as a result of touching the undesirable person or his her clothing, or other possessions

◆ The assimilation can also occur without physical contact—notably by visual contamination

◆ Assimilation/exacerbation can be produced by 'remote' cues, such as television, newspaper stories etc.

◆ In extreme cases the affected person fears that she will lose their own identity and morph into the undesirable personality

◆ The fear of morphing is sometimes accompanied by a belief that there are contagious germs which can carry mental instability from person to person

◆ The affected person feels uniquely threatened

◆ Recognizes the irrationality of the fear

◆ Resists the idea

◆ Is not delusional

◆ Usually (always?) the person has concurrent or past fears of contact contamination

◆ It is usually possible for the affected person to function at least moderately well

◆ The fear is accompanied by shame and/or embarrassment

◆ It impairs the ability to concentrate

◆ It generates avoidance behaviour, mental cleansing, neutralizing, washing

---

The strange and unusual quality of the fear of morphing is itself a source of extra anxiety and can fuel deeper fears of losing one's sanity. Therapists can provide useful and relieving information about the nature and occurrence of the fear of morphing, and reassurance that there is no evidence that it is a way station towards a mental illness. All of our morphing patients have been able to function at least moderately well despite the fear.

Mental contamination and the fear of morphing

Several points, and not a few intriguing questions, emerge from this phenomenon. The connection between the fear of contamination and the fear of morphing, albeit not a full connection, is puzzling. The fear of morphing and *mental* contamination fears share some features, and in particular the transmission of a threat even in the absence of physical contact. Both fears can be evoked by mental events such as memories, images, thoughts. Both fears are generated by contacts with *people* rather than with harmful/dirty substances.

Some cases of mental contamination are generated after the patient has been ill-treated by another person. The affected person perceives that they have been manipulated, deceived, betrayed, dominated—ill-treated in some fashion. In cases of morphing it is not unusual to encounter a history of protracted ill-treatment, but the affected person generally fears contact with *strangers*, or slight acquaintances, not necessarily the specific people who have harmed them. Expressions of anger and resentment towards the perpetrator are common, but the patient tends to fear *a class of people* rather than someone in particular. The person/s are perceived to be of a lower status (almost as if the patient has a personalized caste system) and proximity raises the threat of being tainted by the undesirable characteristics of that group of people (the mentally unstable, dirty, weird, drug-addicted). As mentioned, there usually is an element of (concealed) disgust in morphing. It is an unwelcome and embarrassing fear that causes some shame, as in cases of self-contamination. If proximity cannot be avoided the person feels contaminated and has a need to purify. There are some similarities with caste contamination, discussed in Chapter 5, but caste contamination is socially accepted, even prescribed, whereas patients with a fear of morphing recognize that they alone are vulnerable to the primary sources of contamination, and acknowledge that friends and relations do not share their perceptions or their fears. Moreover, they recognize the irrational core of their fears.

Visual contamination is prominent in the fear of morphing and occasionally features in mental contamination. Mental contamination generally drives compulsive cleaning and although some people who are fearful of morphing also engage in excessive cleaning, they tend to use a wider range of neutralizing tactics, much of it internalized and often described as mental cleansing (e.g. confessions, renunciations, magical counting, making resolutions, debating with oneself, praying, etc.). Mental contamination often has a moral element and in morphing, the people whose appearance or proximity arouses fear are sometimes regarded as undesirable, weird, evil. These common features are sufficient to indicate a link between the two fears, but it has to be admitted that the connection between morphing and contamination is not an obvious one, and few psychologists, including this one, would have predicted such a link *ab initio*.

The link is not obvious and neither is the nature of the connecting mechanisms. In deference to the zeitgeist one's thoughts turn to thoughts. When the fear of morphing and the fear of mental contamination are associated, the cognitive link is a belief that one is vulnerable to contamination which emanates from another person or class of people. So, if I get too close to people who are mentally unstable they will 'infect' me with their mental problems. If I have physical or mental contact with evil people they will induce a feeling of moral contamination, not unlike the feelings that can arise from contact with dirt/disease. The fear of being morally or mentally infected was well-described by the woman who became contaminated after she had been manipulated by a profiteering psychic; she felt threatened by the psychic's 'mind germs' and engaged in extensive avoidance and uncontrollable compulsive cleaning. She believed that the 'mind germs' had adversely affected her mind, and that unless she prevented further contamination, she would suffer a mental breakdown. In both phenomena the underlying fear is a dread of becoming contaminated. 'Unless I take care to protect myself from proximity to these people there is a risk that I will be contaminated and dragged down by them.' The linked cognition is a fear of becoming polluted.

As described earlier there are similarities between mental contamination and contact contamination. They include feelings of uncleanliness, fear of harm, rapid and wide spread of perceived contaminants, urges to clean away the contamination, and avoidance. The similarities between the two, and the familiarity of contact contamination, can cause the manifestations of mental contamination to be overlooked. Additionally, there are circumstances in which contact contamination masks the manifestations of mental contamination. It is common for the mental manifestations to become apparent during the later stages of treatment. The major differences between mental and contact contamination are the occurrence of contamination without contact, the primary source of the contamination (person vs. harmful substance) and perceived vulnerability (uniquely me vs. everyone who has contact with the contaminant).

The need for clarification of the cognitive connections between the different types of contamination is underscored by our limited ability, at present, to provide effective therapy for patients who are struggling with these fears. There are indications that patients with mental contamination derive insufficient benefit from conventional ERP treatment, and we need to develop specific methods for treating patients with mental contamination (e.g. how to tackle the fear of morphing). Proposals and prospects are discussed in Chapter 10. For example, exploratory work indicates that an adaptation of the methods that are helpful in treating obsessions (Rachman 2003) will prove useful in dealing with cases of self-contamination. The patient is helped to appraise whether or not the intrusive thoughts are personally significant, and whether they are a realistic threat. To this end relevant evidence is collected. In cases of morphing, the same general approach is applied, namely the attempt to help the patient modify the damaging cognitions (see Chapter 10). Specific treatments for the fear of morphing are being developed along the lines adumbrated in Chapter 10. Fortunately the fascination of the phenomenon exceeds its low incidence.

The *co-occurrence* of mental and contact contamination is an interesting and potentially revealing phenomenon. It suggests that there might be a common element, even a linking element between the two. It also suggests the probable existence of a common vulnerability. To take a simple example, a patient who had mental pollution that was readily evoked by intrusive thoughts, criticisms and other non-physical sources, was also contaminated if she touched dirt or bodily fluids.

The co-occurrence of mental contamination and contact contamination shows that the two phenomena are related, but the association is lop-sided (see Fig. 4.2). On present knowledge, most patients who have clinically significant mental contamination also manifest some contact contamination. However, only a minority of patients who have clinically significant contact contamination also manifest some mental contamination. To put it another way, the chances of a patient with contact contamination also having mental contamination are small; the chances of a patient with mental contamination also having some contact contamination are high. It is too early accurately to estimate the incidence of each form of contamination, but on present knowledge contact contamination seems to the most common. If this is confirmed,

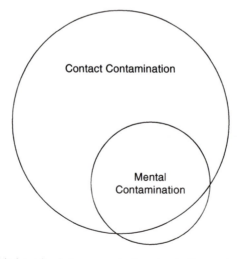

Fig. 4.2 The lopsided overlap between contact contamination and mental contamination

it is bound to influence our construal of the connections between contact and mental contamination.

It seems as if contact contamination is primary; there is more of it, and most people who experience mental contamination also manifest contact contamination. Is contact contamination a pre-condition for the development of mental contamination? At present we cannot answer that question as we require, as a minimum, data on the evolution of cases of both types of contamination. Which comes first, and what is the lag between the development of the first form and the second form of contamination? Given the higher prevalence of contact contamination, and the lop-sided overlap between contact and mental contamination, it does seem that mental contamination is secondary to contact contamination, but there are cases which conflict with this view. For some patients the clinical problem commences with mental contamination. Usually this is followed by the emergence of an ever-widening form of contact contamination, Macbeth style. The development of mental contamination is not automatically followed by contact contamination, but the very occurrence of this sequence suggests that the presence of mental contamination can provide a carpet for other contamination. Possibly the feelings of mental contamination are confusing—subjectively they are similar to the feelings of contact contamination, and both are distinctively different from other feelings—and as a result the affected person begins to attribute the feelings of contamination to familiar sources of ordinary contamination, such as dirty bandages, pesticides etc.

The development of a sense of mental contamination, in the absence of prevailing fears of contact contamination, was observed in the experimental inductions of mental contamination reported by Fairbrother *et al.* (2005) and by Herba (2005). In Herba's study some participants with negligible scores on a scale to measure fears of contact contamination nevertheless developed feelings of mental contamination. To conclude, the clinical evidence indicates that mental contamination is often secondary to contact contamination, but we are not in a position to conclude that contact contamination is a precondition for the development of mental contamination. The experimental evidence suggests that it is possible for contact contamination to develop secondarily to mental contamination. The interplay between contact contamination and mental contamination needs further investigation.

Given the common co-occurrence of both forms of contamination and their subjective similarities, it is likely that people with a *pre-existing sensitivity* to feelings of contamination are vulnerable to mental contamination or contact contamination or both.

Chapter 5

Phenomena of contamination

One of the most remarkable features of contamination is that the perceived contamination spreads so rapidly and widely, from object to object and place to place. All it needs is a single touch. It has a powerful force and *dominates* competing behaviour. Contamination easily becomes pervasive, in large part because it does not easily degrade. These qualities of spread, pervasiveness, and non-degradability, are evident in the rooms that severely affected patients keep locked for years and years in order to seal off the contaminant. In extreme cases the person regards extensive areas as contaminated and, as mentioned, even entire cities can become contaminated. Other important features of contamination include its easy transmissability, and its proneness to return even after initially successful therapy.

In most cases of contact contamination, the feelings of contamination are acquired rapidly, indeed instantly. The contamination spreads rapidly, easily, and widely, transferring from object to object, from person to person, from person to objects, and from objects to persons. The contagious quality of contamination is most evident among patients who fear that they are in serious danger of contracting a disease. As a result of the contagious spread of possible contamination, they live in a pervasively dangerous world. Once the fear takes grip, their vigilance and precautionary behaviour cannot keep pace with the spreading contamination, and if left untreated the fear drives them to avoid more and more places and people. One patient described his shrinking world in this way: 'As soon as I walk out of my front door it is Vietnam'.

Contamination is generally transmitted at full strength. Moreover, a small amount of contamination goes a long way (in both senses). (Mental contamination is an exception to the ease of transmission from person to person, or person to objects, see below.)

The rapid and ever-widening spread of the feeling of contamination has no parallel in fear, except of course in the fear of contamination itself. In these fears the person's construal of the contamination component dominates the path and the shape of the fear. A fear of being contaminated by the AIDS virus shapes the path of the fear, and is different from the path of a fear of being contaminated by pesticides, or from the path of a fear of being polluted by one's repugnant intrusive thoughts.

The transmission of 'ordinary' contamination is determined primarily by physical contact with a contaminated item or place, and secondarily by people who are believed to have had contact with the contaminated material. In specifiable circumstances, some fears can be transmitted from person to person (see Rachman 1990, 2004; and p. 71 for a discussion of the vicarious acquisition of fears) but the large majority of significant fears remain confined to the fearful person; transmission of *abnormal* fears of contamination to another person is not common. Transmission of a feeling of contamination from one object (or person) to another takes place if the patient perceives a significant similarity between the already contaminated item and a neutral but similar item or person. The transmission of fears of contamination is often subject to two prominent laws of sympathetic magic in a manner similar to the transmission of disgust as described by Rozin and Fallon (1987). The laws of contagion and of similarity which operate in the induction or transmission of disgust (see p. 69), can also operate in the transmission of contamination fears. However, there is a curious asymmetry in the spread of contamination. A teaspoonful of contaminated fluid is sufficient to spoil an entire barrel of clean water. However, a teaspoonful of clean water will do absolutely nothing to cleanse the contents of a barrel of contaminated water. Contamination dominates cleanliness.

The same asymmetry, in which the transmission of a sullied substance overwhelms a clean substance, is observed in the transmission of contamination from person to person, or even from group to group. A person from a group believed to be sullied or polluted, such as an 'untouchable' in India, can contaminate a person of a higher and cleaner status by mere proximity. (Sadly, very sadly, untouchability is construed as an inherited impurity.) The reverse rarely occurs; a person of high status cannot 'cleanse' an untouchable person by a direct or indirect contact. The entry of a contaminated person into an unsullied group will contaminate the group but the entry of a clean person into a 'contaminated' group will do nothing to cleanse that group.

The prevalence of such beliefs about contamination makes it possible to deliberately contaminate a rival or enemy. Contamination can be produced in the obvious way by spreading dirt, germs, anthrax, and also by less obvious but equally effective non-physical ('mental') manipulations. Passing on information, correct or incorrect, can produce feelings of contamination—e.g. that dangerous chemicals have seeped into the water supply, or were used in food preparation.

It is also possible to create mental pollution by labelling a person or a group of people (e.g. untouchables) as polluted or contaminated. This method was used in the Soviet Union (Applebaum 2003, p.121) and in Nazi Germany (Gilbert 1986, pp.23–31) to exclude, imprison, or kill political or personal enemies. Describing people as vermin was commonly a precursor of isolation and violence. According to Human Rights Watch (1999) this chain persists in parts of India. Aggressive feelings are common among people who feel that they have been polluted by someone else.

Does contamination degrade?

Feelings of contamination tend not to degrade spontaneously, and even under treatment are slow to degrade. Moreover, contaminants leave traces: even after the contaminated item has been removed, it leaves traces. As Tolin *et al.* (2004) demonstrated in an elegant study, contamination passes from object to object with virtually no loss of intensity. A contaminated pencil was used to touch neutral pencils, and the same level of contamination was thereby transferred from pencil to pencil without loss of intensity. This demonstration is consistent with reports made by patients experiencing feelings of contamination. Objects that were felt to be contaminated 5, 10, even 20 years earlier retain their original level of contamination!

Some patients report that the level of contamination has even increased over time; perhaps mould has grown on the items, perhaps the germs have multiplied. We need to take into account not only the the 'resistance' of contamination to degradation, but also the occurrence of a spontaneous inflation of contamination over time. This inflation can be caused by cognitive changes pertaining to the the particular contaminants, even without renewed contact with the contaminant. *'Spontaneous' inflation of the feelings of contamination* is most evident in cases of mental contamination. Changes in the patient's perceptions and cognitions about the person who is the primary source of the contamination, almost always negative, can cause contamination-inflation. Similarly, changes in the perception/cognition of secondary sources of contamination can also do it, but presumably the largest effects occur in relation to the primary source.

It is probable that the intensity of the contamination and the rate of spontaneous degradation are correlated, with the most intense contamination the least likely to degrade spontaneously. Study of the degradability, and inflation, of contamination will be facilitated by using the concept of *degrees of contamination* referred to on p. 18.

The persistence of a fear of contamination

In most instances it is assumed that the contamination does not, will not, degrade. In cases of significant fear of contamination the person over-estimates the probability and the seriousness of the threat, and the combination of non-degradability and over-estimations is evident in the intensity and persistence of the fear. As a result the locked, contaminated room is sealed off for years. If the room is opened the patient asserts that the objects are still contaminated—little or no degradation has occurred, and the threats presented by the objects are unchanged—or even enhanced by further decay. Many patients are puzzled and troubled by the persistence of their fears of contamination. Why, they ask, does my fear continue, why doesn't it fade away?

Periods during which a person feels a significant degree of contamination are episodic; however, the *fear* of becoming contaminated tends to persist for long periods, often for many years. Cognitively, the fear will persist as long as the affected person attributes the distress to actual or threatened contamination; their estimates of the probability of becoming contaminated and the seriousness of the contamination are elevated. When these cognitive misappraisals are replaced by more appropriate appraisals the abnormal fear tends to decline and disappear. The feeling of being contaminated is unpleasant and at times very frightening, but each episode can be terminated, usually by washing away the contaminant or its traces. However, the *fear* of recontamination persists.

Washing is a dependable, effective method for removing/reducing the feeling of contamination, and is by far the most common response to contamination. The two phenomena are so closely linked that it has become customary to use the terms and concepts interchangeably, as is evident in most psychometric scales for measuring OCD. But for several purposes, and examining the persistence of the fear is one of them, it is necessary to prise them apart. The episodes of feeling contaminated are triggered by perceived contact with a contaminant and they generally persist until the person washes away the traces. The inevitable question of what happens if the contaminant is *not* washed away was investigated in a series of connected experiments, described below. The early explanation of the persistence of the fear of contamination was based on the Miller-Mowrer two-stage theory of fear and avoidance (see Clark, D.A. 2004; Rachman and Hodgson 1980), and it was claimed that the fear is reinforced and consolidated by the short-term success of anxiety-reducing actions, such as vigorous washing in cases of OCD. By deduction from the theory, it was asserted that the compulsive washing which follows on feeling contaminated successfully reduces the person's anxiety but paradoxically strengthens the fear. The learning theory explanation still carries some weight but is best incorporated within a fresh, cognitive explanation.

Whatever the proximal cause of the fear, the persistence of the fear is determined by the person's interpretation of the personal significance of the instigating event/s, namely the contact with the contaminant. If the ensuing contamination is interpreted as a danger to one's physical and/or mental health (e.g. I remain at risk of developing AIDS) the fear of touching the contaminant will persist and become elaborated (e.g. the threats spread ever wider). However, if the contact is interpreted as being insignificant and/or circumscribed, then the fear will fade (e.g. it was a nasty event but a one-off, or, it was a nasty event and we were all equally upset at the time). The maintenance of a fear of contamination is facilitated by the maladaptive cognitions and by the adoption of self-defeating safety behaviour, notably avoidance and compulsive cleaning.

The next questions arise out of the observed persistence, and for irrational reasons, of the washing behaviour. Why does the compulsive washing persist even when it is less than successful, and why and when does it become compulsive? Washing that successfully removes the contaminant, comes to an end and therefore presents no problem. Repeated washing that continues for hours, even up to and beyond causing one's hands to bleed, is an ineffective, demeaning compulsion and warrants re-consideration from a fresh perspective.

The learning theory explanation was that the washing persists because it is partially successful; it reduces some anxiety and is therefore functional. Moreover, there are data showing that partial reinforcement tends to increase the habit strength of a response. The only way to unwind a strongly reinforced pattern of behaviour, such as compulsive washing, it was asserted, is to provide the conditions for extinction; namely, repeated but unreinforced evocations of the response. This line of reasoning provided the rationale for 'exposure and response prevention' treatment, and the experiments described below provided some bolstering evidence. The method, like the rationale, is at least partly justifiable.

The basic idea of the learning theory account of OCD was that compulsions reduce anxiety and hence are strengthened. In cases of contamination fear it was postulated, anxiety is evoked by actual or threatened contact with a perceived contaminant, and the consequent washing is an attempt to reduce the anxiety and, if possible, remove the threat. The washing reduces the anxiety but paradoxically builds up a strong habit, and in some cases the washing becomes compulsive. In this sense the washing turns into a problem because it is so successful at reducing anxiety—Mowrer (1960) described this type of self-defeating behaviour as 'the neurotic paradox'. It was also believed that the anxiety-reducing compulsions serve to preserve the fear because they prevent extinction of the fear itself. A cognitive explanation seems preferable (Chapter 9)—the fear is preserved because the false belief that the contaminant is dangerous is shielded from disconfirmation.

The hypothesis that compulsive washing reduces anxiety was supported by clinical anecdotes, standardized interviews, and later by experimental analyses. In a series of experiments carried out at the Maudsley and Bethlem Hospitals in London, UK, it was demonstrated that patients with a fear of contamination experience an increase in anxiety when they touch a perceived contaminant, and that the anxiety is quickly and sharply reduced by carrying out the appropriate washing (see Fig. 5.1, and Rachman and Hodgson 1980). It was also found that if the washing is delayed for 30 minutes, a small but significant amount of anxiety declines spontaneously during this passive waiting period. The results obtained in the laboratory were essentially the same when the process was carried out in the home of the patient. Contrary to expectation, interruption of the washing behaviour produced no adverse effects, and on the resumption of the washing the anxiety reduced in the usual way. In further tests it was found that the provoked anxiety undergoes a slow but substantial spontaneous decline over a period of 1 to 3 hours after touching the contaminant; washing accelerates the decline of the anxiety. This additional finding that the anxiety will decline even if the person refrains from washing bolstered the rationale for exposure and response prevention treatment. If the patient is guided into planned contacts with the avoided contaminants, and refrains from washing, the anxiety will subside. Repeated exercises of this kind gradually but steadily reduce the anxiety and the compulsive behaviour.

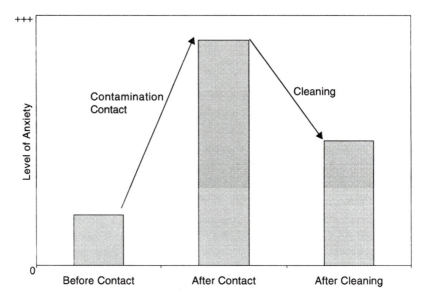

Fig. 5.1 The experimental evocation of anxiety after touching a contaminant

However, the learning theory rationale for exposure and response prevention is less satisfactory when dealing with compulsive washing that persists, even though it fails to suppress the immediate threat or anxiety. It fails to account for the persistence of futile washing. One thinks here of the numerous patients whose compulsively repeated washing leaves them in an unaltered state of distress, but persists nevertheless. One patient had up to eight hot showers in succession and felt as contaminated and miserable at the end as she had at the beginning. Another patient washed himself over and over again, and scrubbed as many of his possessions as he could manage in washing sessions that could consume an entire day, and leave left him exhausted but still contaminated. It seems probable that in these instances and many others, the repeated washing fails because it is misdirected. If the patient is suffering from a form of mental contamination, the site and the source of the contamination are obscure and hence inaccessible. Compulsively washing one's hands, body, clothes, possessions is misdirected and bound to fail. Why then does the washing persist?

Following the cognitive construal of the fear of contamination, it is postulated that the patients' attribute the threats to their health and well-being to physical contamination. Accordingly they resort to the customary and usually effective way of removing contamination—washing. Their misconstrued and therefore misdirected attempts to remove the contamination are futile. In the present analysis of mental contamination, it is argued that the primary source of the sense of contamination is a person not a tangible harmful substance. There is no contaminated substance to remove and therefore, compulsively washing one's bleeding hands is misdirected (*vide* Lady Macbeth). It is of little or no value in the long run, and seldom much good even in the short run. For people who feel polluted, tainted by the person/people who violated them physically or mentally, the compulsive cleaning is not only futile but adds injury to injury. This deplorable state of affairs, feelings of contamination and uncontrollable compulsive cleaning, is evident in some victims of sexual assault. In cases of self-contamination, washing is also misdirected and ultimately useless.

When compulsive cleaning fails to bring relief but nevertheless persists, the possibility of mental contamination is worth considering. In principle, the treatment should focus on the person/s construal of their distress, the origins and basis of their interpretation in terms of contamination, and of course attempts should be made to help them arrive at more satisfactory and realistic appraisals of their distress, as well as coming to understand the reasons for the inefficacy of the compulsive behaviour. In numerous cases the patient's construal of the distress in terms of contamination is understandably complicated because they also experience 'ordinary' feelings of contamination that arise from contacts with harmful substances. This calls for a genuine combination of cognitive and behavioural techniques.

Memory

Most patients retain a precise memory of the nature and exact whereabouts of contaminated material, even going back as far as 20 years or more. For example, a patient was able to recall the exact spot in the hospital parking lot where he had seen a discarded, stained Band-Aid® 10 years earlier. He was still avoiding the affected area. Characteristically he was able to describe in detail the original stained Band-Aid®, its location, and the position of his own car. An OCD participant in an experiment on memory said that he could recall the 'location of every chair at work (restaurant) that has been contaminated, the type of contaminant involved, a description of the person sitting there and what cleaners were used to remove the contaminant, over the last 5 years' (Radomsky and Rachman 1999, p.614). Another participant said 'I can never seem to find my keys but I can surely tell you where the germs are in my home'. Others will recall the exact spot on a shelf on which a container of pesticides was briefly placed years earlier, and so forth. In these common instances one observes a familiar combination of the non-degradable quality of the contaminant and an enhanced memory. If an item is contaminated and presents an unchanging threat, remembering its location makes good survival sense. The results of an experiment by Radomsky and Rachman (1999) are consistent with clinical observations in showing that people with fears of contamination display superior recall of contaminated objects, relative to anxious participants without this particular fear. The OCD participants with a fear of contamination displayed a superior memory for those items which had been touched by a 'contaminated' cloth in an array of 50 items, half of which were free of contact with the contaminant. The mean recall of contaminated items recorded by the OCD participants was 7.8 and for clean items 4.5. The mean scores for anxiety control participants were 4.8 for contaminated items and 5.3 for clean ones. There were no differences between the groups on standard tests of memory.

Incidentally the clinical observations and experimental findings which indicate superior memory among people with OCD, under specifiable conditions, are difficult to reconcile with the idea that these people suffer from a memory deficit, probably attributable to biological abnormalities (see Clark 2004; Rachman 1998, 2004; Tallis 1997).

The contamination and the memory of the contamination both tend to be non-degradable. The patients require no reminders of what has been contaminated and where it lies festering. Interestingly they all appear to know, without the benefit of curious psychological experiments, that (OCD) contaminants are not degradable, and that is why the location of contaminated items, people and places is worth remembering. No doubt they will be less well-remembered if the person comes to believe that the particular contamination has decayed.

Does OCD contamination ever degrade? Some therapeutic interventions can promote the degradation of the contaminant and a reduction of the fear of the contaminant. The best established method is exposure and response prevention (Abramovitz 1997; Barlow 2002; Clark 2004; Rachman and Hodgson 1980) in which repeated, controlled exposures to the contaminants are followed by steady and progressive reductions in fear. This process is facilitated by ensuring that the patient refrains from cleaning away the contaminants. The reductions in fear are accompanied or followed by a degradation of both the original contaminant and the contamination induced during the exposure sessions. The fear and the associated cleaning compulsions decline. Not infrequently this overall progress is punctuated by partial returns of the fear, especially between sessions. Intra-session habituation of the fear generally exceeds inter-session habituation, especially in the early stages of therapy. (Incidentally providing an excellent opportunity to study the patterns of degradation of feelings of contamination.) It is also known that the fear evoked by the exposures to the contaminant, and the accompanying urges to clean, decline 'spontaneously', if somewhat slowly, even when the patient refrains from the customary post-contact cleaning compulsions. In other words, in a controlled planned series of exposures, the fear induced by contamination will tend to dissipate. The question 'What is the degree of contamination now?', is rarely asked but it is safe to assume that in these therapeutic circumstances the level of contamination does indeed degrade. The behavioural changes observed during fear reduction treatment, especially the decline in avoidance behaviour, strongly suggest that the intensity of the contamination has also diminished.

Given the rapid spread of contamination, its resistance to degradability, and the enhanced memory for threats from contamination, it is not surprising that the phenomenon is so powerful, enduring, and dominating.

The relation between contamination and fear

Thus far no distinction has been made between OCD contamination and the accompanying fear; traditionally the two terms have been used interchangeably. It is however possible to make a distinction, and it is not inconceivable that a reduction in an OCD fear may leave the level of contamination itself unchanged but no longer regarded as a source of danger, and no longer fearful. Although contamination is almost always uncomfortable, even distressing, it is not always frightening. Treatment may detach the fear component from the contaminant. It remains to be determined whether the gradual decline of fear is accompanied, preceded, or followed by a degradation of the contamination.

Patients rarely distinguish between their feelings of contamination and their *fear* of contamination. From their point of view the two are intertwined, and they are in good company with many psychologists on this point. Unfortunately for researchers and therapists, analysis of the phenomena is complicated by using the two terms interchangeably.

A determination of the interactions and differences between feelings of contamination and feeling frightened might throw light on the model set forward here, namely that the prospect of becoming contaminated and therefore harmed, maintains the fear. The prospect of being contaminated can be broken down into the two factors of probability and seriousness: the probability of being contaminated, and secondly, the prospect of sustaining a damaging degree of contamination. It is predicted that during therapeutic exposures the severity factor begins to diminish first and is followed by a decline in the probability factor. The other possibility mentioned above, of a detachment of the fear from the contaminant, seems less likely but may occur in some circumstances. The cognitive mediation of contamination fears may produce detachments ('yes, my hands remain contaminated but I now recognize that it is not dangerous; uncomfortable but not a danger').

As with other types of fears, *contamination fears collapse downwards*. For example, during exposure treatment a reduction of the fear of a contaminated item that is high on the patient's hierarchy is generally followed by a spontaneous (i.e. non-treated) decline in contamination fears lower down in the hierarchy. (A reduction in the high level of contamination of an item at the top end of a hierarchy of contaminants may well collapse the items lower in the hierarchy.) The exceptions to this downward collapse of the fears stem from categorical differences; that is, if the patient believes that the non-treated source of contamination is categorically different from the treated source (e.g. a reduction in the fear of pesticides is most unlikely to generalize to a reduction in the categorically different fear of being contaminated by HIV). In circumstances in which the categorical differences, or the similarities, between contamination fears are of experimental or clinical importance it is prudent to bear in mind that the fearful person's verbal report of the similarities and differences may be misleading. The results of an experiment on people with multiple fears revealed a discrepancy between the participants' appraisals of the similarity of their fears and the results of behavioural tests of the similarities of their various fears (Rachman and Lopatka 1986). Moreover, the respondents' predictions of how the reduction of one of their fears would affect their 'untreated' fear/s were no better than chance. A specific test of the 'accuracy' of patients' subjective appraisals of the similarities and differences between their contamination fears would be useful.

Normal and abnormal feelings of contamination

Not all feelings of contamination are excessive, irrational, and unadaptive. Contamination by contact with disgusting or dangerous material is a common, probably universal experience. However, the sense of contamination does not arise until the person passes through the earliest years of childhood. Young children attempt to touch or even eat matter that is known by everyone else to be dangerous or disgusting. Naturally they are ignorant of possible sources of infection, and the conception of infection. They do not avoid infectious people or materials and display no disgust even in contact with excrement. Further, people are tolerant of their own bodily products (and those of their infants) but are disgusted by those of other people. Contact with the bodily products of other people or animals usually produces feelings of disgust, contamination, and consequent urges to clean oneself. As a rule, people believe that anything which the body excretes must not be allowed to re-enter one's body (Douglas 1966).

Beliefs governing the nature of dangerous/disgusting contacts, how to avoid them and how to remove the unavoided contamination, are prevalent in all societies. Davey (1993) plausibly suggested that reactions of disgust have biological utility and protect people from eating or touching diseased/dangerous substances. Presumably this folk knowledge is used to protect the entire community, for example by proscribing the eating of particular foods or substances. (Some food prohibitions are baffling; for example, a curious distinction is made between acceptable, clean, eatable locusts that hop, and unclean, prohibited, uneatable locusts that crawl; Douglas 1966, p.56). Davey's interesting division of animals into those that evoke fear or revulsion has not been fully confirmed (Woody and Teachman 2000).

In any community the construal of contamination is shaped by cultural and religious beliefs and by the knowledge prevailing in the particular society. In some communities folk beliefs prevail, and in others scientific information is dominant. The beliefs are activated when the person comes into contact with a culturally recognized source of danger. Although some beliefs about pollution appear to be extremely widespread (e.g. regarding excrement), there are many and major cultural differences in the perception of pollution. ('Dirt' is derived from *drit*, borrowed from Old Norse, meaning excrement—Ayto (1990)).

In some communities in India, contact with people of a lower caste is regarded as contaminating and assiduously avoided. If contact nevertheless occurs the affected person has to engage in a ritualized cleansing process. The untouchables are required to avoid contact with people of higher status. Despite the fact that untouchability was legally abolished in India in 1950, according to a Human Rights Watch report in 1999, the beliefs and practices persist. 'Untouchables may not cross the line dividing their part of the village from that occupied by higher castes. They may not use the same wells, visit the same temples, drink from the same cups in tea stalls . . . (and) are relegated to the most menial tasks, as manual scavengers, removers of human waste and dead animals . . .'. Before handling the money they receive from untouchables, merchants from a higher caste clean it in water (Anand 1940). An echo of this practice is encountered in clinics; some patients wash the coins they receive before re-using them. Temples can be polluted if an untouchable person approaches, and Anand described a priest's assertion that if an untouchable person comes within 69 yards of the temple it will become contaminated. A fine number 69. Acts of violence against the degraded and ostracized untouchables are common (Human Rights Watch 1999). Aggressive feelings towards people who are believed to be responsible for polluting one are also encountered among patients.

A traditional form of mental pollution that still occurs among semi-literate people in contemporary Egypt, *kabsa*, was researched and described in considerable detail by Inhorn (1994). The pollution takes place when an impure person enters the room of a vulnerable woman of reproductive age during a period of 'reproductive openness', and is regarded as a major cause of female infertility. *Kabsa* is a 'form of polluting boundary-crossing: a ritually violating entrance into the protective room of the sacredly vulnerable female ritual initiate who is still "open" due to important bodily "entrances"... and "exits" ...external intruders who cross the boundaries of her ritual sanctuary unwittingly "re-violate" her bodily boundaries with the polluting substances that they exude' (Inhorn, 1994, p. 503). The 'intruders' who cause *kabsa* are people (mainly other women) in an impure state, especially those who have been exposed to blood. A range of depolluting methods, including purifying bathing, are attempted to restore the woman to normal reproductiveness. In her analysis Inhorn concludes that they are predominantly attempts to reopen the suspended reproductive processes and that the people or items (e.g. blood) believed to have caused the pollution in the first place, are used in attempting to reverse the pollution. *Kabsa* illustrates several interesting features of mental pollution (feelings of uncleanliness, human agent, no actual contact necessary, sense of violation, cleansing and other neutralizing acts) but differs from clinical cases in that it is socially accepted and the methods of depollution are socially prescribed, whereas the clinical form is personal, unique, and recognized by the affected person and others to be irrational and abnormal.

Douglas (1966), Kroeber (1948) and others have observed that people tend to be vulnerable to pollution during transitional states; they are more easily polluted and/or more easily polluting. Typical transitional states include initiation processes, pregnancy, and menstruation. Clinically there is evidence that women experience an increase in unwanted, intrusive thoughts during the post-partum period, and occasionally these turn into obsessions (usually with unacceptable aggressive themes). In Western societies many of the transitional states involve changes in personal relationships. The possibility of contamination-sensitive *states* is considered in Chapter 6.

Sympathetic magic

Two of the prominent features of contact contamination, easy spread and non-degradability of contaminants, have points of resemblance with sympathetic magic as described in Frazer's monumental book, *The Golden Bough*, published in 1922. Beliefs in magic are derived from causal reasoning of a supernatural or paranormal type, and Frazer extracted two principles of sympathetic magic from his mountain of information. The law of contact, also referred to as the law of contagion, states that 'things which have once been in contact continue ever afterwards to act on each other' (Frazer 1922, p.12), even if all physical contact has been severed. They continue to influence each other even at a distance. Once in contact, always in contact. The influences can be benevolent, but mostly are thought to be malevolent. The continuing contact can threaten harm and the affected person makes attempts to remove all traces of the worrying connection, by washing, purification rituals, and so forth. The resemblance to contamination that never degrades is interesting. The law of contagion may also play a part in the wide spread of contamination. If all or most contacts with contaminated materials or places continue to exert their influence even if further physical contact is avoided, and if the influences can operate at a distance, this will lead to a steady accumulation, a steady increase of items and places that are capable of evoking feelings of contamination. The number of contaminants will expand, and the feelings of contamination spread accordingly. Feelings of visual contamination, common in cases of a fear of morphing, are consistent with the observation that the influence of 'things which have once been in contact' will continue, even at a distance; contamination at a distance no less.

Influence at a distance is also encountered in Frazer's second principle: 'The most familiar expression of contagious magic is the magical sympathy which is supposed to exist between a man and any severed portion of his person—whoever gets possession of human hair or nails may work his will, at any distance, upon the person from whom they were cut' (ibid, p.43). The essence of this law of similarity is that 'like produces like'. Enemies can be harmed at a distance by damaging them in effigy or by damaging their possessions (hair, nails, clothing). By extension, people can harm one even from a distance-as in cases of a fear of morphing.

There is an imitative quality in the law of similarity, and Frazer observed that in sympathetic magic people believe they can produce a desired effect by imitation, as in damaging an enemy by damaging his effigy. Frazer also drew attention to the 'magic sympathy' between a person and his clothes. Interestingly, in many cases, clothes—one's own, or one's enemies—are felt to be common 'carriers' of contamination. Patients go to great lengths to keep separate their contaminated outdoor clothes and their relatively safe indoor clothes. There are many compulsions involved in laboriously washing one's clothes, and the clothes of a person who has harmed or seriously upset one are highly contaminated.

Beliefs about contamination are universal and culturally shaped, and they influence the experience and manifestation of feelings of contamination and their consequences. In their context many of the beliefs about contamination are rational—there are harmful substances and avoidance and cleaning are rational acts. However, beliefs about contamination can become extreme and even abnormal. Importantly, patients who are oppressed by intense, abnormal fears of contamination recognize the presence of irrational reasoning in their construal of the dangerousness and ubiquity of the contaminants. They have little difficulty distinguishing between ordinary contaminants that are universally avoided, and their excessive, irrational fears of contamination.

In communities in which the principles of sympathetic magic prevail, the nature and range of potential contaminants are an accepted part of social and personal life, and in context are adaptive. Manifestations of behaviour that arise from these principles are encountered in all societies, even if they go unrecognized. It is possible that the reasoning which underlies beliefs in sympathetic magic also plays a part in the generation and maintenance of unadaptive and excessive fears of contamination.

The obstacle to exploiting the theoretical connections between Frazer's conceptions of sympathetic magic and fears of contamination is that Frazer's laws lack limits. For example, the number of possible points of similarity between, say, different items (or actions or places or people) is extremely large, but the influence of the law of similarity is relatively limited. 'Like produces like', but *which* likes? The same can be said about the law of contagion, 'once in contact always in contact'. Plainly, not all contacts are subject to the law of contagion, not everything remains in contact with everything else; we lack criteria for setting limits.

What causes a fear of contamination?

As there is no a priori reason to assume that the fear of contamination is fundamentally different from other fears, or is caused by unique factors or circumstances, the question of causation is approached from one of the prevailing theories of the development of human fears, namely the three pathways theory of fear acquisition (Rachman 1978, 1990, 2004). According to this theory, the three pathways consist of conditioning, vicarious acquisition, and the transmission of fear-inducing information.

There is a good deal of laboratory evidence that fears can be the product of conditioning, but there are several reasons for discounting an exclusively conditioning explanation for the development of fear (e.g. the skewed distribution of fears, failures to develop fears despite conditioning trials, failures to develop fears after repeated exposures to aerial bombing, significant fears in the absence of relevant conditioning exposures, etc). The neoconditioning theory, advanced during the past two decades, overcomes some of the objections, but lacks adequate limits—there are few circumstances in which conditioning can be ruled out (Rachman 2004). The revised theory set aside the idea that contiguity between the conditioned and unconditioned stimuli is necessary for the establishment of a conditioned response. People and animals do not learn a 'useless clutter of irrelevant associations' but rather, the 'function of conditioning is to enable organisms to discover the probable causes of events of significance' (Mackintosh 1983, p.172).

During the shift towards cognitive explanations of behaviour and experience it became apparent that the conditioning theory must be expanded to incorporate two additonal pathways to fear: vicarious acquisition by observational learning (Bandura, 1969) and by the transmission of threat-relevant information (e.g. 'the water in your cup is dangerously contaminated!'). Incidentally, companies trying to market water filtration equipment sometimes use alarming information; one advertisement listed 30 obscure, supposedly suspect contaminants that may appear in drinking water.

A powerful illustration of the informational genesis of intense fear is provided by recurrent epidemics of *koro* in S.E. Asia (Rachman 2004). Rumours of an outbreak of *koro*, a fear of male genital shrinkage and impending death, caused thousands of people to panic. One epidemic of *koro* was set off in Singapore by a rumour that the Vietcong had contaminated the food supply.

Each of the pathways can be illustrated by case histories. A highly responsible woman was caring for her infant granddaughter, as promised, despite feeling ill. She had what seemed to be a bad cold (actually flu) and was sneezing and coughing but persisted in carrying out her obligations. Late that night the parents realised that the baby was struggling to breathe and rushed her to emergency. She had such a serious fever and respiratory difficulties that she was admitted to hospital for intensive treatment. The cause of the infant's illlness was medically unclear but the grandmother interpreted it as her fault, feeling that she had transmitted her flu to the child. As a result she developed a strong fear of disease contamination and took to washing repeatedly and intensively with the aid of disinfectants. She became preoccupied with the fear that she was at risk of becoming contaminated and possibly die, and unsurpisingly was terrified of transmitting diseases to her family. Another patient developed a vicarious fear of disgust contamination after witnessing a friend slip and fall into a deep puddle of pig manure during a holiday in the countryside. The friend screamed as she fell into the puddle and after climbing out was filthy and distressed for hours. Shortly after this event the patient became highly sensitive to dirt and began washing vigorously and frequently, especially before leaving his home.

A full account of the present status of the fear-acquisition theory is provided elsewhere (Rachman 2004) and for present purposes three points merit attention. Firstly, a fear of being contaminated by contact with a suspect item can be generated by the transmission of threatening information. Secondly, a fear of contamination assuredly can be generated by observing the frightened reactions of other people to actual or threatened contact with a notorious contaminant. Thirdly, conditioning processes can establish disgust reactions in a manner comparable to conditioned fear reactions. It remains to be seen whether fear and disgust can be simultaneously conditioned. There is no barrier to this possibility.

The interesting question of whether people, some or all of us, are predisposed easily to acquire 'prepared' fears (very likely so) re-emerges now because we are predisposed to react with disgust to aversive/dangerous materials such as putrefying flesh, decaying vegetable matter, foul-smelling water, etc. The fact that young children do not display the expected reactions of disgust does not rule out the possibility of a biologically-based predisposition any more than does the absence of certain fear reactions among the very young rule out the likelihood of prepared phobias. Prepared fears, and presumably 'prepared disgusts' as well, can emerge during early maturation. The marked individual differences in prepared fears may be attributable to learning experiences—probably we learn to overcome our prepared reactions by increasing knowledge and self-efficacy. In a seeming paradox, the more experience one has with a potentially fearsome animal or place, the lower the likelihood of of developing a significant fear. We learn to 'not fear' (Rachman 1978, 1990). A telling demonstration of learning to not-fear was provided by Di Nardo *et al.* (1988) who showed that people with lots of contact with dogs, even if it included some aversive experiences with them, were significantly less likely to have a phobia of dogs than people who had few experiences with dogs. The prospect of immunizing people to feelings of disgust by systematically exposing them to disgusting material can safely be left in the realm of lofty academic speculation.

We have also to consider whether some fears of contamination might arise without any relevant learning experiences. It has been suggested that at least a few fears arise in this manner; they have always been present. Poulton and Menzies (2002) set out the case for some of these 'non-associative' fears (see Craske 2003, for a critical view). Subject to new information it seems preferable at this stage to allow for the possible occurrence of prepared fears of contamination.

The causes of a fear of mental contamination include all three of the pathways to fear, especially the role of negative information, plus some distinctive contributors. The critical features of mental contamination are that the feelings of contamination are evoked by direct or even indirect negative contact with a person, and are evocable by mental events. The contamination can be evoked by criticisms, by violations, by the person's memories, images, dreams, intrusive thoughts. The negative personal events evoke feelings of contamination/pollution which are over-interpreted as indicants of potential disaster. A long chain of mental associations is established which then facilitates the spread of the contamination. For this reason the spread of mental contamination probably exceeds even the remarkable stretch of contact contamination. At this point it begins to appear that the spread of concepts and types of contamination equals that of the phenomenon itself.

The consequences of a fear of contamination

The strength and depth of contamination fears is evident from the wide-ranging consequences which follow the emergence of such fears. The consequences are cognitive, emotional, perceptual, social, and behavioural.

Once the fear is established the affected person construes the world and himself/herself in a changed fashion. The parameters of danger are expanded and the areas of safety are newly constrained. The person becomes highly sensitive to possible threats of contamination and hypervigilance is the result. The person believes that they are specially vulnerable to contamination and its anticipated effects, such as infection or the distress of feeling polluted. It is believed that contact with the personally defined contaminants will cause harm and may well be dangerous as well as distressing.

The elevated and directed hypervigilance is concentrated predominantly on external cues, such as dirty bandages, but includes the scanning for internal cues of contamination, dirt/infection. 'Am I now entirely, certainly, safely clean? Does my body feel absolutely clean?' As with other fears, it gives rise to consistent over-predictions of both the likelihood of experiencing fear and of the intensity of the expected fear (Rachman 2004). 'If I visit my relative in hospital I am certain to feel extremely frightened of becoming contaminated.' It remains to be determined whether the general tendency to over-predict one's fear extends to predictions about the likelihood of becoming contaminated in specifiable situations.

The fear of contamination can lead to intense social anxiety and avoidance. Patients who fear their own bodily pollution (e.g. offensive bowel smells) can become acutely sensitive to the effects of their pollution on other people. Given their beliefs about the pollution, it is not unreasonable for them to dread how people will react to it, and they anticipate rejection. People who are especially sensitive to negative evaluations are likely to particularly vulnerable. Another social threat, seen most strongly among people with an inflated sense of responsibility, is the dread of passing the contamination on to other people and therefore endangering them. In these instances the usual fear and avoidance is accompanied by guilt.

Methods of coping

The fear of being contaminated usually generates such powerful urges that they over-ride other considerations. It temporarily freezes other behaviour. The person tries to avoid touching anything until they have had an opportunity to clean themselves. The attempts to clean oneself, and one's possessions such as vehicles, clothing, are compulsive in that they are: driven by powerful urges, commanding, very hard to resist, repetitive, and recognized by the affected person to be extreme and at least partly irrational. The most common form of compulsive cleaning is repeated handwashing, which typically is meticulous, ritualistic, unchanging, difficult to control, and so thorough that it will be repeated again and again even though it abraids the skin. There are instances in which patients continue washing despite the reddening of the water caused by their bleeding hands. Paradoxically the compulsive washing causes dryness of the skin because it removes natural oils and the person's skin becomes blotchy, dry and cracked, especially between the fingers. If the core fear is that one's health might be endangered by contact with contamination material, it is common to over-use disinfectants, supposedly anti-bacterial soaps, and very hot water. When the fear is associated with a feeling of pollution, the use of hot water and much soap is the order of the day and disinfectants are seldom employed. The details of the methods used to achieve a sense of safety and/or non-pollution provide clues to the nature of the underlying fear.

In addition to the need to remove a present threat of contamination by cleaning it away, compulsive cleaning is carried out in order to prevent the spread of the contamination. 'If I do not clean my hands thoroughly I will spread the contamination throughout the house.' Other attempts to prevent contamination include the use of protective clothing (e.g. gloves, keeping outdoor clothing and indoor clothing separated), using tissues to handle faucets, doorhandles, toilet handles, and taking care to remove sources of potential contamination (e.g. removing pesticides, anti-freeze fluid). In the process of avoiding contamination the person steadily sculpts a secure environment, establishing some sanctuaries. As the number of safe places shrinks, one's own room tends to develop into a personal sanctuary and great care is taken to ensure that it remains uncontaminated. The home as a whole is safe but less safe than one's room because other members of the family do not share the patient's super-sensitivity to contamination and are not as careful about taking precautions. At the other extreme there are highly contaminated places, such as public lavatories, clinics for the care of people with sexually transmitted diseases, and so forth. People are also 'ranked' in terms of their contamination threat, and those high in the ranking are vigorously avoided.

When they feel that they have been contaminated, people clean themselves and also attempt to escape from the source of the contamination. The fear of contamination generates elaborate and vigorous attempts to avoid coming into contact with perceived contaminants. An otherwise well-adjusted woman developed an intense fear of being contaminated by any bodily waste matter, animal or human. She became hypervigilant and avoidant but on one fateful day she woke up to find that a dog had defecated on the lawn directly outside her front door. She was shocked and felt thoroughly contaminated. Repeated showers relieved her not, and within days she dreaded leaving or returning to her house (now using only the back door). The fear became so intense that she sold her house and moved into a rented home in another suburb. As this failed to help her, she decided to move to another city, and forever avoided going anywhere near the city in which the trigger event had occurred; she regarded the entire city as contaminated. This example of extraordinary avoidance also illustrates the rapid and uncontrolled spread of imagined contamination. The example is extreme but not different in form or consequences from other attempts at avoidance. It can take the form of avoiding entire groups of potentially contaminating people, such as the homeless, cancer patients, and so on.

Among people who have an inflated sense of reponsibility, a major factor in many instances of OCD (Salkovskis, 1985), their fear of contamination is manifested in the usual compulsive cleaning but they also devote special efforts to prevent the occurrence or spread of contamination. They are strongly motivated to protect other people from the dangers of contamination and strive to maintain a contamination-free environment. They try to ensure that the kitchen and all eating implements are totally free of germs, dirt, and tainted food. One father insisted on sterilizing his baby daughter's feeding bottles at least ten times before re-use. Affected people try to ensure that their hands are free of contamination before touching other people or their possessions. If they feel that they have not been sufficiently careful, anxiety and guilt arise. They try to recruit the cooperation of relatives and friends in preventing and avoiding contamination, but rarely succeed in persuading adults to comply with their excessive and irrational requests.

People who feel that their cleaning and avoidance behaviour have not ruled out the threat from contamination resort to neutralizing behaviour and/or a compulsive search for reassurance. In cases of contact contamination, the main form of neutralizing—cleaning—is overt; the internal neutralizing that is prominent in other types of OCD, is used infrequently, presumably because it is thought to be ineffective in removing the contaminant.

Coping with a fear of mental contamination presents some problems. The content and intensity of the fear can be changeable and puzzling because of the obscurity of the contaminants. What is provoking the feelings and how does the contamination come about without touching dirt or germs? Repeated cleaning is at best only partly effective and therefore the patients resort to other means of neutralizing their feelings and fears. These methods take the form of internal neutralizing, and include counting, praying, and repetitious phrases. Repeated requests for reassurance are common and can be as intense and insistent as in other types of OCD. If the fundamental fear is of a threat to one's health because of contamination, attempts to obtain reassurance, especially from doctors, are common but as transiently relieving as in cases of health anxiety. In some cases of mental contamination, attempts to cleanse one's mind are added to the familiar methods of escape and avoidance. This occurs commonly in instances of self-contamination.

In sum, there are multiple consequences of contamination fear—cognitive, perceptual, emotional, social, and behavioural—and they serve to remind us of the complexity and ramifications of what might at first sight appear to be merely another fear to add to the catalogue. The methods of coping are attempts to maintain safety or to regain safety. The fear of contamination can become so powerful that it dominates the person's life.

Spiritual cleansing and plain hygiene

The anthropological literature is replete with descriptions of cleaning rituals that fulfil symbolic rather than hygienic needs (Kroeber 1948), and the distinction between spiritual cleansing and plain cleaning is evident, for example, among Hindus who achieve spiritual cleanliness while washing themselves in heavily polluted rivers. In a case of severe OCD the patient washed her hands up to 50 times per day, using hot water and antiseptics, but was relatively unconcerned about the dirt that was evident on other parts of her body and clothing. Her compulsive cleaning no longer served a useful hygienic purpose but had taken on some elusive superordinate symbolic meaning.

The sheer repetitiveness and futility of compulsive washing raises the possibility that affected patients may be confusing symbolic cleansing and hygienic cleaning. There are some superficial similarities between compulsive cleaning rituals and spiritual cleansing—stereotypy, repetitiveness—that contribute to the confusion, but the differences between the two are of greater importance. Unlike social cleansing rituals, compulsive cleaning is personally driven, intended to serve a different and unique purpose, and aimed at preventing misfortune rather than promoting a desired event or spiritual state.

In light of the attention now turned towards mental contamination it is worth considering whether patients who are afflicted with mental contamination might be engaged in compulsions that resemble symbolic cleansing more closely than hygienic cleaning, most notably in mental cleansing. If this is correct, therapeutic implications follow: in cases of mental contamination the cognitive analysis should include a search for the (ahygienic) significance of any compulsive washing. The significance probably varies from subtype to subtype, with cases of self-contamination the most accessible. In these cases the symbolic significance of the washing should be easier to fathom. Cases of mental contamination generated by psychological violations are more complex.

Cultural attitudes to hygienic cleaning vary across times and places, and Kroeber (1948) quotes some amusing historical examples. Although the early Romans were enthusiastic about bodily cleanliness, the early Christians 'felt themselves... in conflict not only with the established pagan religion but with many of its attitudes and trends', and baths were part of this unacceptable culture. They considered 'over-cleanliness, and what we would consider minimum cleanliness... to be one of the roads to ruin' (Kroeber, p.600). For periods in European history, people washed little and regarded bathing as dangerous to health. This point of view is encountered among young boys.

Purification and mental cleansing

As feelings of mental pollution often have a moral element, and because theologians recognized mental pollution hundreds of years ago and are the experts in this domain, it is worthwhile considering how they construe it. When pollution occurs after physical contact with an impure place/material/person, the religious advice or requirement is that the person carries out a ritualistic cleansing—of one's body, and secondarily of one's possessions and surroundings. The similarities between prescribed religious cleansing of one's body and possessions, and certain clinical manifestations of compulsive washing and cleaning, led some clinicians to introduce the term 'ritualistic' into their descriptions of compulsive activities, especially washing. It can be objected that this transposition blurs the differences in purpose, form, and observable content of the two types of cleaning activities, but the term is encountered. More interesting is the question of what psychologists can learn from theology about dealing with mental and moral pollution, in which no physical contact with a contaminant has taken place.

The religious tactics to overcome or at least subdue the feelings of mental pollution include prayers, pardons, offerings, resolutions, disclosures, compensations, acts of charity, acts of service, confessions, renunciation, inhibition, exorcism, and repentance. This list is not immediately familiar to clinicians.

The tactics include a range of preventive measures such as the avoidance of polluted places or people, and the establishment and protection of places of safety and sanctity. The sanctuary is clean, safe, calming, ordered, hushed, and tranquil. The sanctuaries have to be kept clean of contamination—impure people or objects are strictly excluded. This is understood by enemies who take pleasure in defiling the sanctuaries during periods of conflict. Defilement in turn produces an angry reaction.

Religious tactics fall into three categories: putting matters right (similar to the psychological concept of neutralizing), making compensation, and preventing recurrences. For those people whose feelings of contamination/ pollution are the result, at least in some measure, of their own thoughts or actions, the advice pertaining to putting matters right—by cleaning, disclosures, inhibition, suppression, prayer—is worth considering. One method of putting matters right is to cleanse one's mind. Patients appear to concentrate on substituting acceptable, moral thoughts for the polluting ones. If that fails, special prayers are said in order to gain strength and support for cleansing the mind. If that too is ineffective, for some prayers are discoloured by blasphemy, patients tend to become resigned and feel that the best they can do is make compensation in other ways, by service, or charities, or scrupulosity.

Patients with OCD sometimes explain the need for a rigidly unvarying form of cleaning by saying that it removes the indecisiveness that troubles them and also provides an end-point in their cleaning; 'Otherwise, how would I know when I have done sufficient cleaning?' Sadly, attempts to clean away feelings of mental contamination by washing are rarely sufficient, even when conducted in a rigidly unvarying manner. Disclosures of a carefully planned kind can be helpful, as in the treatment of obsessions (Rachman 2003). The rationale for these disclosures is that by concealing their obsessions, the patients prevent themselves from collecting the usually sympathetic reactions, information, advice, and support of friends and family. Instead they continue to catastrophically over-estimate how others will react to them; 'If people knew my repugnant thoughts they would recoil from me, reject me, avoid me'. Advice to suppress the intrusive thoughts can produce a paradoxical increase in their frequency, and the failure of attempts at deliberate inhibition is evident from the existence of the clinical problem. If the attempted inhibition succeeds, the problem can perhaps be averted. Prayers can be a source of comfort and strength but their therapeutic value in overcoming feelings of contamination or mental pollution is not known.

Are any of the spiritual methods of purification likely to be helpful for patients struggling to carry out a mental cleansing? Purification and mental cleansing are resorted to when attempting to relieve distress, but spiritual purification has wider uses than mental cleansing. It is carried out in a prescribed, regular, routine manner in preparation for and during religious ceremonies, often involves religious figures, is usually carried out in a public, sanctified place, plays a prominent part in rites of passage or other transitional states, and is used by individuals to reduce guilt and/or remove feelings of contamination. The mental cleansing that patients resort to when they feel mentally contaminated is a private response to an event, and the cleansing is both personal and personally developed, usually by trial and error. Like some of the religious rituals it is an attempt to clean away contamination, feelings of pollution, and guilt. Despite some common aims however, there is no obvious way successfully to absorb tactics for achieving spiritual cleansing into clinical tactics for helping patients to cope with their distressing feelings of mental pollution and contamination. The main obstacle is that spiritual cleansing is a well-established, socially supported or prescribed, publicly advocated method of purification, open to all. The patients attempts at mental cleansing are private, personal to them, not exchangeable, often shameful and concealed, unknown to others, and not supported by custom, teachings or spiritual leaders. It is a private struggle.

When more is learnt about the psychological nature of individual attempts at mental cleansing, and how to promote and facilitate it for therapeutic purposes, most obviously in cases of OCD involving feelings of mental contamination, the dissemination of the knowledge by and to friends, families, and public agencies will make a helpful contribution to the well-being of private sufferers.

Chapter 6

Illusions of vulnerability

One of the most important advances in health psychology was the identification of a prevailing illusion of invulnerability to health threats. Most people function as if they are at a lower risk of health misfortunes or catastrophes than other people. For example, if they rate the risk of a person like themselves having a 10 per cent risk of a significant stomach ailment over the next ten years, they give themselves a rating of say 2 per cent. They assume that they are less vulnerable than other people to health problems. In her account of these positive illusions, which she described as 'adaptive fiction illusions' Taylor (1989), classified them into three categories: self-enhancement, exaggerated sense of personal control, and unrealistic optimism (about one's health and well-being). Of course specific questions about contamination and mental contamination were not asked at the time, but given the wide prevalence of unrealistic optimism, it is highly probable that most respondents would have rated their chances of becoming significantly contaminated as unrealistically low. They would have expressed a degree of personal invulnerability, relative to other, comparable people.

The illusion of *vulnerability to contamination* is opposite to the general illusion of *in*-vulnerability to illnesses. With a few exceptions, the belief that one has a special personal vulnerability to the harmful effects of contamination has no rational basis. Moreover, the affected person believes that that only a small minority, of which they are a member, is at elevated risk. 'Other people will not contract AIDS from using a public telephone but for me the risk is extremely high.' This belief in one's unique and elevated vulnerability is not shared by other people, who recognize its exaggerated quality.

The illusion of elevated personal vulnerability has several components. The first is an extreme over-estimation of the probability that contact with a perceived contaminant will produce harmful effects for me. The second component, an extreme over-estimation of the seriousness of the consequences of the contamination, is contributory to the fear. An extreme over-estimation of the ease of transmission of contamination to one's self or others is contributory to the degree and extent of the fear.

In calm moments the affected person recognizes the irrationality of the beliefs, but in not so calm moments, particularly when exposed to a perceived contaminant, the intensity of the belief is powerful and the level of conviction in the belief approaches maximum. Beliefs in one's unique vulnerability to harmful contamination are not ordinarily responsive to contradictory evidence, and hence they are inclined to persist and may even become permanent.

The power and persistence of beliefs about one's unique vulnerability were particularly evident in a patient whose irrational fear of being contaminated by the HIV virus was so strong that when he was admitted to hospital for an emergency operation, which he acknowledged was essential, he tried to prevent the the staff from touching him or using any instruments on him.

Abnormal beliefs and feelings about contamination can reach delusional levels. They often have a bizarre quality, are impervious to contradictory evidence, and tend towards permanence. Some clinical examples include: a belief that one is vulnerable to contamination from contagious 'mind germs', or from the sight of physically handicapped people, or can develop gangrene from touching any patients in hospital. In these cases, as in others, the bizarreness of the belief is all the more remarkable because many of the people holding such beliefs are well-educated and acknowledge that their beliefs are strange and restricted to themselves.

These beliefs predispose the person to the acquisition of fears of contamination. A comprehensive account of how these beliefs are formed and consolidated is not yet available, but numbers of patients describe extraordinary parental beliefs and practices that must have sensitized them to the pervasiveness of danger. 'The world is full of dangers', 'Pollution and disease inhabit the world', 'All public facilities are cesspits', 'Godliness is second only to cleanliness', 'I must wash all of your toys in lysol repeatedly'.

Clinicians are well aware of the difficulties involved in trying to determine whether intensely held abnormal beliefs are delusional or not (Chadwick and Lowe 1990). There is no simple divider and the tendency is to base one's assessment on the presence and intensity of a few criteria: uniqueness, bizarre qualities, resistance to disconfirmatory evidence. From a clinician's point of view it is the last-named quality that presents the greatest obstacle to treatment. In tackling a patient's delusional beliefs about contamination and contaminants some guidance can be obtained from the gradual, encouraging progress made by clinical researchers who are using psychological methods to reduce the abnormal beliefs and cognitions of patients with psychotic disorders (Chadwick and Lowe 1990; Garety et al., 1994; Tarrier et al., 1993, among others).

Sensitivity to contamination

The common co-occurrence of contact and mental contamination raises the possibility of a broad sensitivity to contamination, and presumably there are identifiable individual differences in such sensitivity. In considering the idea of a general sensitivity to feelings of contamination/pollution, the research on apparently comparable sensitivities to anxiety (Taylor 1999) to disgust (Haidt *et al.* 1994), and to pain, are useful guides. Scales for assessing anxiety sensitivity and disgust sensitivity are widely used, and the coherence of the constructs has been confirmed by statistical analyses. The constructs are measurable, show the expected continuum of individual differences, and have acceptable validity. None of this is an enthusiastic call for the introduction of one more scale, to measure sensitivity to contamination, but it is unavoidable. At a minimum a statistical investigation of the two divisions of contamination is necessary (see Appendix). Is it possible to distinguish between mental contamination and contact contamination, can the common elements be teased out, what is the extent of their correlation, do they show different degrees of correlation with other scales/variables (e.g. anxiety sensitivity, disgust sensitivity, depression, social anxiety, responsibility, obsessions, cleaning complusions)?

There are some indications of an association between contamination and sensitivity. The report by Ware *et al.* (1994) of a significant correlation (0.34) between disgust sensitivity and the washing subscale of the MOCI was an encouraging first step, especially as disgust did not correlate with the other subscales of the MOCI (e.g. checking). On similar lines, Sawchuk *et al.* (2000) found a correlation of 0.49 between disgust sensitivity and the contamination subscale of the revised MOCI scale, the VOCI. The next step is the investigation of the associations betweeen the two divisions of contamination, contact and mental, and anxiety/disgust sensitivity. It is to be expected that the correlation between contact contamination and anxiety sensitivity will be larger than the correlation with disgust sensitivity. Mental contamination probably correlates with both tests of sensitivity, but to a slightly higher extent with disgust than with anxiety sensitivity. The hypothesis is that the two divisions of contamination share a common element—sensitivity. It is deduced that the sensitivity to contamination is related to other types of sensitivity, beginning with anxiety sensitivity and disgust sensitivity, and this prediction is under investigation using the research scale for assessing sensitivity to contamination that is reproduced in the Appendix.

The idea that there is a general sensitivity to feelings of contamination is plausible but presents an interesting problem. If the propensity is *general* how do we explain the lop-sided association between contact contamination and mental contamination? There is more contact contamination in cases of mental contamination than instances of mental contamination in cases of contact contamination. It might be argued that if contamination sensitivity is a general quality then the co-occurrence of the two divisions of contamination should be equal rather than lop-sided. The postulated sensitivity to feelings of contamination cannot be the sole predisposing factor. Particular life experiences and cognitions are bound to play a part as well.

The common cognitive factor across contaminations appears to be a threat to one's well-being and/or health arising from contact with a tangible contaminant, or by association with specifiable mental contaminants. In contact contamination the threats are predominantly physical, especially pertaining to one's health. In instances of mental contamination there are additional threats to one's sanity, self-esteem, and social acceptability.

It is to be expected that differences in responsibility will be found, with greater concerns expressed by people experiencing contact contamination in comparison to mental contaminators. The people who are prone to feelings of mental contamination will feel less responsible for others because they believe that they are uniquely vulnerable to the source of their (non-physical) contamination, and correspondingly that they are less likely to spread their particular contamination to other people. For example, people who feel polluted by their vile blasphemous thoughts do not believe, nor *behave* as if they believe, that their pollution is transmissable to others.

Another difference between mental contamination and contact contamination is encountered in the reaction to social criticism, humiliation, or social distress. In cases of mental contamination the duration and intensity of a period of compulsive cleaning tends to be prolonged by social distress, and occasionally is even triggered by such distress. In cases of contact contamination the purpose is to remove the tangible threat to one's health/well-being. Disturbances of mood may prolong the cleaning, not because of the inaccessibility of the contaminant but because the person feels dissatisfied with the quality of their cleaning (e.g. too upset to concentrate well enough). The site of the contaminant is known and usually the affected person is able to decide when it has been removed. The site and the nature of the contaminant are relatively independent of social distress— e.g. 'the lavatory that I used during my visit to the hospital may have been infected, and regardless of my prevailing mood, it is essential that I completely and safely clean myself'. Periods of compulsive cleaning associated with mental pollution/contamination are more influenced by mood and mental state, than are the periods of cleaning that are intended to safeguard oneself from physical harm or remove tangible dirt.

In clinical work the co-occurrence of contact contamination and mental contamination can lead to confusion when trying to determine whether a patient who dreads touching diseased or dirty items is also experiencing mental contamination/pollution. They are not mutually exclusive. In order to facilitate the analysis the Structured Interview Schedule can be used (see Appendix).

Contamination-sensitive states

There is anthropological evidence of beliefs in the existence of contamination-sensitive *states*, and there are indications that people who hold these beliefs are indeed more likely to develop feelings of contamination during unusual states. It is worth considering the possibility that in cases of abnormal fears of contamination, there are two types of sensitivity to contamination, probably correlated but with independent properties. The first possibility, discussed above, is that people vary in their sensitivity to acquiring feelings of contamination and also in their perceived vulnerability to acquiring the associated fears of contamination. This sensitivity to contamination is assumed to have stable properties and to be an amalgam of constitutional and environmental factors. It is akin to a *trait*.

It is also possible that there is a second, less stable, episodic type of *state* sensitivity. In particular states a person is at elevated risk of acquiring feelings of contamination, and of acquiring the associated fears. (There might be an opposite state in which the the likelihood of acquiring a feeling of contamination is minimised, but that is of less interest at present.) The anthropological example of *kabsa* is an example of the belief in contamination-vulnerable states. Nubile young women in a transitional state are believed to be at risk of reproductive failure if they are contaminated by contact, direct or indirect, with impure people or objects (Inhorn 1994). If contact takes during this period the woman feels contaminated and has to carry out elaborate cleansing rituals. This is an excellent example of the causal interplay between a belief about contamination and the occurrence of feelings of contamination. Something similar is at play in clinical instances of contamination—beliefs about contamination and contaminants predispose people to develop these feelings, and the associated fears. Of course the beliefs governing *kabsa* contamination are socially supported and the preventive and cleansing behaviour are prescribed. Clinical contamination is personal, unique, irrational, and regarded by others as abnormal. Nevertheless the identification of socially recognized *states* of elevated sensitivity to contamination, as in *kabsa*, is important.

From a clinical point of view, postulating the existence of elevated states of sensitivity contamination is appealing. It might help to make sense of those cases in which strong feelings of contamination erupt suddenly. Not infrequently they erupt fullblown, and many neutral cues are immediately converted into contaminants. It might also help to make sense of those occasions in which disproportionately strong feelings of contamination are evoked by relatively mild contaminants, by cues that ordinarily produce minimal contamination. There is no shortage of clinical examples of sudden, rapid onsets and disproportionately strong reactions. There are several circumstances in which particular states might predispose a vulnerable person to sudden, rapid onsets, or exacerbations. In light of the anthropological evidence of heightened sensitivity to pollution during states of transition, attention should be paid to psychological transition states.

Given the connections between OCD problems and depression, patients who have a general sensitivity to contamination may be at an elevated risk of becoming contaminated during states of low mood or frank depression. In the state of shock that occurs after many instances of trauma, the victim might be in a state of elevated risk for feelings of contamination, and here the cases of PTSD and OCD described by de Silva and Marks (1999) are relevant. In their series, the two patients who had been raped developed feelings of contamination but those who had been the victims of robbery or accidents did not. The high rate of mental pollution reported by victims of sexual assault (Fairbrother and Rachman 2004) suggests that after a sexual assault, in addition to the polluting violation, the victims might be especially sensitive to the development of feelings of contamination Non-violent instances of psychological violation, particularly those which span a long period of time, are more likely to engender a stable, trait-like sensitivity to contamination rather than sensitive states. During unusual mental states, such as those associated with street drugs, the person's sensitivity to contamination can be elevated. Over and above these contributors to contamination sensitivity, significant cultural beliefs and practices can easily induce states of high sensitivity to contamination (e.g. during religious rituals, during important religious meals, and so on).

The interaction between contamination-sensitivity and periods of heightened vulnerability to contamination remains to be examined in depth.

Irrational over-estimations of contamination

With the exception of health professionals, accurate and authoritative information about the threats from invisible germs and viruses is not easily available, notwithstanding the internet, and prevailing uncertainty about the dangers can lead to considerable over-estimations of the probability and seriousness of the contamination. Patients consistently overestimate the danger of touching or even approaching a wide range of harmless substances and places. Theirs is a dangerous world.

The correlation between overestimations of threat and OCD in general, was confirmed in a report from the large international study being conducted by the Obsessive Compulsive Cognitions Working Group (OCCWG 2003). The Working Group developed two major instruments for assessing the cognitions—The Obsessional Beliefs Questionnaire (OBQ) and the Interpretation of Intrusions Inventory (III)—and have been and are collecting data from many parts of the world (Frost and Steketee 2002; OCCWG 2003). The two scales have reasonable psychometric properties and are clinically valid, but are too closely correlated, and not sufficiently distinct from other clinical phenomena such as depression. Among other interesting and useful findings, they showed that overestimations of threat correlated with total scores on the Padua OCD scale (0.55), and with scores on the self-report version of the YBOCS (0.40). The 248 patients with OCD returned a mean score of 54.1 on the overestimation of threat scale, significantly higher than the means of the two non-clinical groups (20.5 and 10.7 respectively). However, the anxious control group mean of 50.2 was not significantly different from that of the OCD patients. The overestimation of threat is not specific to OCD. This is understandable but is a reminder of the need to move from general to specific hypotheses. Given that OCD and anxious patients both overestimate threats, how do we account for the different clinical manifestations of these over-estimations?

In addition to the basic overestimations of probability and seriousness, some specific and notably irrational thoughts and expectations are woven into the fear of contamination. Even health professionals are not invulnerable to these fears, and most patients do recognize in calm moments that their fear is baseless. They also recognize some of the inevitable inconsistencies in their fear. Even those patients who seal away the dreaded contaminants in 'that' room are embarrassed by their behaviour, and concede that many of the sequestrated items cannot still be contaminated. They recognize some degradability but maintain a belief that most of their contaminants are affected for ever, regardless of the opinions of others, and regardless of the approach behaviour of others. The contamination is perceived as non-degradable.

The Working Group divided the cognitions into two types, beliefs and interpretations. Belief is acceptance of the truth of a proposition, or in psychometrics, the endorsement of a proposition; it goes beyond observation of a true fact. For present purposes, 'belief' refers to the endorsement of a truth proposition. In the Obsessional Beliefs Questionnaire (OBQ), these two examples are belief propositions: 'There is only one right way to do things',

'I believe that the world is a dangerous place'. Regrettably however, a number of items in the Beliefs scale involve interpretations. For example: Item 76 is, 'Having violent thoughts means I will lose control and become violent', Item 64 is, 'Having bad thoughts means I am weird or abnormal', and Item 51 is, 'If I don't do as well as other people, that means I am an inferior person'. All of the items that ask the respondent to say what the statement *means* for them, are interpretive. Other items are also interpretive even though they do not explicitly ask the respondent to say what the statement means for them. The unfortunate wording of some items is evident in the similarity of questions in the OBQ and in the Interpretation of Intrusions Inventory (III). Item 2 of the III is, ' Having this unwanted thought means that I will act on it'. Item 22 is 'Having this thought means I am weird or abnormal' (very similar to Item 64 on the Beliefs Scale). The second scale, the III, which addresses interpretations of intrusions, is consistent and most of the items directly solicit interpretations—*means* appears in many of the propositions. A number of the items are presented as assertions but they do go beyond observations and imply interpretations.

The Working Group recognized the difficulty of making a 'distinction between beliefs and appraisals' (OCCWG 2003, p.875), but notwithstanding, the beliefs were regarded as 'enduring trait-like conceptions'...and the 'appraisals on the other hand, are thought to reflect the immediate, situational cognitive processing of specific intrusions' (p.875). Unfortunately however, the III interpretive scale turned out to be highly *stable*, with retest correlations that ranged between 0.69 and 0.77, and mostly exceeded the retest correlations of the putatively trait-like OBQ scales.

The assumption that OCD appraisals/interpretations are episodic and restricted to immediate, situational circumstances, is difficult to sustain, and not in keeping with cognitive theories of anxiety disorders e.g. Clark's theory of panic causation (1986), the theory of obsessions, (Rachman 1997, 1998) etc. These and like theories assume that the tendency to seriously misinterpret specifiable events is enduring, and the aim of treatment is to put an end to it. Moreover, it is not only the tendency to misinterpret that is stable—specific misinterpretations are also stable.

The difficulty in separating beliefs and interpretations is also evident in the factor structure of the III scale. All three factors of the III—Responsibility, Control of Thoughts, Importance of Thoughts—also appear as factors in the OBQ beliefs scale. Furthermore, the factors from the two scales are highly correlated. For example, the Control of Thoughts factor in the OBQ correlates 0.70 with the Control of Thoughts factor in the III. This repetitiveness leads one to question the value of attempting to separate the beliefs and interpretations into two scales as the same factors occur in both.

The inability to come up with scales that distinguish between obsessional beliefs and the interpretation of intrusions is disappointing, but provides an opportunity for considering the aims and achievements of the project. The primary purpose, to collect important information about the cognitions involved in OCD, was very well-chosen and the major factors in the two scales have been identified.

The high correlation between the scales can be reduced somewhat by re-writing items in the OBQ to ensure that they are truth propositions and exclude all suggestions of interpretation, but the other problems, such as the contrast between trait-like beliefs and episodic interpretations, and the repetitive factors, remain. An alternative would be to forego attempts to separate out the two types of cognition on the grounds that it is impractical and perhaps misguided. Some propositions inevitably are a mixture of belief and interpretation. Moreover, in the matter of thought–action fusion for example, the very concept incorporates belief and interpretation, and little would be gained by trying to prise apart the two elements. It is of some academic interest certainly, but the clinical implications are not obvious, and it might be preferable instead to develop a single scale for measuring OCD *cognitions*. Among other advantages the preparation of a single scale would simplify the factor structure, leaving only one factor of say, Responsibility, that would incorporate beliefs and intepretations. The clinical advantages of separating beliefs and interpretations are not evident at present.

Beliefs about contamination

Prior to the growth of cognitive clinical psychology, the assessment of patients' beliefs and cognitions about their disorder was an undistinguished part of the assessment process. The purpose of the assessment was to collect information that would enable the therapist to form a plan for treatment, and as the available treatments were essentially behavioural, the focus was behavioural. Three types of information were collected: responses to specialized tests such as the Maudsley Obsessional Compulsive Inventory (MOCI), the patient's account during interviews, and planned observations of the patient's behaviour, notably behavioural avoidance tests. Information about the patient's beliefs and cognitions was gathered, but in an incidental manner. The infusion of cognitive concepts gained momentum in the 1980s and inevitably led to the need for improved, focused methods of assessing the newly promoted cognitions. As part of the shift towards cognitions, the *content* of the patient's fears and beliefs became critically important.

The progress accomplished is relevant and helpful for the present analysis of the fear of contamination, but understandably limited because the scales address OCD in general, not contamination specifically, and it all rests on the familiar 'ordinary' type of contact contamination. Nonetheless, it is possible to combine clinical observations of contamination with findings extrapolated from the OCCWG research to compile an account of cognitions involved in all forms of contamination, including mental contamination.

Insofar as the OCCWG scales incorporate information about contamination, it is based on contact contamination, and therefore the present compilation had to be extended to include mental contamination. Four compilations of beliefs and appraisals were constructed, to cover contact contamination, mental contamination, self-contamination, and morphing. The two manifestations of contamination that follow episodes/periods of violation are embedded in the compilation of cognitions pertaining to mental contamination. In the Treatment section, Chapter 10, shortened lists of 'personalized' versions of the cognitons, comprising beliefs and appraisals, are included as an aid to therapy.

The OCCWG Beliefs scale encompasses six 'domains': inflated responsibility, intolerance of uncertainty, overestimation of threat, over-importance of thoughts, importance of controlling thoughts, and perfectionism. The domains that seem most relevant for contamination are the overestimation of threats of contagion (especially in cases of contact contamination) and the exaggerated or unadaptive significance attached to one's cognitions about contamination and its effects. Extrapolating to the different manifestations of *mental* contamination, this is how the six (OCCWG) domains may be relevant. The overestimation of threats is especially relevant in cases of mental contamination that arise from psychological or physical violations, and in cases of a fear of morphing. The over-importance attached to one's thoughts and to controlling them is most relevant in cases of self-contamination, mental pollution and morphing. Inflated responsibility comes into contact-contamination and self-contamination, but not morphing. Perfectionism may play a part in self-contamination and mental pollution.

Beliefs and appraisals concerning contact contamination

+ To avoid illness I must always handle garbage and garbage bins very carefully
+ I wash my hands after handling money because it is so dirty
+ I am sure to pick up a sickness whenever I travel
+ I avoid public telephones because they are sources of contamination
+ I worry that I might pick up contamination that will affect my health years from now

- Once contaminated, always contaminated—it doesn't go away
- Daily use of a cell-phone (mobile) is definitely harmful
- If I get sick, I must make absolutely sure that I never pass it on to other people
- Some types of contamination can cause mental instability
- I pick up infections very easily
- It is important for me to keep up to date with the latest information about germs and diseases
- I never ever feel properly clean, all over
- To be safe it is essential for me to wash my hands very thoroughly and frequently
- I am allergic to almost all chemicals
- I worry that if I get sick, I won't be able to cope
- I need to be very careful to keep away from people with an obvious cold
- If I eat food that is past the due date, my stomach will get seriously upset
- To keep safe from germs it is essential to use powerful disinfectants
- When I get an illness it takes me a very long time to recover
- One can pick up sicknesses on buses because they are very dirty
- Contamination never fades away
- When I get sick, I get really sick
- For reasons of safety it is essential for me to keep everything very clean
- It is safest to avoid touching animals because they are are sources of contamination
- If I thought that I had passed my sickness on to others, it would make me extremely upset
- I am much more sensitive to pollutants than most other people
- Any contact with bodily fluids (blood, saliva, sweat) can lead to infections
- To be safe I try to avoid using public toilets because they are highly contaminated
- If there is any sickness around I am sure to pick it up
- I am highly sensitive to radiation from microwave ovens
- Unless I am careful to wash thoroughly I may become ill

Beliefs and appraisals concerning mental contamination

- Many things look clean but feel dirty
- People should be pure in mind and in body
- Some people think I am weird because I am a clean freak
- When people are under stress, they are far more sensitive to feelings of being contaminated

- I must always avoid people with low morals
- Before leaving home, I need to to make sure that I am absolutely clean
- If I think about contamination, it will increase my risk of actually becoming contaminated
- Seeing disgusting pornographic material would make me feel sick, dirty
- If I touched the possessions or clothing of someone who had treated me very badly, I would need to have a good wash
- People who do something immoral will be punished
- Sometimes I have a need to wash even though I know that I haven't touched anything dirty/dangerous
- If I was touched by someone who had treated me very badly, it would make me feel unclean
- People who read pornography must be avoided
- On returning home after work it is essential to change one's clothing
- Mixing with immoral people would definitely make me feel unclean
- I will never be forgiven for my horrible thoughts
- If I am touched by a nasty or immoral person, it makes me feel very unclean
- It is quite possible to feel contaminated even without touching any contaminated material
- It is immoral for me to use bad language at any time
- Simply thinking about contamination can make me feel actually contaminated
- No matter how hard I try with my washing, I never feel completely clean
- If I cannot control my nasty thoughts I will go crazy
- Simply remembering a contamination experience can make me feel actually contaminated
- It is completely wrong for me to tell dirty jokes
- When I am in a low mood, I am far more sensitive to feelings of being contaminated
- I will never get rid of the feeling that I am unclean, dirty
- I definitely avoid movies that contain foul language and explicit sex scenes
- I have a hard time getting rid of the feeling that I am unclean
- People think I am weird because of my worries about dirt and diseases
- When I feel bad about myself, having a shower makes me feel better
- I fear that one day I will completely lose control
- Having to listen to someone making disgusting, nasty remarks makes me feel tainted, dirty
- People will reject me if they find out about my nasty thoughts
- If a nasty, immoral person touched me I would have to wash myself thoroughly

- I completely avoid anyone who uses bad language
- If I do not overcome my feelings of dirtiness, I will become sick
- If I did something immoral it would make me feel unclean
- If I was touched by someone who behaved badly, I would need to wash myself
- People who use disgusting language make me feel dirty, tainted
- If I was touched by someone showing off disgusting pornographic pictures I would need to wash myself

Beliefs and appraisals concerning self-contamination

- I believe it is important to be clean in body and in mind
- Having bad, unacceptable thoughts means that part of me is immoral
- It is very difficult for me to block unacceptable nasty thoughts
- If other people knew about my repugnant thoughts and urges they would regard me as evil, wicked
- Unacceptable aggressive thoughts are always unworthy and unkind
- In trying to deal with unwanted and unacceptable sexual thoughts it really helps to have a good wash
- It is wrong for me to have unwanted unacceptable thoughts or impulses
- An unwanted objectionable thought is as bad as an objectionable deed
- My unwanted unacceptable thoughts mean that there is something wrong with my character
- When I am under stress, I am far more sensitive to feelings of being contaminated
- If other people knew about some of my nasty habits they would reject me as evil
- I feel tainted or dirty if I have a disgusting dream
- Is it important for me to keep my repugnant thoughts secret from other people
- It is important for me to control my thoughts better
- I must always keep my mind clean
- Unacceptable sexual thoughts or impulses will make me feel unclean
- I believe that having a good wash helps to get rid of nasty unwanted thoughts
- When I am in a low mood, I am far more sensitive to feelings of being contaminated
- Having unwanted unacceptable thoughts or impulses means that I might lose control of myself one day
- If I have a truly disgusting thought it makes me feel tainted

- I must try harder to control my thoughts
- I must never ever have disgusting thoughts or impulses
- Having repugnant thoughts makes me feel like a bad, wicked person

Beliefs and appraisals concerning a fear of morphing

- It is best to avoid staring at people who look weird
- I am too easily influenced by some people who behave badly
- It is easy to pick up germs from mentally unstable people
- Quite a few people think that I am weak-minded and ineffective
- My own identity might be affected if I spend too much time with mentally unstable people
- It is best to wash very carefully if you touch the possessions or clothing of a weird person
- I often think that I have a weak personality
- It is best to avoid coming close to people who look mentally unstable
- My own identity might be affected if I spend too much time with weird people
- I worry that someday I will have a breakdown and be completely unable to cope
- It is best to avoid touching a person who seems to be mentally unstable
- Coming close to a weird person makes me feel unclean even if I don't actually touch the person
- Mentally unstable people can influence me without my knowledge
- It is best to avoid touching a weird person
- Some forms of mental instability are contagious and can be picked up by contact
- I am very easily influenced by other people
- Staring at a nearby person who appears to be mentally unstable can make me feel unclean
- Weird people can influence me without my knowledge
- It is best to avoid coming close to people who look weird
- At times I worry that my fears about weird, shabby people might give me a breakdown
- It is best to avoid staring at people who appear to be mentally unstable
- It is best to wash very thoroughly if you touch the possessions or clothing of a mentally unstable person
- Sometimes I fear that I might lose my identity

Chapter 7

Disgust and the DSM

Fear and disgust share some common features and at times overlap, but most often they are independent of each other. Fear/anxiety is the central and necessary feature of the several clinical problems that comprise the DSM category of Anxiety Disorders. Disgust is a common and often intense emotion that frequently defies control, but has no pre-ordained place in the DSM. There are no clinics for the treatment of disgust and the ever-vigilant drug manufacturers show no interest in developing and marketing anti-disgust medications. The intense, uncontrollable emotion of fear is considered to be a clinical problem but disgust is not. Why not? This question is best tackled by analysing their common and distinct qualities.

Fear and disgust are intense and unpleasant emotions. With a few exceptional instances of pleasurable fear, these emotions are aversive and people exert considerable efforts to escape from or avoid them. A clinical overlap between fear and disgust is observed in selected cases of OCD and in animal phobias. The connecting link between the two emotions is a dread of contamination.

In both fear and disgust the emotion can be provoked by direct or indirect contact with a perceived contaminant. In both instances the observed consequences—cognitive, behavioural, and perceptual—are similar and most prominently, both disgust and contamination-fear generate compulsive cleaning. If it is disgust contamination then soap and hot water will do, but if there is a threat of infection by contamination, disinfectants may be added. However, the attempt in both instances is to remove the contaminant. In both instances it is believed that after contact the contamination can be spread, and in both of them attempts are made to limit or prevent this contagion. Some stimuli (e.g. dirty bandages, decaying food) can provoke both disgust and a fear of contamination. Others can provoke one or the other but not both. The feeling of contamination is the main connecting link between fear and disgust.

There are innumerable stimuli or situations capable of provoking disgust that convey no threat and produce no fear; there is far more disgust than contamination fear. Likewise, in the large majority of fears there is no element of disgust. The cues for disgust generally are visual and olfactory and include putrefaction, the stench from bodily waste, and decaying vegetable matter. Smell plays little part in fear. In instances of disgust the distress is readily removed by cleaning and once it is completed, no threat or discomfort persists. The successful removal of the contaminant can be confirmed visually and by the disappearance of the smell. In those instances of contamination which threaten one's health, and they probably are the majority, the problem and the fear are relieved but not removed even after full cleaning. The possibility that one might have been infected by contact with a disease contaminant cannot be adequately resolved by cleaning, as in fears of AIDS. Disgust contamination and fear contamination run different time courses. Unlike disgust contamination, the triggers for the fear of being infected by contamination, are not always identifiable. The suspect viruses or germs are invisible and hence difficult to remove with certainty. Disease contamination is accompanied and followed by considerable doubting in a way that is rarely seen in disgust contamination.

The facial expressions associated with disgust and fear differ as do the physiological reactions that accompany the two emotions. The physical reactions to stimuli that evoke disgust include an array of gastric sensations such as nausea, gagging, and vomiting. Fear reactions include a pounding heart, sweating, trembling, and shortness of breath.

Health-endangering contamination resembles the disorder formerly called hypochondria and now preferably described as health anxiety (Salkovskis and Warwick 1986), in a number of ways. The threats are similar, temporally remote, often ambiguous, felt to be very serious, and difficult to resolve. The threats give rise to comparable behaviour, including repeated attempts to gain reassurance, an unrealistic striving for total certainty. Health anxiety and fears of disease/infection contamination are characterized by episodic spikes in fear that leave a residue of lingering anxiety.

The subject of disgust was re-introduced in a wonderfully stimulating analysis by Rozin and Fallon (1987). Their original paper was limited to oral disgust (subsequently expanded by Rozin et al. 1993), but nevertheless their creative ideas inspired a great deal of interest and research, and in recent years not a small part of it has dwelt on the relations between fear and disgust (McKay 2002; Olatunji et al. 2004; Sawchuk et al. 2000; Woody and Teachman 2000, among others).

Rozin and Fallon discerned the operation of some laws of sympathetic magic in the evocation and transmission of disgust (see Chapter 5). The first of these, the law of contagion, transmission by contact, is straightforward and occupies central stage in virtually all discussions of disgust, including the present one; it is summarized as 'once in contact, always in contact' (Rozin and Fallon 1987, p.30). The second of the laws is similarity—contagion can pass from object to object, or from person to person, on the basis of a perceived similarity; 'like produces like, that is, resemblance in some properties indicates a fundamental similarity or identity,' (ibid, p.30). The law of similarity probably plays an important part in the genesis and spread of mental contamination

Rozin and Fallon bolstered their argument with a series of imaginative, curious demonstrations of the play of disgust (e.g. they provoked disgust by inviting people to eat a piece of fudge shaped as dog faeces). Rozin and Fallon also noted the important role of interpersonal factors in disgust. In fears of contamination, contagion by contact is prominent but contamination can be evoked or spread without physical contact, notably in instances of mental contamination. In these cases the operation of the law of similarity is evident and often involves magical thinking.

Although the law of similarity is most evident in the transmission of contamination, and in the resulting fear and avoidance, in rare cases the same law appears magically to negate the contamination. An intriguing example of this reversal of the usual pattern was encountered in the treatment of an in-patient who suffered from an intense fear of contamination and consequent hand washing. She received daily sessions of exposure and response prevention, and was as ever, strongly encouraged to refrain from 'illegitimate' washing between sessions. The first four sessions were slow and difficult for her because the contaminants evoked such high levels of fear that she was able only to touch a few items and those swiftly and minimally. The patient would touch an item with the tip of one finger and then rapidly withdraw her hand. When the therapists arrived for the fifth session they were pleasantly surprised to discover a considerable improvement in the patient's mood and engagement in the exposure exercises. She readily touched the full range of contaminated items, using her hands in a normal manner, and reported only slight fear. However, on the following day her fear had returned to its original high level. Once again she completed the exposure tasks without difficulty. This pattern continued for a few more days until the therapists stumbled on the explanation for her inconsistent behaviour. A nurse happened to mention in passing that the patient no longer dreaded the treatment sessions because she now had a special cloth which she used to get over the exposure to the contaminated material. The patient had imbued a piece of cloth with 'supernatural powers' that instantly cleaned away all contaminations. Interestingly the magical power of the piece of cloth was confined to contaminated items used in the sessions; the patient was unable to extend its powers to remove naturally-occurring contaminations. A pity.

The analysis of disgust introduced by Rozin and Fallon in 1987 was widened by Rozin *et al.* in 1993 and provided the basis for a scale to measure sensitivity to disgust (see the revised version by Haidt *et al.* 1994). It has been used successfully in various studies (McKay 2002; Sawchuk *et al.* 2000; Woody and Tolin 2002). In clinical studies, especially those pertaining to the fear of contamination, the scale is best accompanied by measurements of anxiety sensitivity. Presumably, in cases of fear of contamination the scores on both scales of sensitivity will be elevated. It will be useful to determine whether the use of these scales can help to elucidate any factors that predispose people to develop these fears; conceivably there is a pre-existing sensitivity to disgust and to anxiety in cases of contamination fear. The potential value of a scale to measure contamination-sensitivity is considered on p. 83, and the Scale itself is provided in the Appendix.

To return to the original question of why fear but not disgust features in the DSM, the stimuli that provoke disgust are easily identifiable, circumscribed, and can be dealt with promptly by straightforward cleaning or by removal of the cues or the person. The removal of the cues is easily confirmed by visual inspection and the disappearance of any offending smells. Disgust is therefore manageable and hence transient. It seldom outlasts the contact with disgusting material. It leaves no residue of problems and does not interfere with one's life. Fear and anxiety are decidedly less manageable and long-lasting. The cues are less easily identified and all too often have irrational qualities (that tend to be unmanageable). It can be very difficult to remove or control fear and anxiety, and there is no easy method for confirming that they have been dealt with. Fears and especially anxiety persist and often are disruptive, even incapacitating, and a continuing source of distress. They warrant inclusion in the DSM.

However, even disgust can develop irrational properties. As described above, some people develop irrational fears of disgust contamination and clinicians encounter these in the context of OCD. A fear of contamination from bodily products, especially one's own, occurs in some cases of OCD. Patients become preoccupied with the fear that they might pollute others and/or exude offensive smells because of bodily pollution, and spend many hours cleaning themselves before going out (see case illustrations in the Appendix). Not surprisingly dirt/disgust contamination is associated with social anxiety. 'People are generally careful to avoid evoking disgust in others, and failing to be properly fastidious can do just that' (Woody and Teachman 2000, p.307). Their observation brings to mind George Orwell's remark in *The Road To Wigan Pier*—'However well you may wish him, however much you admire his mind and character, if his breath stinks, he is horrible' (Orwell 2001 edn., p119). The belief that one is bodily polluted, and that the olfactory and visual signs of one's polluted state are evident to other people, can generate serious anxiety and an ultimate fear of rejection. Non-physical stimuli, including accusations, memories, and even one's unwanted intrusive thoughts, can provoke a sense of disgust and of internal dirtiness, a sense of mental pollution. The involvement of disgust in cases of mental contamination is considered below.

Similarities between fear and disgust

1. Contact with fear-evoking or disgust-evoking stimuli can produce feelings of contamination.
2. Fear and disgust can co-occur and even overlap; putrefying meat can be fearful and disgusting.
3. Contamination is associated with negative emotions.
4. It is believed that the contamination spreads.
5. Contamination provokes urges to avoid or escape and to undertake preventive actions.
6. Contamination provokes attempts to clean away the contamination; these attempts are prone to become repetitive.

Some differences between fear and disgust

1. Disgust-contamination is seldom perceived to constitute a threat to one's health or well-being; in fear-contamination this is usual.
2. Feelings of disgust-contamination tend to present a social threat, even a fear of rejection.
3. Sight and smell are prominent triggers for disgust; the triggers for fear are predominantly visual and auditory, and a sense of smell rarely features.
4. In disgust the contaminant is tangible and the site of the contamination is evident
5. In fear the contaminant is tangible but the site of the threat is wider and has uncertain boundaries.
6. As a result, cleaning away or avoiding a fear contaminant is less manageable (e.g. the germs are not visible).
7. Attempts to avoid or escape from fear-evoking contaminants, especially by cleaning, are seldom wholly satisfactory because the boundaries of the contaminants are wide and unclear, and it is therefore difficult to achieve certainty about the efficacy of one's efforts (invisible germs again). Disgust contamination tends to be circumscribed.
8. It is easier to achieve certainty that one has removed a disgusting contaminant.

9. Fear contamination is associated with doubting.
10. Disgust contamination tends to be relatively short-lived; fear of a contaminated threat to one's health tends to persist.
11. The predominant physical reactions of disgust are nausea, gagging, vomiting, faintness; the predominant reactions in fear are pounding heart, tremor, dry mouth, shortness of breath.
12. The facial expressions of fear and of disgust are different.
13. A feeling of dirtiness is more common in disgust than in fear.
14. These distinctions between disgust and fear are blurred in cases of mental pollution.

The interaction between disgust, aversion, and mental contamination

There is a strong possibility that fear and disgust interact importantly in mental contamination. We already know that mental contamination can be produced without physical contact, and that people are the primary source of the contamination. People are also a common source of disgust. To take a glaring example, feelings of contamination after a sexual assault almost certainly have an element of disgust, mixed in with feelings of aversion and anger. It is suggested that there are elements of disgust and aversion in most, or all, instances of mental contamination caused by physical or psychological violations. In many of the case excerpts described here, these elements were explicit or implicit (e.g. in the cases of betrayal, humiliation, assault). Understandably, in such cases it is a feeling of angry disgust. Exactly how these feelings of disgust, and the associated feelings of aversion and anger, contribute to the production and maintenance of mental contamination, remains to be elucidated. The important influence of interpersonal factors in feelings of disgust described by Rozin and Fallon in 1987 was recently encountered in Herba's (2005) replication of the 'dirty kiss' experiment. The experimentally-induced feelings of internal dirtiness were significantly correlated with scores on a scale that measures the fear of negative evaluation.

Predispositions

Are there any factors that might predispose people to develop fear and/or disgust reactions, and in particular, are there any factors that might predispose people to develop a fear of contamination? In addition to the predisposing factors that are thought to increase one's vulnerability to significant fears (Barlow 2002; Craske 2003), there are some indications that a specific sensitivity to disgust might play a role in fears of small/slimy creatures with snakes and spiders attracting most interest (see Woody and Teachman 2000). It has also been suggested that disgust might contribute to blood-injury sensitivity (Koch *et al.* 2002). The several findings of a relation between disgust sensitivity and animal phobias, and blood-injury reactivity, are interesting but can be said to beg the question. What is the basis of the sensitivity in the first place?

The accumulating evidence of a correlation between the commonly-used measures of disgust sensitivity and anxiety sensitivity (Woody and Teachman 2000) inevitably raises the possibility of a generally elevated sensitivity (neuroticism perhaps?), and one that is bound to be a predictor of anxiety problems. As far as the fear of contamination is concerned, elevations of both measures of sensitivity are to be expected; in cases of predominantly disease contamination the anxiety scale is likely to be particularly high, and in cases of predominantly dirt/disgust contamination the disgust scale should prevail. Presumably the scores on the scales of sensitivity should decline after successful treament. As to the origin of the sensitivities it is difficult to avoid speculation about the influence of a biologically-based sensitivity that is manifested during exposures to the threat of contamination and is then consolidated or not, depending on the outcome of the exposures and the person's interpretation of these events. In keeping with developments in the subject of psychopathology, it is advisable to consider the role of cognitions in the appearance and persistence of fears of contamination.

The demonstration of individual differences in sensitivity to disgust and to anxiety is a useful step but there is a gap in our knowledge of the cognitions involved in contamination. We need systematically to collect information about the beliefs involved in contamination, and the appraisals that people make about their actual or anticipated contamination, with or without direct contact (see pp.90–94). It is suggested that a fear of contamination will arise if the affected person interprets the feelings of contamination as a significant danger to their physical and/or mental health, or as presenting a significant social threat.

One reason to pursue the overlap between fear and disgust arises from the possibility that the presence of a significant disgust factor might impede the successful treatment of anxiety disorders. The results of an experiment by Edwards and Salkovskis (2005) have a bearing on the question and suggest that the fear inflates the disgust—an experimentally-induced increase in fear of spiders was followed by an increase in disgust. However, an increase in disgust left the level of fear unaffected. They concluded that 'disgust reactions are magnified by fear, but fear is not magnified by disgust'. In their thorough review of the connections between disgust and fear, Woody and Teachman (2000) found little evidence that disgust reactions impede treatment of anxiety disorders (e.g Merckelbach *et al.* 1993). Some caution is in order because most of the information pertains to small animal phobias and to blood-injury sensitivity (sometimes called blood-injury phobia, perhaps misleadingly). Significant disgust may well influence the course of treatment of mental contamination.

It is probable that in instances of mental contamination, fear can inflate disgust, in the manner shown in the experiment on contact contamination by Edwards and Salkovskis (2005). However, on theoretical grounds, it seems equally likely that disgust can inflate the fear in mental contamination. We know from sociological and anthropological evidence that people react with anger and aversion to anyone who pollutes them or their sanctuaries. The clinical information about mental contamination caused by violations, described in Chapter 4, leads one to postulate that disgust can do more than inflate fear; in association with the reactions of aversion and anger, it can even *produce* mental contamination. The fascinating interconnections between fear and disgust (plus aversion and anger) in cases of mental contamination are inviting.

Disgust and therapy

Fortunately, the main method for reducing fear, repeated exposures, appears also to reduce any circumscribed and associated disgust; however, broad and unrelated feelings of disgust were not altered when a fear of snakes, which is associated with disgust, was reduced (de Jong *et al.* 1997; de Jong *et al.* 2000). It is probable that in cases of contamination-fear, a reduction of the fear will be accompanied by circumscribed reductions in any associated disgust. There is no reason to expect broad reductions of disgust after a fear tinged with disgust is reduced. There is a possible exception however, it is possible that a reduction of mental pollution may be followed by a broader decline in feelings of disgust.

As early as 1987 Rozin and Fallon presciently suggested that disgusts can be unmade by a process of 'extinction by frequent exposure', but that overall, 'conceptual reorientation might be a more effective method' (p.38). If it is confirmed that the exposure method is indeed capable of reducing disgust, and to reduce the fear simultaneously in most cases, then from a therapeutic standpoint the distinction between fear and disgust may be one of those differences that make no difference. However, our exploratory clinical research on the cognitive treatment of mental contamination, including feelings of disgust, suggest that Rozin and Fallon's original expectation may be confirmed.

Given the role of disgust contamination in some cases of OCD, it is necessary to consider the therapeutic implications of this fact. The emphasis throughout the therapeutic research on OCD has been on the fear component while the disgust component has been ignored or regarded as part of the fear or simply secondary to it. It remains to be studied adequately but on present information it appears that any feelings of disgust do diminish after the fear is reduced by exposure treatment. In recognition of the role of mental pollution/contamination in some cases of OCD, and following the opinion of Rozin and Fallon (1987), if disgust persists in these cases, a cognitive form of therapy might help to deal with the disgust component. To modify the examples given by Rozin and Fallon, can the disgust be undone or reduced by cognitive reorientations such as by informing the person that what they thought was rotten milk was actually yogurt, or that the forbidden pork was actually lamb after all? To illustrate, a young woman developed feelings of disgust contamination that were evoked by any direct or indirect contact with her loathed former husband. On returning from work one evening she found a package outside her front door containing a take-out meal and a pair of woollen gloves. Believing that they had been left there by her ex-husband, she felt disgusted and knew that she could never eat the food or wear the gloves. She pushed the package aside and avoided touching the contents. Shortly afterwards she telephoned her parents to tell them about this objectionable intrusion, but was surprised to learn that it was her father who had left the package. Instantly, the feelings of disgust disappeared and she ate the meal and tried on the gloves. (Cognitive reorientation can almost certainly act in the opposite direction; it can induce feelings of pollution. To use the lamb example again, 'the meat you ate was not lamb but forbidden pork'.)

Can mental contamination, and especially mental pollution, be reduced by changing the patient's interpretation of the significance, and threat value, of the feelings of contamination? By doing an anti-Macbeth, if the feelings of pollution are reinterpreted as a manifestation of disgust, or aversion, or shame or guilt, rather than the consequence of touching a dirty object, the compulsive washing at least, will be seen to be misdirected and ineffective. If the analysis of the interactions between disgust (plus aversion and anger) and mental contamination, set out above, gains support, it will encourage attempts to develop clinical methods for promoting the desirable 'cognitive reorientations'.

Chapter 8

Assessing contamination

Behavioural assessments

The behavioural manifestations of a fear of contamination—compulsive washing and extensive avoidance—are so distinctive that they have become emblematic of OCD. From the outset of their work on OCD the early behaviour therapists creditably recorded the compulsive behaviour. The behaviour of patients receiving treatment in hospital was recorded by psychologists and nurses, and the patients completed self-recordings. This was the first attempt to assess the behavioural effects of a psychological treatment for OCD. The collection of behavioural self-recordings from out-patients depended on the person's cooperation and conscientiousness, but in practice this information was incomplete and sometimes of doubtful accuracy. The introduction of behavioural avoidance tests, consistent with Lang's (1985) clarifying construal of fear, was a simple but important advance. In the course of his pioneering research into the reduction of human fears, he replaced the outdated idea of 'fear as a lump' with a three-component analysis of fear—behaviour, psychophysiological reactions, and verbal reports. In his first experimental analysis of the desensitization of a fear (of snakes), he introduced a behaviour test in which the snake-fearful participants were asked to walk towards a live snake and report their fear on 0–10 scale at each point. The main measures were the closeness of the approach to the snake and their fear ratings. These tests were administered before and after desensitization training, and at a follow-up. This first systematic method for collecting behavioural evidence of the effects of treatment was widely adopted (e.g. Rachman *et al.* 1979) and remains an important measure of change in OCD, especially in cases of contamination fear. A review of behavioural tests in OCD is provided by Taylor (1998).

The use of behaviour tests, pre- and post-treatment, is strongly recommended in research and treatment of the fear of contamination. This information should be supplemented by patient self-reports of avoidance and the frequency/duration of compulsive cleaning, notwithstanding the problems involved. In recent years, behavioural experiments have been introduced into CBT, predominantly as a method for encouraging patients to collect direct, personal information that is pertinent to their unadaptive cognitions (e.g. Rachman 2003). They can also be used to assess changes during a course of therapy.

As described on p.29, simple (cognitive) behavioural tests can be used as probes to elicit useful information about mental contamination. After establishing a baseline level of contamination, the therapist asks the patient to form vivid, realistic images involving the person who is the primary source of the mental contamination, the 'violator'. After approximately two minutes of each such 'exposure' the patient reports the degree of dirtiness/contamination experienced and any urges to wash.

In addition to behaviour and verbal reports, Lang recommended psychophysiological measurements. They are employed in research projects but rarely taken during cognitive therapy for contamination-fear. However, with the expansion of the concept to include mental contamination it might prove useful to reintroduce psychophysiological measurements (e.g. pulse-rate) especially when the patients are perplexed about the source and site of their feelings of pollution and contamination.

Psychometrics

The early psychometric scales, such as the widely-used Maudsley Obsessional Compulsive Inventory (MOCI), were constructed during the behavioural era and virtually all of the items addressed observable behaviour (Hodgson and Rachman 1977). The scale established the existence of two major factors, checking compulsions and cleaning compulsions. The fact that the these two major factors mirrored the two most common forms of clinical manifestations of OCD was reassuring. The major findings were replicated in subsequent scales but the inventory became dated, and as the limitations of a narrowly behavioural approach became apparent, a full revision became necessary. The revised scale, the Vancouver Obsessional Compulsive Inventory (VOCI), includes a wider range and includes much-needed cognitive items (Thordarson *et al.* 2004). For present purposes, the change from a subscale that measures compulsive washing (MOCI) to a subscale that measures fear of *contamination* (VOCI) is an improvement that provides a tool for more precise investigations of the two phenomena.

The original MOCI had sound psychometric properties, and the washing subscale had high internal consistency, plus satisfactory criterion, convergent, and discriminant validity (Taylor 1998, p.234). Encouragingly, when scales that measured a fear of contamination were introduced (e.g. in the Padua

Inventory, Sanavio 1988) they correlated significantly with the MOCI washing subscale. Sawchuk *et al.* (2000) found a correlation of 0.90 between the Padua and VOCI contamination subscales. On the new VOCI, the contamination subscale is modestly and appropriately correlated with other OCD subscales, such as checking. The contamination subscale gives distinctive scores, and unlike earlier scales and the Obsessive-Compulsive Inventory (OCI, Foa *et al.* 1998), is not associated with measures of general distress, namely, depression or anxiety. In the new VOCI, contamination is the second of six factors, and OCD patients whose primary problem was compulsive cleaning scored very highly on this subscale—a mean of 25.26 versus 11.72 in patients with other forms of OCD problems (Thordarson *et al.* 2004, p.1305). A non-clinical sample of community adults had a mean of 1.74. All of this suggests that the subscale gives specific information about contamination (see Appendix for the items). Another welcome result was that the VOCI contamination scores correlated 0.83 with the washing subscale scores from the original MOCI. The assumption that a fear of contamination is closely related to compulsive cleaning appears to have been justified. (Despite the overlap, the fear of contamination and compulsive washing are different and should be differently regarded and named; not all fears of contamination are followed by or associated with washing, and compulsive washing can occur in the absence of a fear of contamination.) The VOCI showed high test–retest reliability in an OCD sample. Although some psychometric scales are sensitive to treatment affects (MOCI, Padua, YBOCS self-report), the analyses of the outcomes are based on general scores derived from these scales (Taylor 1998). Following the present line of thought, reports on treatment and other effects should include sub-scale scores, and in the present case, scores on the contamination sub-scale. The VOCI and the Padua contain such contamination sub-scales. Basic information about the VOCI is provided in the Appendix.

Now that the conception of contamination is being expanded and elaborated, the introduction of the VOCI scale, and in particular the contamination subscale, is likely to become a useful tool in the interim. The introduction of the new scale is timely because earlier versions, from the MOCI onwards, were based on a view of contamination that was rooted in an outdated conception of the phenomenon—namely that all contamination arises from physical contact with a contaminant. Actual or perceived contact with a contaminant so frequently leads to cleaning behaviour that in the early scales the presence of feelings of contamination was inferred from the reports of washing behaviour. In order to carry out investigations of mental contamination, the VOCI contamination subscale will have to be supplemented by measures that collect information about mental pollution, self-contamination, and morphing. A scale to promote this development, The Mental Contamination Subscale, which was the strongest predictor of self-reported dirtiness and urge to wash among the 'contaminated' participants in the Herba (2005) replication experiment, is provided in the Appendix. The Structured Interview Schedule has a wider range and should also facilitate this process (see p.174 in the Appendix).

The Interview Schedule is designed to be used flexibly and as the interview proceeds, some questions can be expanded and others omitted, depending on the particular patient's responses. It covers the following topics: the cues that produce feelings of contamination, the onset of the problem, attempts at coping, washing and cleaning, avoidance, contamination without contact, sense of internal and/or diffuse dirtiness, evocation of feelings of contamination by mental events such as memories and images, inflated responsibility, feelings of morphing, proneness to the thought-action-fusion bias. The complete schedule is given in the Appendix, and these are a few examples of the questions.

Do some things look clean, but feel dirty?

Do you ever look clean, but feel dirty?

Do you get really bothered by sticky hands?

If your hands feel very sticky does that scare you?

Are your feelings of contamination ever set off even without touching a dirty or contaminated object/substance?

Are your feelings of contamination ever set off by an upsetting remark or a criticism of you?

Do you ever feel dirty under your skin?

Do you ever wake up feeling contaminated?

If you stand close too close to people who look weird or mentally unstable, do you ever worry that you might pick up some of their habits or problems?

Mental contamination, self-contamination, morphing, and mental pollution are more complex than physical contact contamination. Certainly, compulsive cleaning often follows mental or self-contamination, but the nature of the fear is less clearcut—the source and site of the contamination are unclear. Hence, the very close relationship between physical contact with a contaminant and subsequent cleaning is not to be expected in cases of mental contamination. It is highly probable that the range and types of neutralizing behaviour instigated by mental contamination include but go well beyond compulsive cleaning. In time the expanded conception of contamination will require an extension of the psychometric scales to include the occurrence of mental contamination, self-contamination, and so forth.

Conclusions from the psychometric data

- Contamination is a coherent concept, and is measurable.
- In all scales designed to measure OCD, contamination/compulsive cleaning and compulsive checking emerge as major factors.
- (Compulsive cleaning and compulsive checking are the most common behavioural manifestations of OCD).
- Contamination/washing subscales are modestly, and appropriately, correlated with other OCD subscales, such as obsessions and checking, but not with hoarding and slowness.
- In some recent scales the term has been changed from compulsive washing to *contamination.*
- Contamination scales meet the standards for reliability and validity.
- Contamination scale scores are associated with clinical manifestations of fear of contamination, and with compulsive cleaning.
- The early indications are that the VOCI contamination subscale is satisfactorily specific.
- Unlike other tests of OCD, the VOCI contamination subscale is not blurred by associations with general distress, especially depressions and anxiety. The 'purity' of the contamination scale, if confirmed, will be an advantage in future research.
- In future psychometric and other research a distinction should be made between the fear of contamination and compulsive washing.
- The two terms should be distinguished, and so should the two concepts.
- The sensitivity of the VOCI, and especially the contamination subscale, as a measure of therapeutic change, needs to be determined.
- Scales to measure contamination need to be expanded to include feelings of mental contamination.

Assessing mental contamination

Formal assessments of mental contamination, by questionnaire and standardized interviews, can incorporate the sensations, beliefs/cognitions, and feelings described above (e.g. internal dirtiness) These are supplemented by items dealing with behaviour (especially cleaning), avoidance, prevention, unwanted intrusive thoughts, and concealment (Newth and Rachman 2001), plus appraisals of the probability/seriousness of harm arising from contamination. Test probes using images involving the human source of the mental contamination can be revealing. The rationale for these test probes is based on the experimental induction of feelings of contamination by imagery (the 'dirty kiss' experiment), and from spontaneous reports of imaginal/memorial evocations of contamination given by patients during treatment. Patients are asked to form a variety of vivid images involving the source of the contamination, the 'violator'. These include images of the person, images of being touched by the violator, images of touching or wearing clothes belonging to the violator, images of sharing a drinking glass with the violator, and images of handling a sweat-stained garment belonging to the violator. The expectation is that the images will induce feelings of contamination and urges to wash. As an illustration, a patient who had severe fears of contamination and associated avoidance, was initially reluctant to talk about, let alone imagine, the person who was the primary source of her fears, the uncle who had humiliated her throughout most of her childhood. She was able to form vivid images and all five of them (the uncle, his clothing, a shared drinking glass, being touched by him, and handling his sweat-stained shirt) evoked strong feelings of dirtiness/contamination and an urge to wash. She toned down the unpleasant feelings by cleansing her hands with antiseptic hand wipes.

The use of psychophysiological measures is most suitable for research purposes, but can be useful in some cases, especially when the patient is confused about the source and site of the contamination. For clinical purposes, the following procedures are most suitable: Standardized Interview, VOCI questionnaire, Yale (YBOCS), Beck Depression Inventory (BDI), Behaviour avoidance tests. In cases of self-contamination, a scale to measure the patient's interpretation of his unwanted intrusions (the Personal Significance Scale, PSS, can be administered at the beginning of each session in order to track the changing appraisals—see Appendix). The contamination TAF scale should be administered if the patient reports thoughts that smack of a cognitive bias. Self-recordings of compulsive behaviour and avoidance are introduced at the start of therapy.

The scale to measure sensitivity to contamination (see Appendix) is primarily a research instrument, and most relevant for questions pertaining to vulnerability, but occasionally is useful in treatment. As stated, it is modelled after the measures that assess vulnerability/sensitivity to disgust, and to anxiety. The scale to measure thought–action fusion (Appendix) can be useful clinically but is most relevant for research into cognitive processing of the fear of contamination. Details of the conduct of a clinical assessment are given in Chapter 10.

Chapter 9

Towards a cognitive theory of contamination

The main premise of cognitive theories of anxiety is that disorders develop when a person misappraises the significance of external or internal threats to their health or well-being. The person overestimates the probability and the severity of the threat. The theories are constructive, and being testable, are undergoing evaluation. Methods of treatment derived from the theories are also underdoing rigorous testing, and some encouraging results have been reported. Some of the theories are ambitiously causal and, therefore, unusual.

However, the weakness of the main premise is that it too general. It applies across the board, to all forms of anxiety disorder, and is too blunt. Satisfactory theories of anxiety disorders need to go beyond the general, and at a minimum try to explain the specific factors that lead to the development of each of the major types of disorder. The classic example of a specific, and causal, theory is Clark's cognitive theory of panic.

He argued that panics are *caused* by a catastrophic misinterpretation of certain bodily sensations (Clark 1986). For example, if a person misinterprets his laboured breathing as signifying an impending heart attack, a panic ensues. If it is correctly interpreted as a consequence of climbing stairs too rapidly, no panic occurs. Similarly, Salkovskis's (1985) highly influential cognitive theory of OCD attributes the psychological problems to the person's misappraisal of threat, combined with an inflated sense of responsibility; these two factors are crucially involved in the genesis and maintenance of OCD problems. The cognitive theory of obsessions continues in this line, proposing that obsessions develop and persist if and when the person makes catastrophic misinterpretations of the personal significance of his unwanted intrusive thoughts (Rachman 2003). The utility of this cognitive approach in tackling the fear of *contamination* is worth exploring.

Cognitions and contamination

Fear is a response to a perceived threat. The physiological reactions to the threat, and the behavioural consequences, are similar across all fears. The distinguishing characteristics of the different fears arise out of the nature of the particular threat, and how the person interprets the threat. The threats come down to three possibilities, or combinations of the three: a fear of physical harm, a fear of mental harm, and/or a fear of social harm. 'I fear that I will get seriously ill, be injured or killed. I fear that I will lose control of my mind/behaviour and become insane. I fear that I will be rejected and isolated from other people.' All three of the threats can arise in the fear of contamination, but one or other of the three is predominant in response to particular contaminants.

The threat in fears of disease contamination is clearly enunciated; contact with the contaminant will infect the person and cause serious bodily damage, even death. A secondary threat cognition in disease contamination, sometimes even more intense than the fear of harm to oneself, is the threat of being responsible for passing the danger on to other people. The threat of being contaminated by dirt may have the two elements discussed earlier, an anticipation of disgust and distress, and a secondary dread of the negative social consequences of being dirty or polluted. 'I feel polluted/dirty, others can sense it, they will reject and avoid me.'

The threat in mental contamination is one of losing control of one's thoughts and behaviour, and hence a possible fear of becoming mentally unstable, especially as the feelings of internal dirtiness/pollution appear to have a mean-ingless quality, are intangible and puzzling, out of control, and often repug-nant. Unwanted, intrusive, repugnant thoughts (e.g. incestuous images) and urges can induce feelings of pollution. Even though the thoughts are contra-dicted by the available facts they remain unyielding, elusive, and uncontrol-lable. They are upsetting, perplexing, frightening, and morally repellent. The inability to control these objectionable thoughts, which clash with the person's values, raises self-doubts about character, misgivings about the ability to control one's behaviour, and ultimately to a fear of having a breakdown or even of going insane. Feelings of mental pollution/contamination can also be provoked by external events that leave one sullied, for example after a sexual assault. The cognitions associated with external provocations of mental con-tamination resemble some of the cognitions that are common in PTSD (see Ehlers and Clark 2000). The victims of a personal violation, whether a physical assault or prolonged humiliation, may come to believe that they are irreparably damaged/polluted by the event and that their life is blighted. The very symp-toms of their distress, uncontrollable intrusive images, hyper-arousal, and irrational feelings of pollution/contamination, reinforce their fears of the future. Feelings of inadequacy and hopelessness are to be expected.

In cases of self-contamination the personal evaluations tend to be gloomy, self-critical and frequently have a moral element. 'I am impure, sinful, out of

contol', 'I will never get rid of these thoughts and the feelings of contamination', 'I can't control my thoughts' (but I should, I must), 'I am losing control
of my mind', 'I will be and/or am being punished'. 'These repugnant thoughts
and urges, and the associated pollution, are of great personal significance, and
mean that I have a nasty hidden flaw in my character.'

All people experience concern or anxiety if they touch a substance which
they believe to be contagious and/or dangerous, and if it is not possible to
remove the contaminating material, stark fear can erupt. However, if the belief
is incorrect and/or the perceived threat is exaggerated, the resulting fear is
outside the normal range. If the person removes the threatening contaminant,
say by a thorough wash, but the perceived threat persists, that too is beyond
the normal range. A fear of contamination can be abnormally generated and/
or abnormally persistent. The root is traceable to a significant, even catastrophic, misinterpretation of the probability of the threatened harm occur-
ring and/or the seriousness of the anticipated harm is grossly over-interpreted.

Shaping these premises into increasingly specific propositions is complicated by the diversity of the fear. There is a division between contact contamination and mental contamination, and within these divisions are eight sub-
types of the fear. Fears of contact contamination are less complex and invite a
single explanation. The person fears that contact with specifiable contaminants will cause him physical, mental, or social harm. In cases of disease
contamination, there is a clear connection between the particular contaminant
and the feared consequence. In recent years there has been a large rise in fears
of contracting AIDS, and a decline in fears of syphilis. Extreme avoidance of
dirt can be driven by a dread of the social consequences of contamination and/
or a fear of disease. A fear of mental harm tends to be secondary to the fear
of contamination. The abnormal level and spread of the dread of touching a
contaminant, and the acknowledged irrationality of the compulsive cleansing
and avoidance, promote doubts about one's mental stability, doubts that can
be reinforced by the reactions of other people.

Why this person, why this fear?

The outstanding questions are why *this* person and why *this* particular fear? In
addressing the first question, it is well to begin with individual differences in
predispositions to develop the fear. As discussed earlier, it is probable that
some people have an elevated sensitivity to contamination, and this in turn is
correlated with sensitivities to anxiety and to disgust. The postulated sensitivity to contamination is a combination of beliefs/cognitions about the
probability and seriousness of threats to one's physical and mental health

and a biological reactivity to stimuli that evoke disgust and/or fear. This predisposition is ignited into a fear of contamination by specifiable experiences, for example, rape. The growth of the disposition into a significant fear occurs as a result of observational learning, conditioning, negative information—one or more of the three pathways to fear (Rachman 1990, 2004).

In most cases it is possible to construct a cause and a path of development for the particular fear. The fear of contamination by contact with HIV started for a highly 'sensitive' patient after he shared a wineglass and cigarettes with an unfamiliar person at a large, well-lubricated, rowdy, all-night party. The fear of picking up unspecified but pervasive germs led another patient to live a secluded life and wash compulsively. She had been raised by an extremely anxious mother who was constantly watchful for dangers and every day warned her to avoid touching suspect items. Clothing was washed three or four times before use, the kitchen was scrubbed down with disinfectants every day, travel was treacherous. A reclusive patient had a dread of dirt that kept her virtually housebound. The problem arose when she had a prolonged bout of digestive problems in early adulthood and developed a fear of losing control of her bowels in public and/or exuding unpleasant smells in public. For many years, long after the digestive difficulties had been overcome, she showered compulsively and limited her excursions to a minimum. The patient carried out her shopping at unsocial hours, usually late at night. She feared a social catastrophe and attempted to avert the threat by compulsive cleaning and wide avoidance. An 18-year-old man developed a fear of touching pesticides, anti-freeze fluid, and then most other chemical products. It began when he heard that the father of a friend had committed suicide by drinking anti-freeze and was found dead in his garage. He was so shocked and frightened that he became preoccupied with the story, even though it may well have been inaccurate, and took to washing his hands intensively. He avoided all contact with chemicals and places where chemicals were stored. Because of the fear he avoided garages and had to arrange for other people to refuel his car.

These cases illustrate the three pathways to fear—by conditioning, observational learning, and provision of negative information. The patient who dreaded touching anything even remotely connected to AIDS had developed a conditioned fear, the person who had a pervasive fear of germs was exposed to a frightened model throughout her life and was given a daily diet of frightening information. The reclusive patient's fear was a combination of conditioning and negative information that she had picked up when attempting to cope with her medical problem. The person who avoided contact with chemical products developed a fear of chemical contamination as a result of disturbing, negative information.

The manifestations of mental contamination are complex, and even though they can be reduced to three underlying fears—a fear of physical, mental or social harm—they play out in diverse ways. A fear of mental contamination can be caused by physical violation. A prime example of this causation is seen among people who have been sexually assaulted. The initial feelings of contamination are comprehensible but in many instances they persist for months or years after the assault. Victims describe feeling an inner dirtiness (e.g. 'it is under my skin') in addition to the external signs, and it is these *persisting* feelings of inner pollution which have the characteristics of mental contamination. The primary source of the pollution is a person, the dirtiness is internal and difficult to localize, is easily re-evoked by memories or other mental events, often has a moral element, and is not properly responsive to washing. In cases of physical violation the instigating event involves some form of contact, but re-evocations of the feelings of contamination occur without physical contact. There is a common overlap between this type of mental contamination and PTSD, and a probable overlap in causes and consequences. Ehlers and Clark (2000) attribute the persistence of symptoms of PTSD to the victim's sense of a continuing and current threat. The threat/s can be an external threat to their safety or an internal threat to themselves or their future. They suggest that the person's appraisal of the trauma plus the memories of the event combine to produce the sense of current threat. The threat is accompanied by intrusive images and memories, heightened arousal and re-experiencing, and these signs reinforce the victim's feeling of a current threat.

Mental contamination, often associated with feelings of mental pollution, can also be caused by psychological violation, even without any physical contact. The list of violations, including degradation and betrayal, is lengthy and not easy to classify. The extensity of the possible types of violation raises the question of limits. Why are we not over-run with an epidemic of cases of mental pollution and contamination? Are all distressing emotional experiences possible triggers for a sense of contamination? Which particular experiences will do it, and which particular people are vulnerable to becoming contaminated? In clinical assessments of a fear of contamination, particularly when there are indications of mental contamination, it is worth enquiring into the possible role of the perceived 'violator'. The source of mental contamination is other people, and patients generally attribute the violation to a particular person. The nature and circumstances of the violation are important, and patients tend to regard the violator as a source of contamination, with consequent avoidance. In the Standardized Interview Schedule patients are asked whether any particular person ever caused them serious harm and/or upset them very deeply.

Current knowledge is insufficient to permit confident theorizing about how exactly a distressing emotional experience, a sense of being violated by someone, is transformed into a feeling of pollution/contamination, but we do possess some clues.

In the cases of PTSD caused by assaults that are described by de Silva and Marks (1999), only two patients developed feelings of contamination, and both were victims of sexual assault. None of the the patients who had been attacked, robbed, or stabbed, reported such feelings. Sexual assaults are especially intrusive and perhaps the most severe instances of a breach of someone's personal boundaries. The assaults are carried out by people and inflicted on the victim (very different from contact contamination caused by touching an inert, harmful substance). There is in addition a moral element in sexual behaviour, and also in cases of mental contamination. In cases of psychological violation the victims generally recognize the injustice, and immorality, of the way in which they have been treated, and consequently feel anger towards the perpetrator, sometimes mixed with disgust. The perpetrator is regarded as morally repugnant. No doubt there are many instances in which the victim feels anger, repugnance and disgust towards the perpetrator even before the trigger event/s; being touched, or manipulated, or humiliated by a person one loathes may well trigger feelings of mental pollution. After being psychologically violated the victim experiences emotional distress that may include fear, anger, and disgust, and it is no surprise that they take steps to avoid seeing or hearing about the perpetrator. When these attempts fail a feeling of contamination may resurge. Sexual violations and betrayals are often involved in cases of mental contamination that contain an element of mental pollution. Another source of mental pollution arises from repugnant, blasphemous thoughts and impulses.

The cognitions associated with mental contamination and mental pollution tend to include moral precepts, the necessity to maintain fastidious habits, the need to control one's thoughts and to exclude the naughty ones. The associated cognitions are on the themes of moral and physical purity, the unacceptability of unwanted thoughts, the need to exclude and suppress unacceptable thoughts, the dreaded moral and psychological consequences of lapses in purity.

Self-contamination is caused by contacts with one's bodily products (wastes, sexual emissions) or by the occurrence of unwanted, intrusive repugnant thoughts/urges, and is associated with shame and guilt. In common with other forms of mental contamination, self-contamination can be evoked without physical contact with a contaminant, the primary source is a person (self) not a tangible substance, it is easily evoked or re-evoked by mental events, and is restricted to oneself. Feelings of pollution are prominent in self-contamination and not properly responsive to washing. The intrusive thoughts that give rise to self-contamination resemble obsessions (Rachman 2003) and the two disorders do appear to overlap somewhat—the thoughts involved in self-contamination are obsession-like, but only a minority of obsessions produce feelings of contamination. To the extent that cases of self-contamination share some features of obsessions, the treatment prospects are favourable (Freeston et al. 1997), as progress with CBT is steady.

The fear of morphing is best approached from the observation that all, or most, of these patients have concurrent or past fears of contact contamination or mental contamination. The fear may arise out of a belief that undesirable characteristics are transmissable by physical contact or by visual contamination, and the belief generates cognitions about the personal threat to the believer. Under threat, the person becomes vigilant and learns to avoid people and associated places that are potential sources of contamination by morphing. The people who are regarded as threatening are marginal and include those who are perceived as mentally unstable, weird, and/or unkempt. People of elevated status are rarely, if ever, the source of a fear of morphing.

The reason for the appearance of morphing, almost like a modern manifestation of imitative sympathetic magic, is not always clear, but in some instances it is associated with a belief in the possibility, or even probability, of the contagiousness of mental instability. If one believes that weirdness, mental instability, are transmissable and that contact increases the risk of contagion, then avoidance is understandable. An additional factor is a distaste for contact with strangers who appear to be unstable or weird, and the dirtiness and disgust that can be experienced after unavoidable contacts. Some patients had a history of being seriously disvalued and repeatedly told that they were failures and would come to nothing. They absorbed the fear of becoming a failure, followed by a decline into hopelessness. Contact with dysfunctional people triggered their dread of personal failure, and a fear of becoming similarly dysfunctional.

The cues that provoke neutralizing or cleaning are touching a person who is regarded as a primary source of contamination or any secondary associations with that person, especially their clothing or other possessions. Visual contamination is a particular feature of morphing; the mere sight of the undesirable person is sufficient to evoke feelings of contamination. In most forms of contamination, including a dread of picking up someone's undesirable characteristics, unavoided contacts are generally followed by washing. However, people who fear that they might actually morph into someone else are more inclined to engage in covert neutralizing activities.

The implications for therapy are two-fold. As ever, the beliefs and unadaptive cognitions need to be ascertained and modified by didactic sessions and by the accumulation of personal evidence that bears on the validity of the main misinterpretations. Secondly, the past or present occurrence of more familiar forms of contamination-fear should be gone into, and the connections between them and the fear of morphing examined. It is too early to say, but it is possible that giving priority to the treatment of the familiar, contact contamination might weaken the fear of morphing and make it more amenable to modification. Interestingly, some patients respond readily and easily to the therapist's advice to eliminate avoidance of potential morphers. The therapist's assertions that morphing does not occur produces a welcome and effective reassurance, and then the avoidance diminishes. In unyielding cases the use of behavioural experiments is recommended. For example, does planned proximity to the feared people actually produce any manifestations of mental instability?

Cognitive biases

Cognitive biases operate in various forms of OCD (Rachman and Shafran 1998; Shafran and Rachman 2004), notably in the generation and maintenance of obsessions, and so far most attention has been paid to thought–action fusion (TAF). The person believes that certain of his thoughts can have external effects: the belief that one's thoughts about a possible misfortune actually increase the probability that it will occur, is called 'likelihood (probability) TAF', and the belief that having a morally unacceptable thought is equivalent to an immoral action is called 'moral TAF'. A second cognitive bias observed in OCD is the responsibility bias, namely that if I am responsible for preventing a misfortune, that very responsibility increases the likelihood that the misfortune will occur. The woman who dreaded passing on disease contamination to her granddaughter, was convinced that she in particular presented the greatest threat to the child (p.72). She avoided being alone with the child because her threatening thoughts surged in the presence of the little girl, and the grandmother believed that the probability of the girl being infected was raised by her frightening thoughts. Other examples of the operation of a TAF-contamination bias include these propositions: 'If I have thoughts about getting contaminated, it increases the risk that I will actually become contaminated', 'Having a thought that I might pass on contamination to a child is almost as bad as actually passing it on'. A short scale designed to measure contamination-related TAF, the CTN–TAF Scale, is provided in the Appendix. For purposes of research the total scores, their stability and relations to other scales are of primary interest, but clinicians will find that patients' responses to specific questions can be of therapeutic relevance. The same is true of the other scales for measuring contamination and mental contamination.

Thought–action fusion is prominent in instances of self-contamination. When unwanted intrusive thoughts evoke and promote feelings of self-contamination the TAF bias may come into operation. For example, incestuous images/thoughts are capable of evoking self-contamination, and may well trigger both types of TAF, the moral and the likelihood biases. 'Having these repugnant incestuous thoughts is as immoral as carrying out an immoral action', 'Having violent images increases the probability that I will act in a violent manner'. Blasphemous intrusions can trigger moral TAF, so that, for example, a person who has intrusive impulses/thoughts about making obscene remarks and gestures in church interprets the thoughts as the immoral equivalent of committing a sin in church. It is to be expected that there is at least a modest correlation between mental contamination and TAF. A comparably modest correlation between a fear of morphing and TAF is possible. 'If I repeatedly think that I might morph into, or pick up unwanted qualities, from undesirable people then I will increase the probability of such changes.' However, there is a distinct possibility of the operation of a form of TAF that is specific to fears of contamination.

It follows from the possibilities and examples that patients who are prone to these troubling cognitive biases will try to block the intrusions if they can, and suppress them if they can't. Their attempts at coping are seldom satisfactory and may even exacerbate matters (Clark 2004; Rassin 2005). Subject to confirmation of the connections between TAF and the various forms of contamination, therapeutic possibilities follow from the present analysis. Despite the tenacity of cognitive biases, including TAF, useful small steps have been made in tackling the problem. The cognitive behavioural treatment of obsessions includes a didactic component that provides corrective information about cognitive biases, and Zucker (2004) showed that TAF can be reduced in sub-clinical OCD students by providing a few group educational sessions. Of course, clinically significant biases present a far more difficult prospect, but the introduction of anti-bias tactics into the treatment of contamination should be helpful for those patients who endorse items on the Contamination–TAF Scale (Appendix). The tactics proposed by Arkes (1981) can be effective: avoid dichotomous judgements, take into account the non-occurrence of events, collect disconfirmatory evidence, consider alternatives, think Bayesian.

Self-perpetuating cycle

There is an outstanding question about why fears of contamination persist. The main premise of cognitive theories of anxiety is that the affected person significantly misappraises the probability and seriousness of perceived threats, internal and external. This is the puzzle: why do patients persist in overestimating the probability/seriousness of the threats of contamination despite frequently repeated disconfirmations? They experience the fear of being harmed by contamination hundreds or thousands of times, but nothing bad happens. In most cases the patient is frightened by perceived contaminants on a daily basis, but no harm ensues. In fears of disease-contamination they never catch the dreaded disease. But they continue to fear that they will—why does the fear persist despite the total absence of harm?

The original behavioural explanation for the persistence was based on the associated compulsions. It was argued that the fear (say of contamination) persisted because the person compulsively washed away the contamination and therefore experienced a reduction of anxiety. In accordance with the prevailing drive-reduction theory of reinforcement, it was claimed that the compulsive behaviour maintained the fear. The main premise of contemporary learning theory was that all behaviour is reinforced by drive-reduction. Hence, washing reduces the anxiety/drive and this reinforces the compulsive behaviour. The explanation was supported by experimental results which showed that anxiety is indeed reduced if the person washes away the contamination (Rachman and Hodgson 1980), but in retrospect the results may have been misinterpreted. The results can explain why the compulsive behaviour persists—because it reliably reduces anxiety—but the results did not explain why the *fear* persisted.

Whenever the perceived contaminant was re-presented the fear reaction was dependably re-evoked. Patients who are struggling to overcome their fear of contamination gain temporary relief from washing their hands, but the fear persists, often for years and years, even though nothing bad happens. It is time to think afresh about fears that persist despite thousands of disconfirmations (Seligman 1988).

In recent theoretical analyses of compulsive checking, it was found necessary to introduce the concept of a self-perpetuating mechanism in order to account for the persistence of the checking (Rachman 2004). The problem in compulsive checking is similar to the problem encountered in fears of contamination. Why do the patients continue compulsively to check the safety of the house, doors, windows, stove—thousands and thousands of times—even though no disasters occur? Why does the checking behaviour persist despite thousands of disconfirmations? It is possible that a self-perpetuating cycle or mechanism is also operating in the maintenance of fears of contamination.

It is proposed that two forms of cognitive bias, one major and one minor, generate a self-perpetuating cycle that maintains the fears. The first bias is the *ex-consequentia* bias, according to which, people infer the presence of danger from their feelings of fear. 'If I feel anxious, there must be danger' (Arntz *et al.* 1995). It was suggested that neurotic patients engage in 'emotional reasoning', i.e. draw invalid conclusions about a situation on the basis of their subjective emotional response, and most important for the present analysis, infer the presence of danger from their emotional reactions in the situation.

When the patient encounters a perceived contaminant, it evokes fear and this is interpreted as a signal of present danger. This resembles the faulty cognition, mentioned earlier, that is expressed in the phrase 'It looks clean, but feels dirty', and here it is experienced in this way—'It looks safe, but *feels* dangerous'. The same *ex-consequentia* bias operates in the fear of dirt-contamination. The perceived contaminant evokes strong feelings of fear/disgust and these are interpreted as signalling the presence of significant pollution/danger. The fear reaction is originally acquired by one or more of the three pathways to fear.

The bias also helps to explain how patients construe their abnormal fear. They are aware (i) that other people do not fear the perceived contaminant, and (ii) in calm circumstances, they know that contaminant is not truly dangerous. In their fearful moments however, they feel in danger. 'Yes, it might look safe, but for me it feels very dangerous.' And I certainly will not touch it. Incidentally, this analysis leads to a new view of the clinically familiar term, 'in calm moments'. Talking to a patient about an abnormal thought/fear in a clean, safe clinical interview room, they usually say, 'Yes, it is nonsensical, I know it, but...'. In contrast, if you ask the same patient the same question when they are inches away from a major contaminant, they are decidedly less confident that the fear is baseless. Similarly, a person who is snake-phobic will agree in conversation that garter snakes are harmless but be very frightened if one is brought within inches. In calm moments, in the absence of fear, estimations of danger are minimized. Inferring a present danger from one's feeling of fear can be demonstrated in laboratory conditions; participants will give elevated estimates of danger when they feel frightened by the presence of a perceived contaminant, and relatively low estimations of the danger of the same contaminant when they are feeling calm and the actual contaminant is not present. The cognitive bias is illustrated in Fig. 9.1 below.

Among patients, the fear of contamination is regularly evoked whenever the contaminant is encountered. In these circumstances, the arousal of the fear is interpreted to mean that the contaminant is dangerous (I am frightened, so it

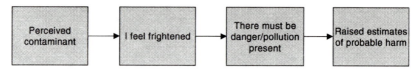

Fig. 9.1 *Ex-consequentia* appraisals

must be dangerous). With frequent repetitions, and in cases of contamination-fear this generally means thousands of repetitions, the patient's estimates of the probability of danger are confirmed and reconfirmed. So, the fear of contamination persists because the appearance of the contaminant always evokes fear that is appraised as a threat of being in danger. The main premise of cognitive theories of anxiety is that they are caused by persistent overestimations of the probability and seriousness of a perceived threat. It is argued here that the repeated interpretations of fear as signalling a present danger of contamination ensure that the person's estimations of probable harm from contamination remain unchanged, at a very high level.

The cycle can be illustrated by the fear of morphing. 'When I see a disreputable or unstable person, I feel frightened—hence, there is danger present.' Furthermore, my fear rises steeply as the person comes closer; the danger has increased. 'I must escape, I must wash away the danger.' In cases of contamination provoked by violation, 'When I see the violator my fear rises steeply; there is danger present'. Again, 'I must escape, and wash away the danger'.

If the *ex-consequentia* cognitive bias is reduced, say by therapy and reeducation, the overestimations of the probability and seriousness of the threat will decline. On the same lines, if the fear reaction to the contaminant is repeatedly weakened, by whatever means (e.g. deep relaxation, tranquilizing drugs), then the inference of danger will weaken, and the estimated probability of future threats will diminish.

This analysis helps to understand the great difficulty which many patients encounter when they attempt to carry out at home the exposure exercises that they manage tolerably well in the clinic. They complain of the frustration they experience when they are unable to repeat the seemingly simple exercises of touching contaminated items at home—even the very items that they successfully touched in the clinic. 'I can't seem to do it on my own; I need someone there with me.' In part this curious difficulty occurs because the patients feel significantly less fearful in the safe, protected clinic, supported by the staff. They experience less fear, and hence the contaminated items are *appraised as less dangerous*. In contrast, alone at home their fear is not dampened and hence the contaminated items are appraised as very dangerous. *The (appraised) dangerousness of the same item varies in the two sites*, except in instances of particularly severe/intense fear. It is moderately dangerous in the clinic but very dangerous at home.

It is now possible to return to the original question of why the fear of contamination persists even though nothing bad ever happens. It turns out that something bad does happen, actually two bad things happen, and worse, they happen on every encounter with the perceived contaminant. Similar to the unpleasantness of recurrent episodes of panic, the recurrent episodes of contamination fear are unpleasant (bad event) and the recurrent feeling of being in considerable danger is very unpleasant and unsettling (bad event). Each encounter with the contaminant strengthens the belief in, and the expectation of, danger. The original question was baffling because we focused exclusively on the explicit fears expressed by the patients—e.g. a fear of contracting a deadly disease etc. The fears were never realised, but still persisted. The cognitive view is that the dread of contamination persists because of a regular misinterpretation of feelings of fear as signalling present danger.

The second, lesser, cognitive bias that enters in to the self-perpetuating cycle is thought–action fusion (TAF). Patients report that having significant, recurrent thoughts about contamination increases the probability that they will actually become contaminated, and also that having contamination thoughts about other people increases the risk that these other people will actually become contaminated. The TAF bias can increase the person's estimations of the probability of harm, and the probable seriousness of the anticipated harm. Among patients with an inflated sense of responsibility for preventing harm to others, the TAF bias significantly raises the estimations of contamination-harm, followed by increased guilt and anxiety. The inclusion of the TAF bias into the self-perpetuating cycle is illustrated in Fig. 9.2.

The self-perpetuating cycle has therapeutic implications. Discussion of the cycle and its putative operation in the particular case is recommended, and attempts should be made to undo or at least weaken the *ex-consequentia* bias. The same is true of the TAF contamination bias.

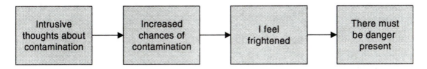

Fig. 9.2 Thought-action cognitive biases contribute to the self-perpetuating cycle

Why do fears of contamination ever decline?

At the risk of seeming excessively analytical, the important question of why the fears of contamination are so persistent, is followed by the equally interesting question of why they ever *decline*.

With few exceptions, the feelings of contamination do not degrade, and they spread widely and rapidly. This formidable combination of non-degradability and wide spread of the contamination should lead to an ever-expanding and stable net of contamination, with the associated fears and avoidance. The unchecked feelings of contamination and fear can indeed grow ever wider until the person comes to avoid entire cities which have been contaminated. These extreme cases illustrate the ultimate extent of unchecked contamination. There is no obvious braking mechanism to prevent the spread of the contamination, and no spontaneous process of decay. (The non-degradability of contamination is reminiscent of the anthropological principle of contagion, *once in contact, always in contact.* The spread of contamination recalls the principle of similarity, *like affects like.*)

Fortunately the extreme cases of contaminated cities are rare, but the easy spread and non-degradability are at play in most cases of contamination fear. What prevents the ultimate spread of contamination in the majority of instances? People oppressed by their feelings of contamination try to control and contain the spread and disabling effects of the contamination by elaborate tactics of avoidance and escape, notably by washing. At best these are exercises in damage limitation. The tactics often are successful in *containing* the spread of the contamination. However, there is little reason to expect them to eliminate or even reduce the fear of contamination. (Among other reasons, we need to remember that contamination is not degradable, and simply avoiding the contaminants, will leave the contamination unchanged.) To the contrary, it is argued that 'safety behaviour', the avoidance, escape, washing tactics, may preserve the fear. Cognitive theorists would add that safety tactics prevent the collection of disconfirmatory evidence, and hence, preserve the patient's unadaptive misinterpretations.

Containment is an extremely common, perhaps universal, reaction to the fear of contamination and regardless of whether or not it preserves the abnormal behaviour and cognitions, it is most unlikely that containment does the opposite, namely diminish the fear. The fact remains that in many instances the fear of contamination does decline, and is capable of elimination. Treatment, by psychological and/or pharmacological methods, can be reasonably effective. As mentioned earlier, control trials have demonstrated that psychological methods are moderately effective in treating OCD, and in these trials many of the patients suffered from contamination fears. The specific efficacy of the methods for contamination fears is not clear yet, but over many years and trials, numbers of patients reported and showed significant clinical benefits that included a reduction, even elimination, of their fears of contamination. Pharmacological methods have also been shown to be moderately effective, at very least in the short-run, and need to be taken into account. How do these methods change the fear of contamination? Do they prevent the spread, and if so, how? Do they promote the degradation of the contamination? This is an enticing idea, but improbable. Instead, the drugs appear to reduce the *fear* of the contamination by damping down the person's reactions. The typical description given by patients is that the medications 'take the edge off' the fear, and make life more tolerable. If during this damping down period the patient engages in approach behaviour, the fear-reduction may become lasting. It is also possible, but remains to be tested, that during the damping down period the patient is significantly less likely to experience further spreading of the contamination, or to acquire new contamination fears. Even though the non-degradability of the contamination is most unlikely to be affected by the drugs, patients probably would add that they are less upset by the contaminants.

Psychological treatments that are predominantly behavioural and depend almost entirely on exposure exercises are intended to reduce fear, and in cases of fear contamination that is a common outcome. To the extent that the treatment succeeds, no spreading of a fear of the contamination is to be expected. In respect to the degradability of the contamination, little change should occur but, as with drug therapy, the contaminants should be tolerated better; specifically, cause less fear.

The prospects for reducing the fear and the spread of contamination, especially in cases of mental contamination, are greater with CBT. In these cases CBT may also succeed in promoting the degradation of the contamination. If the patient succeeds in replacing the catastrophic misappraisals of probability/seriousness of the perceived threat from a 'contaminated' source, the fear and the spread should decline sharply and even disappear. This is well-illustrated in cases of self-contamination. If the patient succeeds in replacing the catastrophic misinterpretations of their unwanted intrusive thoughts by adaptive and benign appraisals of the significance of the thoughts, the feelings of mental contamination evaporate. No spread of contamination is expected or observed. The question of whether the patient's feelings of contamination are degradable is no longer relevant. There are other examples of the potential power of CBT in these cases.When the patient described earlier (p.103) discovered that she had mistakenly attributed the 'contaminated' food to her despised former husband, the feelings of contamination, and avoidance, disappeared as soon as she learned that the gift had come from her father. A corrective reattribution can alter the contamination; it will not spread and it degrades completely. Another example was provided by a patient whose fear of a contaminated bottle of pesticide disappeared as soon as he learnt that that the bottle had contained spring water and never held any chemicals. In cases of mental contamination the primary source is a person and therefore, when our CBT focuses on promoting a deep reappraisal of the person-source of the contamination, significant improvements can be expected.

Given the combined effects of non-degradability and easy spread, fears of contamination should flourish. It is unclear how and why intense/ abnormal fears of contamination sometimes decline *spontaneously* (spontaneous elimination is most unusual). In the broadest terms, we can speculate that the acquisition of evidence which disconfirms the person's inflated appraisals of the probability and seriousness of the threat emanating from the contamination will diminish the fear. The best evidence comes from direct personal experiences ('Handling the bottle of pesticide did not make me ill'). Other disconfirmations arise from observational learning ('My brother did not become ill after handling the bottle of pesticide'), and from public sources of information. Also, fluctuations in mood, levels of stress, and perceived responsibility, can affect the tolerance or intolerance of bodily sensations that are interpreted as signals of threat. The deliberate or unplanned reduction of safety behaviour also provides opportunities for obtaining potentially disconfirmatory evidence. For someone who has a strong fear of contamination, a coincidence of these potentially disconfirmatory experiences and thoughts would be fortunate, but not perhaps common. In which case the fear of contamination would persist and even expand. It usually does.

In cases of mental contamination, spontaneous improvements can be anticipated if and when the affected person arrives at a major reappraisal of the person-source of the contamination and/or the circumstances in which the violation took place.

Cognitive co-morbidity

It has been suggested that the study of *cognitive* co-morbidity is likely to prove more fruitful than the traditional approach to co-morbidity which is based on statistical associations between disorders (Rachman 1991). Analyses of cognitive co-morbidity involve a search for *psychological* links between disorders and begin with a consideration of the affected person's primary cognitions pertaining to the disorder. The basic cognition in the fear of disease contamination is that contact with specifiable contaminants will threaten one's health. The underlying, and overlying, cognition in health anxiety (formerly, hypochondria) is also a threat to one's health. In the light of this central common cognition we should observe common beliefs and behaviour in these two disorders. In both of them the threats are perceived to be serious, even life-threatening, are temporally remote, blurred by uncertainty, difficult to cope with, and hard to eradicate. In both, the affected person feels specially vulnerable and at significantly greater risk of illness than other people. However, the risks perceived by a sufferer from health anxiety range more widely than do those who suffer from a fear of contamination. Another difference is that in the fear of disease contamination the perceived source of the danger is predominantly external and identifiable; in health anxiety most of the sources of perceived danger are internal and can be ambiguous. Both disorders are notable for persistent hypervigilance. In the fear of contamination the elevated vigilance is directed towards the identification and avoidance of external threats in the form of contaminants. In health anxiety the hypervigilance generally takes the form of internal scanning for signs of trouble, such as perceived lumps, irregular heart beats, etc. The source of the threat differs in the two disorders. In cases of health anxiety the patient believes and/or fears that they already have symptoms of an illness and hence repeatedly requests medical examinations and testing. People who dread contamination are concerned about future threats and their energies are focused on prevention, avoidance, washing. The cognition common to both disorders is a perceived threat to one's health, a present threat in cases of health anxiety, and a prospective threat in the fear of contamination. In both disorders steps are taken to protect one's health and the exact form of the safety-seeking is determined by the perceived nature and location of the threat. The uncertainty and doubt that pervades health anxiety promotes compulsive checking and reassurance-seeking, whereas the need to remove a threat of contamination promotes compulsive cleaning. In both disorders the background level of anxiety is subject to episodic surges in reaction to specific threats that leave behind the residue of uneasiness and uncertainty.

The physiological and behavioural similarities between phobias and a fear of contamination were noted some time ago (Rachman and Hodgson 1980). The linking cognition appears to be an exaggerated prediction of serious harm coming from the phobic object, person or place. Both disorders are disorders of fear but with differing threat content; the simplest course is to fold the fear of contamination into the general category of phobia. For most purposes this is a satisfactory step, especially from a therapeutic standpoint ('exposure treatment rules'), but it runs the risk of losing some subtle variations. In the present analysis for example, a workable distinction is made between the fear of disease contamination and the fear of dirt contamination. Folding mental contamination into phobias is a less satisfactory fit because of the complexities of the various manifestations of mental contamination.

The main cognitive link between contact contamination and compulsive checking can be traced to an inflated sense of responsibility. If a sufferer from intense fears of disease contamination is also prone to feelings of inflated responsibility, compulsive checking can be expected. (Incidentally, this connection may be a major contributor to the significant correlation between scores on the two major subscales of most OCD inventories, washing and checking.) Given a high score on responsibility, anyone who develops a fear of contact contamination will almost certainly engage in repetitive checking. The role of a few key variables, so-called 'multipliers', in determining compulsive checking is considered in Rachman (2004). In sum, in the presence of inflated responsibility cognitive co-morbidity between contact contamination and compulsive checking can be predicted.

Next, there appears to be a cognitive link between obsessions and mental contamination, and self-contamination in particular (Fig. 9.3). It has been proposed that obsessions are caused by a catastrophic misinterpretation of the personal significance of one's unwanted intrusive thoughts (Rachman 1997, 2003). Unwanted thoughts/images/impulses are extremely common but can be transformed into obsessions as a result of misinterpretations of their significance. Additionally, obsessions are accompanied or even promoted by negative self-appraisals. Mental contamination also can be promoted by pre-existing negative appraisals, and comparable to obsessions, can be precipitated by unwanted intrusive images or thoughts or impulses. An example that covers both disorders can be found in incestuous images and urges. If the incestuous images are interpreted by the person as evidence of lurking, unacceptable, repulsive tendencies they can turn into recurrent, uncontrollable obsessions. They can also produce feelings of mental pollution, a sense of internal, inaccessible, and moral dirtiness. There is a cognitive link between repugnant obsessions and self-contamination. (By deduction, the most appropriate treatment for cases of self-contamination that arise from repugnant obsessions is the cognitive-behavioural method, Rachman (2003)). Mental pollution/ contamination is most often associated with blasphemous and sexual obsessions and less often with harm obsessions. As mentioned earlier, mental pollution is likely associated with a fear of dirt contamination; they share the

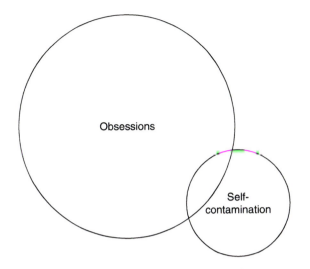

Fig. 9.3 The overlap between obsessions and self-contamination

behavioural manifestations of disgust, cleaning, and avoidance. An important cognitive link between obsessions and mental pollution/contamination in general is the catastrophic misinterpretation of the significance of one's unwanted, intrusive thoughts.

Other precipitants of contamination include sexual assaults (Fairbrother and Rachman 2004), psychological or physical violations (domination, oppression, betrayals, manipulation, memories, humiliations, insults, accusations). The undoubted links between OCD and PTSD (de Silva and Marks 1999; Gershuny *et al.* 2003) are important but complex and challenging. It is troubling that in some cases at least, therapeutic progress in reducing one of the problems was followed by an exacerbation of the other problem (Gershuny *et al.* 2003). These reports make it advisable to incorporate a full cognitive analysis of both problems, and also to assess the presence of mental contamination when formulating a treatment plan. In some of our cases the treatment of the PTSD-associated feelings of mental contamination greatly facilitated the subsequent reduction of the remaining OCD problems. Careful studies of how best to tackle co-morbid OCD and PTSD are needed. As ever, it is important to address the question of why the person feels under current threat.

Given the probable cognitive links between contamination arising from physical violation and PTSD, the theory set out by Ehlers and Clark (2000) provides a firm foundation for such analyses. Contamination arising from psychological violation probably has cognitive links with social phobia and with PTSD, but at present the relative frequency and seriousness of the various precipitants can not be estimated.

A probable cognitive link between the fear of dirt contamination and social phobia is the dread and expectation of social disapproval or outright rejection and isolation. The troublesome cognitions involved in social anxiety are described by Clark and Wells (1995). Fears of contamination by contact with dirt have at least two elements, a dread of the unpleasantness of the feelings of disgust induced by the contact (nausea, vomiting etc.), and a dread of the social consquences of one's state of pollution. People who fear social rejection feel compelled to avert this awful possibility by making concentrated afforts to convey a good impression of themselves in company. The beliefs associated with social anxiety include the conviction that other people tend to scrutinise one intensively and to do so in a critical manner. In addition it is commonly believed that the scrutineers can detect one's anxiety and uneasiness easily and accurately, and that they therefore downgrade one as being weak, boring, stupid, and/or inadequate. Interestingly, a similar belief is encountered among patients who fear mental pollution/contamination. Often they report that other people can sense when the patient is contaminated/polluted. Similar cognitions are also encountered. 'When people sense that I am dirty/polluted they will be disgusted and reject and avoid me.' 'Other people can readily detect my dirtiness/pollution, my bad breath/flatulence/body odour/smelly socks, they can tell.' And it follows that I must ensure that all possible signs of my pollution are eliminated or masked before entering the company of others—or social disaster will occur. Typically this takes the form of compulsive cleaning, especially after bowel movements, urination, masturbation, handling dirty products, and so forth. Some patients are reluctant to venture out unless and until they empty their bowels. Repeated checking to ensure that one is free of pollution is common. The possible involvement of a social component in feelings of pollution/dirtiness is supported by the finding of a significant association between feelings of pollution and a fear of negative evaluation in the experimental induction of mental pollution (Herba 2005).

Socially phobic people tend to engage in post-event processing after social events (Clark and Wells 1995), and it will be interesting to determine whether people with fears of pollution/dirtiness do the same. They might 're-play' upsetting social events and ruminate on whether or not other people were aware of and responding to their feelings of mental pollution. There are of course differences between fears of contamination and social phobias but they do appear to share important beliefs about the transparency of their 'abnormalities' and the associated cognitions about being subjected to critical scrutiny and rejection by other people. In both there is a threat of a social disaster.

Why is it a *current* threat?

Following the example set by Ehlers and Clark (2000) in their cognitive explanation of PTSD, writers who tackle specific anxiety disorders should attempt to explain why the affected people feel that they are under *current* threat. The fear of contamination expressed and displayed by people who dread contracting a disease because of physical contact with a perceived source of infection, presents no problem. The person feels under current threat because contact with a diseased contaminant can produce a serious illness. The threat is real and tangible. In many cases the current threat goes beyond a fear of incurring damage to one's health, and extends to a fear of harming other people by spreading the contamination. In some instances, as in the case of the grandmother who went to extraordinary lengths to clean and disinfect herself and her belongings in order to protect her young granddaughter (p.72), the dread of being responsible for contaminating other people is the dominant current threat.

In cases of a fear of being contaminated by physical contact with a dirty pollutant, the threat may yet contain an implied threat to one's health (e.g. contamination from animal or human waste products), but the cases in which it is essentially a fear of dirt as such, the current threat is not easily evident. There are several possibilities. The person may dread the tension and discomfort produced by touching particular types of dirt, and also dread the considerable time, effort, and concentration that will be required in order to carry out the compulsive cleaning—it can take many hours of concentrated effort to complete the process of decontamination. In addition to the obvious dread caused by these two related threats—deep discomfort and compulsive urges—the uncontrollability of one's abnormal reactions to the contamination often stirs a more sinister long-term threat to one's mental stability. In one case the patient's unhappy life was completely distorted by his intense fear of becoming contaminated by his own urine. Despite his recognition that the fear was abnormal, his compulsion to wash was so compelling that he spent up to two hours per shower and on a bad day, repeated the process several times. The immediate effects on his life can be imagined, but in addition he developed a fear that the contamination might be the early stage of a mental breakdown that would result in his admission to a long-stay mental hospital. For him the current threat was a mixture of immediate distress and the fear that he was losing his mind. The fear of contamination by dirt also has social ramifications. For some patients who dread dirt-contamination, the primary current fear is that of social rejection. (There are early indications that the fear of negative evaluation is high among people who dread possible contamination.) They expect that other people will be revolted if they learn that the patient is 'dirty', and they will be ostracised. These patients are super-sensitive to how they are perceived and take great care to ensure that they are always tidy and clean. Some are especially worried that they might be malodorous. As a result they carry out intensive washing and are inclined to use, or over-use, soaps, deodorants, mouth washes, antiseptic wipes, or cleansing lotions. In cases of a fear of becoming contaminated by contact with dirt there are related current fears; a dread of social disaster, a dread of the immediate consequences on one's behaviour, and a dread that the recognizably out of control, irrational pre-occupation with dirt is a sign of impending mental instability.

Unfortunately, for patients who are afflicted by feelings of mental contamination the dedicated washing and cleaning is ultimately futile. Their inability to remove the feelings of internal contamination/pollution is a cause of distress, and for many, contributes to the sense of current threat. They dread the persistence of unbearable feelings of uncontrollable pollution; they are defeated and resign themselves to a state of hopeless misery. They are threatened by the prospect of being trapped in an insoluble, chronic state of distress.

Similar beliefs are expressed by victims of physical violation who develop feelings of pollution. As in cases of PTSD (Ehlers and Clark 2000) they may come to believe that they have been permanently damaged, and polluted, by the (sexual) assault, and may even abandon the hope of having a normal life. In addition to the general belief that they have suffered irreparable psychological damage, they may also believe that they have been permanently polluted. This belief is liable to be reinforced by the repeated failures of their dedicated washing. Patients who think that they are vulnerable to a recurrence of the violation become highly vigilant, and any person or cue that is perceived to be polluted or contaminated provokes a sense of current threat.

In cases of a fear of morphing, the current threat is that contact, direct or indirect, with an 'undesirable' person will lead to personal changes of a damaging kind, or in extreme cases, even up to a total loss of identity. There are few fears so fundamental as that of losing one's sense of identity. In cases of self-contamination the cycle of repugnant thoughts/habits leads to compulsive washing, and the fear is that they are destined to be permanently twisted by their own nature. The primary source of the contamination is always present. As in other cases in which feelings of pollution are prominent, the current fear is that they are trapped in state of mental distress that is unavoidable, uncontrollable, and chronic.

Identification of the patient's current threat is a pre-condition for formulating a *precise* treatment plan. The main thrust of therapy is directed at removing the current threat, supplemented by whatever means necessary to deal with any remaining fears. Treatment can proceed in the absence of such identification but will be hobbled and it is difficult to promote full improvement.

Chapter 10

Treatment

The prevailing treatment for the fear of (contact) contamination, exposure and response prevention (ERP), is well-established and moderately effective in many cases (Barlow 2002; Clark 2004). In most instances the provision of programmed exposure exercises is indispensable. As the method is familiar and widely used, the present analysis is concentrated on the cognitive elements in the therapy, with special reference to the treatment of mental contamination.

The expansion of the concept of fear of contamination to include mental contamination in its various forms, raises the need to develop new methods of treatment that can supplement ERP. Mental contamination is essentially a cognitive disorder and therefore a cognitive form of treatment seems to be the best fit. Work on the integration of cognitive methods with ERP in the treatment of fears of contamination is underway and progress has been made. It is worth mentioning that in the early stages of the process of therapy some patients are perplexed by the therapist's keen interest in seemingly unrelated and often remote 'mental events'. They question the relevance of these events to their fear of contamination and their compulsion to wash repeatedly and vigorously. As one patient expressed it, 'How on earth can my fiance's betrayal have anything to with my fear of becoming contaminated if I touch my own clothing?' Good question.

General principles

The general principles of cognitive behaviour therapy (CBT) are applicable in cases of fear of contamination. The treatment is a combination of cognitive analysis and modification plus exposure exercises and response prevention. The intention of the treatment is to assist patients in recognizing and then modifying their unadaptive, cognitive misinterpretations/beliefs. In parallel, behavioural exercises are carried out to reduce the fear evoked by the stimulus situations and overcome unadaptive avoidance behaviour and related problems. The early part of the treatment includes a didactic component in which patients are provided with corrective information about the operation of cognitive biases such as TAF, the universality of unwanted intrusive thoughts, and the *ex-consequentia* bias. For instance, 'Your fear reaction when you see a contaminant has become a very strong habit, but that feeling of fear does *not* mean that you are now in danger. It is not a danger to you, nor is it a danger to me or to other people.' And, 'Your thoughts about contamination are mere thoughts and cannot contaminate you or me, or anyone else; they are harmless'.

A full cognitive analysis, supplemented by behavioural avoidance tests, is then carried out. Information and evidence pertaining to the cognitive mis-appraisals/beliefs is collected and assembled in a way that enables the patient to evaluate them (see the Standardized Interview Schedule in the Appendix). The evaluations are then retested by incorporating the personal evidence collected from behavioural experiments. The significance of the new evidence is fully discussed, and, where necessary, additional evidence is collected The importance of behavioural experiments is that they give patients the opportunity to collect direct personal information pertaining to their key cognitions. The evidential value of such direct information exceeds statistical information, therapist's accounts, or second-hand stories about the experiences of other people.

In cases of contact contamination the emphasis is on ERP exercises, and the results are reasonably satisfactory. The exercises can be facilitated by the use of therapeutic modelling. It is explained to the patient that watching someone else engage the contaminant in a calm, gradual manner will take the edge off their fear and enable them, slowly and carefully, to copy the actions of the therapist. A hierarchy of contaminated items is jointly compiled and the therapist begins by calmly modelling the approach to the lowest items, while reassuring the patient that modelling sessions are a combined enterprise and the patient will be encouraged to imitate the approaches but will never be coerced in any way. They are also reassured that there will be no surprises and that all of the modelling steps will be discussed and agreed before the exercises are undertaken. They will never be confronted by a hidden contaminant or one they are not ready to face. Instead they will be supported throughout and gently encouraged to make graded, gradual progress in touching the contaminants.

The inability and/or unwillingness of patients to undertake exposure and response prevention treatment is attributable to overriding fear or to their scepticism about the likelihood of the treatment helping them, or both of these obstacles. It is evident from the failures that encouragement, support, and persuasion are not sufficient. The provision of modelling by the therapist produces some reduction in fear and also demonstrates the harmlessness of the contact. Some patients are so highly motivated and conscientious that they carry out the homework part of the exercises fully. Most patients practise irregularly or erratically, and in problem cases one or more domiciliary visits are indicated. The domiciliary treatment is used to promote the patient's home exercising, and it is necessary to avoid the development of a dependency on the presence of the therapist. Before and during domiciliary treatment sessions the therapist elucidates the connection between overestimations of danger, and how they impede ERP exercises, especially at home.

Guidelines for the treatment of cases of mental contamination are proposed for each of the five forms of the phenomenon, recognizing their common and distinctive features. The treatment combines cognitive and behavioural components, but the cognitive analysis and modification take precedence. Targeting the behavioural manifestations first can be a slow and at times puzzling process, but success on the cognitive side usually facilitates improvements in fear behaviour.

Notwithstanding the common elements in the treatment of contact contamination and mental contamination, there is an important difference between the two in the focus and direction of the assessment and treatment. *The treatment in cases of mental contamination focuses on the primary source of the contamination—the source is human*, a person or persons. Consequently the assessment is concentrated on identifying the person/s, and the circumstances in which the contamination arose (e.g. violation). The treatment then focuses on the patient's present appraisal of the person and circumstances, and why it is perceived as a *current* threat. The reasons why it is a current threat are unearthed, and the evidence to support or disconfirm that appraisal is assembled. The intention is to assist the patient develop an alternative, more adaptive, and up-to-date appraisal of the current threat. Naturally, much of the therapy is concerned with the patient's feelings of contamination and why it is persisting long after the critical events, and generally, long after contact with the violator has ceased. Why does the contamination persist and why does it remain a threat?

Clinical assessment

What is the current threat? Generally, people who are being assessed for treatment of a fear of contamination have completed a general psychological evaluation, and received a diagnosis of OCD. In deciding whether a course of CBT is advisable clinicians evaluate the contamination problem by means of the standardized interview, behaviour tests, and specific psychometric tests. The assessment consists of the following tests and generally takes about 2–3 hours to complete.

- Standardized Interview for Contamination
- Present status: a detailed account of the present status of the fear and its development
- Behaviour avoidance tests
- Test probes using imagery
- Vancouver Obsessive Compulsive Inventory (VOCI)
- Mental contamination subscale, appended to the VOCI
- Contamination sensitivity scale
- Contamination thought-action fusion scale
- Yale Obsessive Compulsive Scale Interview (YBOCS)
- Beck Depression Inventory.

Daily recordings of level of fear and any associated washing are started if treatment is to go ahead. Almost invariably it is essential to compile a hierarchical list of the items, places, and people that evoke the fear, and rank the intensity of the fears on a thermometer (0–100). The fear hierarchy is complemented by a similar hierarchy dealing with avoidance behaviour. Depending on the information collected, supplementary tests may be needed. For example, if the person is affected by a fear of morphing or of self-contamination, it is necessary to collect information about the personal significance which the patient attaches to their unwanted, unacceptable intrusions at the beginning of each session, and the Personal Significance Scale is useful for this purpose (see Appendix).

The treatment plan

Armed with this formidable array of information, the clinician determines what type of contamination fear is involved, identifies the current threat/s perceived by the patient, and formulates the treatment plan. An ERP component is primary in cases of contact contamination and secondary in cases of mental contamination. This order of importance is reversed in cases of mental contamination. As stated, the present account of treatment is concentrated on the less familiar forms of contamination, the manifestations of mental contamination.

The first part of therapy is informative and educational. The nature of OCD is explained and the main manifestations, obsessions and compulsions, are described. The universal occurrence of some fear, and much avoidance, of dirty and/or dangerous contaminants is explained and a distinction is made between socially acceptable and endorsed cleaning behaviour and cleaning that is excessive or inappropriate. The connections between fear and compulsions are set out, and examples of abnormally strong fears are given. The compulsive power of the fear of contamination is acknowledged and the concept of response prevention is explained, including the slow but regular spontaneous weakening of compulsive urges to wash during the prevention period.

An account is given of the nature of mental contamination and how it resembles contact contamination in some respects, but differs in that it can be produced and re-evoked even without any physical contact. 'It can be produced by emotional distress and re-evoked by upsetting images, unhappy memories, criticisms. It is mainly associated with people but can develop into a dread of tangible substances that are dirty or germy or dangerous (e.g. chemicals). In order to deal with the fears and compulsions it is necessary to talk about important people in your life and analyse important events in your life, even if at first they appear to have little connection with your present fears. We will also need to find out as best we can, exactly what are your greatest fears and worries at present.'

In the next stage of therapy, attention is focused on the patient's key cognitions, guided by the information collected in the assessment. The cognitions of prime importance are those that explain and sustain the person's sense of present threat. Asking the patient to respond to the list of beliefs/cognitions most pertinent to their particular form of contamination, say self-contamination, facilitates the process of elucidation. In the next few sessions evidence for and against the key cognitions is collected and assembled, along the lines described in the following case.

Treatment of the fear of morphing and contamination

There are three components in this treatment—didactic, cognitive shifting, and behavioural changes. The fear of morphing rests on some odd beliefs that often diminish in the light of fresh authoritative information. The didactic component can be powerful. An underlying assumption is that one can pick up undesirable characteristics from proximity to weird/abnormal/freakish people. The common 'undesirable' characteristics—mental instability, immorality, mental deterioration, freakish physical features—are believed to be transmissable by physical contact with people who manifest these characteristics, or by close proximity to them, or even by visual contamination. They are believed to be transferable from person to person. Fortunately these beliefs usually are amenable to modification by the provision of corrective information, along the following lines.

Patients are informed that 'most feelings of contamination arise from direct contact with dirt/disease or dangerous substances, and the unpleasant feelings are easily removed by washing. Worries about becoming contaminated by mental instability/immorality are somewhat different, and are not picked up by direct contact. The problem arises because some of the troubling feelings that one experiences when coming close to a strange or weird person are similar to the feelings caused by touching a dirty or dangerous substance, and this can be confusing. Actually, the troubling feelings you feel when you get close to a weird person are different from feelings of ordinary contamination caused by touching a dirty/dangerous *substance*, and in important ways. The undesirable, even dreaded characteristics of these people can not be transferred from one person to another. You cannot pick up strange or weird behaviour from seeing or even coming close to a disturbed person. It never happens'. (In the course of therapy, the didactic component is returned to in order to incorporate the patient's own experience in the corrective information. It has never happened to a relative of yours, or a friend of yours. It has never happened to you. If a friend or relative came close to or touched a disturbed person they would not pick up any strange or weird behaviour.)

'The troubling part of encountering a disturbed/weird person is that the very idea of mental instability or mental deterioration can be upsetting. That is why merely seeing a disturbed person can be upsetting, even without any contact, even when seen at some distance. Mental instability is not picked by touching or seeing a disturbed person. Do you think that your relations can pick up mental instability in this way? Do you worry that your family or friends might be transformed by seeing or walking by an unstable/weird person during the day? Most affected people believe that they are *uniquely* at risk of picking up undesirable characteristics or frank mental disturbance by mere proximity. There is no medical evidence that this is true.'

'The health care workers who care for mentally disturbed people on a daily basis, the nurses and doctors, do not pick up mental instability from their patients. No transfer occurs. The same is true of undesirable characteristics. We do not pick them up by physical contact with people who manifest such characteristics. Personality characteristics, desirable and undesirable, evolve gradually from childhood into adulthood. They are not transferable by an incidental physical contact with a person one happens to comes across.'

'Almost all people who develop a fear of being adversely changed by contact with undesirable characteristics or people nevertheless cope well and live ordinary lives. The thought that one might be changed adversely through physical contact can occur frequently, on most excursions, but it never actually takes place. The problem is a problem of your *thoughts*, not a problem caused by a horrifying transformation into another person.'

'People who are affected by a fear of morphing recognize the curious nature of their beliefs, and that friends and relatives are dismissive, but remain puzzled by the inconsistency between their beliefs and their strong reactions when strange/weird people do come close. Not uncommonly they try to explain it by resorting to the notion that there are "mental germs" which are capable of transmitting mental illnesses or mental disturbances. They are reassured that this notion does arise in cases of morphing but there is no scientific evidence to support it.'

'Some people get so concerned about picking up undesirable or harmful characteristics by proximity to a person who appears to be mentally unstable that they begin to fear they will contract a contagious mental illness and be ruined. But there is no medical evidence that mental illness is contagious, in the way that flu, measles, and chicken pox can be transferred by contact. Nurses and doctors who care for patients with a mental illness do not pick up the illnesses.

'If there was a possibility of picking up undesirable personality characteristics from proximity to a disturbed person, it is hard to see how repeatedly washing your hands would solve the problem. Washing one's hands, however vigorously, has no effect on one's personality. The idea of being affected by coming too close to a weird/strange person can be upsetting, but it is an idea, and upsetting ideas are not easily washed away.'

(Occasional patients raise the transmission of certain diseases, such as syphilis, which if left untreated can eventually damage the CNS and cause mental deterioration. This potential source of confusion can be dealt with by explaining the cause of the disease, by sexual contact, its treatability, its rarity nowadays, and the impossibility of contracting the disease by incidental proximity.)

The didactic component is followed by cognitive analyses designed to shift the unadaptive and erroneous cognitions, and as always consists of a compilation of evidence and arguments for and against the person's construal of the threats they face (why is it a *current* threat?), and an evaluation of the efficacy of their tactics for coping with the threats. On the basis of the cognitive analysis and the experiments, the behavioural component of therapy is introduced. The patient is encouraged to engage in planned exposures to the threat figures and places. The tactic of response prevention (inhibit the washing, neutralizing, mental cleansing) is incorporated into the plan. The neutralizing tactic of 'mental cleansing' is often resorted to in cases of mental contamination, especially self-contamination, morphing, and mental pollution. Patients are advised to refrain from such cleansing, and inhibit their urges to avoid people and places in which they anticipate worrying about morphing, and to refrain from any compulsive cleaning away of the effects of a visual contamination.

Adjusting the programme of exposures as required, the anxiety, avoidance behaviour, and neutralizing progressively decline. The strongest fear of morphing is evoked by physical contact with the 'undesirable' person, and hence a reduction of this part of the fear should also weaken the effects of non-physical contacts. During therapy the interplay between the familiar fear of contamination and the fear of morphing is worth studying, especially in the light of knowledge about the summation of fears (Rachman 1990). As fears generally collapse downwards, the therapist should attempt to turn to the strongest fears as soon as some progress has been made and the patient's motivation and expectations are judged to be sufficiently high. In treating cases of contamination it is necessary for the therapist, and patient, to titrate the exposure exercises. Patients refuse or defect from treatment because of the very strength of the fear, and the anticipated spread and duration of the contamination that is provoked during treatment. It often becomes a matter of making speed slowly.

Cognitions selected from the list of common beliefs and appraisals in cases of morphing, set out on p.94, have been 'personalized' for use in the assessment and cognitive analysis stages of treatment. The therapist should pay particular attention to the patient's belief, whether expressed directly or implied, that people can be morphed, transformed. Careful and repeated conversations about the belief and its basis can be most helpful.

This transcript comes from the treatment of a 35-year-old accountant suffering from a fear of pesticides/diseases, compulsive washing and checking, religious obsessions, and a fear of morphing. This extract from the full transcript concentrates on the features of morphing, the provision of information about the disorder, and the collection of evidence about the nature of the patient's perceived threats. Her OCD started at the age of 15 during a period of family stress in which she was persistently criticised and denigrated by her parents, and persisted into adulthood. In addition to the OCD, she suffered from low self-esteem, anxiety, and chronic pessimism.

She experienced unpleasant feelings of contamination and threat whenever she encountered 'unfortunate' people, those who looked weird or disturbed and/or shabby and dirty. The feelings were evoked by the sight of such people, by visual contamination, or by physical proximity, and were especially intense if she touched them or their possessions. She avoided such people and the places where she was likely to encounter them. The feelings evoked by contacts were intrusive and unpleasant, and she dealt with them by vigorous washing.

'When you see them how does that make you feel?
Fifteen feet away I'm comfortable, but 5 feet away I avoid them and even avoid their air-space.

What happens if you can't avoid, or it is too late to avoid them?

It is usually outside, so there is nowhere to wash. I feel the need to touch an unrelated object or recite a safe phrase under my breath until I can have a good wash.

If you are near a washroom what do you do?

Well, if I have physical contact, it would depend. If the person touched my hands I would have to wash them, and if she touched my jacket, I'd have to wash that.

What are you thinking of when you wash?

I'm getting a sense of relief. Uhmm, from any real or imagined germs. ... And I know that it will trouble me until I do wash. Can't get it out of my mind. Here is an example: an odd-looking man dropped his parcel, a sort of blanket affair, as he tried to climb onto the bus and I picked up his stuff and helped him get on. I had to wash my hands before I could do anything else. I was like catatonic. I absolutely had to wash before doing anything else. One good long wash.

What were you thinking? Were you protecting yourself?

Yes.

From what?

From what? Misfortune.

So that is why you avoid them?

Because I get frightened if they come near me.

What happens if you fail to avoid them?

I get upset and rush to the nearest washroom to clean myself.

Does that help you?

Usually, but it can take quite an effort.

Why does washing give you some relief?

Because I am cleaning away the germs.

Are these ordinary germs?

No, they are thought germs.

The kind that you can pick up without any form of contact?

Yes, even from walking in a person's air space.

What do think is the evidence for these germs?

Touching these people gives me the same feeling I get from touching, say, a dirty bandage.

The feeling is the same?

Yes.

Any other evidence you can think of?

It's not really evidence, but mental illness is an illness.

I see. Is there a reason to expect that it is a contagious illness?

I don't see why not.

Is there any evidence that people who work with mentally ill patients pick up the mental illness?

Not that I am aware of.

Any one at all?

No.

How much do you know about mental illness?

Not a lot.

Do you know anyone who is mentally unstable? Or ever hear about an acquaintance or friend who turned mentally unstable ?

No.

Have you ever read about someone turning mentally unstable after walking into contaminated airspace? The sort that worries you?

No, I haven't

If you encounter a person who is well-dressed and clean, no germs, but behaving strangely, say talking aloud and making weird gestures, what would your reaction be if he came close or touched you?

I would have to wash. He is having some problem. Well, I might become like them, mentally unstable and end up in a psychiatric hospital.

What theme is running through this—people who appear mentally disturbed or shabby or having bad luck? Why does it make you so uncomfortable? Even if there is no physical contact, although that makes it worse.

Whatever their problem it can be transferred to me. Thinking about it logically I don't believe in this stuff. It is exhausting talking about this stuff. But I know it helps and I feel better afterwards. I even have to avoid their airspace.

Now, to take another example. How would you react if you saw a woman, who looks shabby and even dirty, but successful, happily talking to a group of her friends who are obviously at ease and enjoying her company. What would happen if she touched you as the group walked past?

Wouldn't bother me, might even wish to talk to her.

Take it a step further. You get upset at the sight or touch of someone who is enduring misfortune, but not if they are seemingly successful, even if they are less than clean

That's right. I can pick up misfortune from homeless, disturbed people. I can even pick up the flaw that has brought them misfortune. Here we go into goof germs again.

When you are out with your husband and son, do you worry that they too might pick up thought germs from weird/shabby/unstable people?

Not really.

And when they are going out without you, do you worry that they might pick up the germs?

No.

I wonder, why is it that they are not at risk?

Yes, its crazy isn't it

Often the people who develop the sort of fear that troubles you so much come to believe that they alone are at risk, they are specially at risk. And that seems to be true for you.

Yes, yes, I suppose it is. Even my family is not affected. So strange.

To recap so far, The positive evidence of picking up thought germs is that proximity or contact with these people gives the same feeling of fear that you experience when you touch germ-contaminated material. On the other hand, the feeling that these people have thought germs and that they are contagious, has little or no positive evidence. Health workers do not seem to pick up mental illnesses from their patients. Your husband and child are not vulnerable to picking up the thought germs. There are no antibiotics or similar medicines for treating mental illness. Come to that, do you know of anyone who picked up a mental illness or became mentally unstable as a result of coming into contact with people carrying thought germs?

Let's write all of this evidence on the board. How can we explain the fact that proximity makes you feel so anxious?

I think it might have something to do with my fear of mental illness, well not mental illness exactly but more what you might call mentally unstable or weird.

How long has that troubled you?

A long time.

Before or after you developed a fear of contamination?

About the same time, about 16.

Why did it worry you so?

That was my reputation in the family, that I was nervous, and weak. A follower, not a leader.

Your whole family?

Well, really my mother. My father said very little.

What led her to call you nervous and weak?

I was quiet, and she said that I was easily influenced. I didn't have a mind of my own. In a way she was right. About being weak.

At work, are you weak? Are you easily influenced? What is your reputation at work?

A good reputation. I am dependable, know my job well, manage my team well. I have been promoted and carry considerable responsibility.

What about your husband, and friends. Do they regard you as weak and easily influenced?

No, I really don't think so. I have a good marriage and my husband and I get on well. My friends? No, they treat me in the normal way that friends do. I help them, they help me. We do things together.

None of this sounds to me like a person on the edge of becoming weird, does it?

No. Except for this problem of mine, with the fear.

And by the way, you had an enjoyable and successful 3 years at college. No bad luck, no bad luck germs, no goof germs. There was a long period in your life when you were free of the beliefs about mind germs, and free of the fear of picking up a serious misfortune by proximity to unfortunate people.

Yes, that's true. I really enjoyed myself at college.

And during your years at college you were well and relatively untroubled by the horrible thoughts and fears—and all this without repeated washing or other rituals. Without mental neutralizing. In recent anxious years you have relied on these rituals etc. to defend yourself but, as you say, they are not too helpful are they?'

As the didactic work and cognitive analysis proceeded the patient was encouraged to refrain from her customary avoidance of proximity to the troubling people. After six sessions of treatment, she reported some progress.

'During the past month have you encountered any of the troubling, 'undesirable' people?

Yes, a few. Quite a few. I am keeping it in mind.

And what happened?

I felt uncomfortable, and a few times had strong urges to wash.

Did you wash?

No, I managed without washing.

Did you avoid any of these people?

No, I'm training myself to not avoid.

Excellent. Keep it up. It's important. Excellent.

The urge is to get away, but I don't.

In earlier conversations we talked about the basis of your fear of picking up unfortunate characteristics from these people, or of changing into them.

Yes, we did

It was the bedrock of your fear of being affected by them. What is your present thinking about this, your present belief?

I no longer believe it is true. I no longer believe it can happen. I don't believe it, but just react that way.

Do you now believe that you can change into such a person, or become like them in any significant way?

It is not true. Except in the movies...

Another reason to go to the library instead...It is the belief, and the consequent urges to avoid, and to wash yourself, that promote the fear and keep it going. It appears to be related to your more obvious and familiar fears of being harmed by touching pesticides or other nasty substances. It seems that these familiar fears of being contaminated spread from nasty substances to certain people. They might spread illnesses, or immorality. It seems to be a form of contamination.

It is the same thing. Exactly the same feeling.

Are the urges similar?

Yes.

Is the urge to avoid the same?

Yes it is. Well, I might become like them, mentally unstable and end up in a psychiatric hospital.'

The patient responded favourably to CBT. Her fear of morphing diminished, and she was increasingly able to inhibit any urges to avoid such people. Her handwashing declined to a low level. The belief that proximity to unfortunate people would harm her faded to a feeling of uneasiness that she was able to control, and she no longer felt the need to avoid their airspace. She reinterpreted the conviction that she is vulnerable to mind germs as a harmless superstition.

As far as the morphing is concerned, her current fear was the threat of becoming mentally unstable/weird, and this led her to avoid, and to wash compulsively. Further discussions and analysis were integrated into behavioural experiments, and a programme of exposure exercises was carried out. Initially some behavioural experiments were designed to ascertain whether her analysis of the ups and downs of the fear was consistent with her actual experiences (they were), and also to uncover any new information about the fear. Then experiments were set up to test her expectations about the consequences of planned, specific encounters with threatening and non-threatening people. She learned that the expected anxiety was evoked by closeness to threatening people, but that the anxiety gradually diminished without washing or other neutralizing acts. She also learned that the planned contacts were not followed by any changes in her personality or mental stability. After the new information was analysed she felt a decline in the fears and in her conviction that she was in danger when she encountered odd, unstable, shabby, weird people. The current fear, of becoming mentally unstable, was reduced. Her ordinary fears of contact contamination were treated by standard ERP exercises with reasonable success. During the assessment, her score on the Contamination–TAF scale revealed a high degree of thought-action fusion, including endorsements of these statements: 'If I have a thought of a friend/relative becoming contaminated, it increases the risk of them getting contaminated', 'If I get an image of myself being contaminated, it will make me feel contaminated'. In light of this, the didactic early part of the treatment included information about the TAF phenomenon and tactics for overriding the bias.

Before we started to talk about your fear of coming close to these people, did you make a connection between this fear and your various fears of becoming contaminated by contact with nasty substances, pesticides?

No, I didn't. I thought of it as just one more anxiety that was causing such difficulties in my life.

Well, contact with these people still makes you a bit anxious—but you are no longer washing compulsively and you are no longer avoiding, even though you still get the urge to do so. What is helping?

I think the non-avoiding is important, and of course the belief has gone. You assured me that people do not change in that way. It never happens. And that helped. I can't think of anyone who was changed in this way; people are never transformed into others. The sight of some of these people still makes me uneasy but I carry on as normal—no avoiding and no more washing. I can think of the mind germs as quirky and illogical.'

In this case, the nature of the fear of becoming tainted by proximity to 'undesirable' people was clarified. It was explained that the fear is not delusional and the person knows full well that the thoughts are irrational. 'This kind of fear is an unusual manifestation of OCD, which is a well-recognized psychological problem. Despite dozens or hundreds of encounters with 'undesirable' people, you have not been harmed. You have not picked up any of their characteristics or weaknesses. You have had the fearful thoughts many, many times but they have never been followed by the harm that you fear. Nothing has happened to you, you have not been changed. *The problem you are dealing with is one of thoughts*, not events or actions or undesirable changes or misfortunes.'

'The thoughts and the fear they produce are not symptomatic of impending mental illness. Nurses and doctors who care for people who are mentally unstable or suffering from a mental illness do not become unstable and nor do they pick up a mental illness. It is not contagious, and there are no 'thought germs' or 'mind germs'. Most of us encounter 'undesirable' people at one time or another, but no one known to me has ever been adversely changed by such an event. Presumably none of your friends or family have ever been changed in this way. You cannot be transformed in this way; it does not happen.'

'These thoughts and fears are a sort of contamination, but not ordinary contamination, not the kind that occurs when we touch a dirty or diseased substance. It is called mental contamination and can be caused even without any physical contact with a dirty substance. It certainly is a feeling of dirtiness, but of a different kind. Even the mere sight of particular people can cause feelings of mental contamination; so can television shows, pictures, memories, images. Mental contamination produces the same reactions as ordinary contamination—the need to wash and/or neutralize, and to avoid the source of the contamination. Your fear of picking up some undesirable or harmful characteristics from coming close to shabby/weird/unstable people is a form of mental contamination.'

'People who develop this fear generally have past or current fears of contamination, especially contact contamination, which is a common manifestation of OCD. Mostly they manage to live a moderately satisfying occupational, personal, and social life despite the intense uneasiness and fear of being tainted which they experience in the presence of particular people. It is a distressing but not disabling problem. When an encounter occurs it produces unpleasant feelings of contamination and an urge to wash away the contaminant, or to neutralize the feelings by going in for mental cleansing by counting or similar tactics. At best, the washing and neutralizing bring temporary relief, but leave the fear intact. However, the fact that washing/neutralizing brings some relief confirms the presence of fear/anxiety. The washing does not ensure safety from the threat of changing, of morphing, but simply eases the present anxiety. It is best to inhibit the urges to avoid the 'undesirable' people, and it is best to inhibit the urges to wash and neutralize.'

Beliefs and appraisals

- It is best for me to avoid staring at people who look weird.
- It is easy for me to pick up germs from mentally unstable people.
- I must wash very carefully if I touch or come close to the possessions or clothing of a weird person.
- I must avoid touching or coming close to people who look mentally unstable.
- At times I worry that my fears about weird, shabby people might give me a breakdown.
- Sometimes I fear that I might lose my identity.

- Coming close to a weird person makes me feel unclean even if I don't actually touch the person.
- If I touch or come close to someone who seems to be mentally unstable, I must cleanse my mind.
- I must avoid touching or coming close to a weird person.
- Some forms of mental instability are contagious and can be picked up by contact.
- Weird people can influence me without my knowledge.
- I must wash very thoroughly if I touch or come close to the possessions or clothing of a mentally unstable person.
- If I touch or come close to a weird person I must cleanse my mind.
- I worry that some day I will have a breakdown and be completely unable to cope.

Contamination after physical violation

The best guide for assessing and treating contamination fears that occur after a physical violation/s comes from the literature on PTSD. In that disorder, common cognitions are that the trauma has caused irreparable damage to one's mental stability, or personality and/or to one's brain. As a result, the person's ability to cope is compromised. The persistence of the PTSD symptoms of re-experiencing, hypervigilance, and disturbances of memory, is interpreted as confirmation of permanent damage, and reinforces the patient's pessimistic expectations about their future. The intrusive symptoms and hypervigilance produce a prevailing feeling of vulnerability and dread.

In some cases of PTSD a fear of contamination is embedded in the disorder, particularly if the traumatic event/s involved sexual violation. The connections between this fear and PTSD are most evident among the victims of assault, especially sexual assault (see de Silva and Marks 1999). As mentioned earlier, a large proportion of victims of sexual assault described feelings of mental pollution/contamination (Fairbrother and Rachman 2004). Victims become hypervigilant to the recurrence of distressing cues that are associated with the assault, and that includes feelings of mental pollution/contamination. These polluted feelings are evocable by visual, verbal cues, memories, and images. They are distressing and stir up urges to decontaminate, to wash and clean. If the victim's PTSD symptoms are accompanied by feelings of unusual intangible dirtiness, mainly internal, hard to localize or remove, easily evoked by memories or other mental events, then the presence of mental contamination is likely. This element of contamination is assessed in the usual manner by a combination of interviewing, behaviour tests, and psychometrics, especially the scale for measuring mental contamination.

Given the large number of victims of sexual assault who reported signs of mental contamination in the Fairbrother and Rachman (2004) study, clinicians treating victims of sexual assault would do well to be alert to the possibility or even probability that their patients are also experiencing mental pollution/contamination. It might even be advisable routinely to assess victims of sexual assault for the presence of feelings of mental pollution and mental contamination. In passing, these PTSD feelings of contamination are occasionally associated with compulsive ordering and arranging and are simply assessed with the SOAQ self-report scale (Radomsky and Rachman 2004).

The treatment for patients with mental contamination associated with PTSD should follow the guidelines for treating victims of trauma, as derived from the Ehlers–Clark theory (2000), supplemented by some measures that are specifically directed at removing the elements of contamination. The Ehlers–Clark method comprises three components: a constructive integration of the disturbed and broken memories, plus a modification of misplaced negative appraisals, and the reduction of unadaptive methods of coping (e.g. inappropriate avoidance behaviour). The early results are most encouraging. The treatment effects are large and stable and dropout rates are remarkably low. Three goals are set out: 'Modify excessively negative appraisals of the trauma and its sequelae; reduce re-experiencing by elaboration of the trauma memories and discrimination of triggers; drop dysfunctional behaviours and cognitive strategies' (Ehlers et al. 2005, pp. 415–18).

The key cognitions pertaining to the fear of contamination need to be analysed and adaptive interpretations promoted. After some progress on the cognitive side, a graded, gradual course of ERP is directed at the contaminants. In the course of cognitive therapy for PTSD it is often necessary for the patient to recall, and sometimes even 're-experience' the traumatic events, but these procedures can also revive or intensify the feelings of mental pollution/contamination, and care needs to be taken to dampen any such resurgences. In some cases of PTSD resulting from sexual violation, the feelings and cognitions about mental contamination are paramount, and accordingly the CBT is focused on the patient's appraisals of the violation and its psychological consequences for them.

It is highly probable that the Ehlers–Clark guidelines can be adapted for the treatment of mental contamination arising from various types of violations. Links between their theory of PTSD and the proposed explanation for particular forms of mental contamination remain to be explored.

Contamination after psychological violations

It is difficult to develop specific, detailed techniques for treating fears of contamination that emerge after periods of psychological violation because of the diversity of such violations, ranging from betrayals to humiliations, degradations, and beyond. In helping patients whose fears of contamination are connected to these violations, clinicians are bound to call on their broad knowledge and clinical experience, supplemented by some specific tactics that flow from the present analysis.

The treatment of the actor described on p.22 illustrates the gradual recognition of elements of mental contamination in what appeared at first to be a straightforward problem of contact contamination. The patient complained of uncontrollable urges to repeatedly wash his hands and shower, in order to remove his strong feelings of contamination. He was preoccupied with the risk of contracting a serious disease and/or becoming polluted as a consequence of touching contaminated materials and showered 2–5 times each day and washed his hands up to 20 times a day. He tried to protect himself by avoiding many items, places and people, and was insistent on restricting visits to his flat because visitors brought contamination into his home and he was compelled to watch their every movement and subsequently clean everything they touched. The fears of contamination were a recurrence of a problem that he had first experienced at the age of 22, and which had lasted for 4 years before fading in intensity when he started taking medication. When he gained some relief from the original problem the patient moved to another city and made a fresh start.

The fears and compulsive cleaning had returned, in his new home, after he found out that he had been betrayed by his partner who deceived him by having a secret relationship with one of his neighbours. He was extremely upset and immediately ended the relationship. At work, and on the journeys to and from, he avoided contact with potential contaminants such as public lavatories, shabby-looking people, and changed out of his work clothes immediately on returning home. He avoided all contact with the former partner and her friends, and reported that even talking to her on the telephone made him feel contaminated. She had become a contaminant.

As the cognitive analysis of his problems continued, therapeutic modelling and ERP exercises were introduced and he made some early progress. In the usual manner he was encouraged to bring contaminated items to the sessions for modelling/exposure exercises. For the third session he brought some articles from his bathroom as agreed in advance, and a few family photographs. All of the articles were highly contaminated, but it was unclear why the old photographs triggered the fear.

It turned out that he had felt rejected throughout childhood, and endured ill-treatment in the family. He was asked to form a vivid image, in turn, of his father, mother, and three other relatives. The images provoked strong feelings of contamination, almost as strong as handling the family photographs, and left him with an urge to wash. Forming an image of his former partner evoked such strong feelings of contamination that he insisted on washing his hands immediately. These signs of mental contamination, notably aroused even without direct physical contact, or in the case of the images without any contact at all, spawned urges to wash, and were evocable simply by recall. It led to a re-analysis of his original fear of contamination, experienced several years earlier. After full discussions of the surrounding events, supported by asking his friends and mother for their recollections of what had happened, and rereading his diaries, it emerged that the fears had developed when he was in a state of despair after enduring a betrayal by his fiancé at the time. The connections between the betrayal and the development of the fears had been obscured by a 3 month 'delay' in the emergence of the fear of contamination and associated washing. It appeared that his problems were triggered by betrayals, against a background of a life-long sense of rejection. After lengthy analyses of these events and their relation to his fears of contamination, he concluded that he was suffering from 'a kind of emotional contamination'. It was set off and maintained by direct or indirect contacts with the primary source, the former lover, by reminders of her and of childhood humiliations, by photographs and images.

Cognitive analyses led him to the conclusion that these cues were emotionally upsetting but not dangerous. Moreover, using anti-bacterial wipes and hot showers was misguided. At best they provided a measure of temporary relief and relaxation, but did not and could not have any effect on the emotional core of the problem. After repeated discussions of this interpretation of the fear of contamination, he was better able to carry out the exposure exercises, but some anxiety and hesitation persisted. As is common in cognitive reanalyses, the resulting behavioural changes took place gradually, over time (Booth and Rachman 1992). The effects of the reinterpretation of the fear also had a salutary effect on his avoidance behaviour and his cleaning compulsions declined slowly but steadily.

The mechanism by which betrayals, such as these, trigger intense feelings of contamination and mental pollution is not clear. Certainly there are elements of fear and disgust involved, but exactly why it takes the form of feelings of *contamination*, rather than some other psychological problem, remains to be explained. One possibility is that the offender is transformed into an enemy who arouses anger, aversion, and disgust—and we know that enemies often are regarded as sources of pollution. There is a strong aversion to touching an enemy or their belongings, and people would rather freeze than use clothing that has been worn by an enemy. It is a source of pollution.

The delayed onset of the contamination fear might be explained by the consolidation of disturbed cognitions, especially those which are based on the very persistence of the post-event distress. 'My feelings of distress and of self-abasement, intensified by each reminder/contact with (X—the primary source) of the distressing events, show that I remain abnormally sensitive to the person and events involved, and mean that I have been permanently harmed. I can no longer cope and am at risk.' This is similar perhaps to the unadaptive cognitions which develop in cases of PTSD—'These nasty, intrusive experiences are persisting and will not cease; I have been irreparably harmed, and remain vulnerable'. The repeated evocation of these distressing reactions in the presence of the primary or secondary sources of the contamination is likely to consolidate the appraisal that one is in danger of pollution and/or harm—*ex-consequentia*.

This selection of personalized versions of beliefs and appraisals common in cases involving mental contamination after experiencing a violation, is provided as an aid to therapy:

Beliefs and appraisals concerning mental contamination

- If I touch the possessions or clothing of someone who treated me very badly in the past, I need to have a good wash.
- For me, many things look clean but feel dirty.
- If I am touched by a nasty or immoral person, it makes me feel very unclean.
- When I am under stress, I feel sensitive to feelings of being contaminated.
- Before leaving home, I need to to make sure that I am absolutely clean.
- If I think about contamination, it will increase my risk of actually becoming contaminated.
- Pornographic material makes me feel sick, dirty.
- Sometimes I need to wash even though I know that I haven't touched anything dirty/dangerous.
- If I was touched by someone who had treated me very badly, it would make me feel unclean.
- I will never be forgiven for having nasty, horrible thoughts.
- Sometimes I feel contaminated even without touching any contaminated material.
- No matter how hard I try with my washing, I never feel completely clean.
- Simply thinking about contamination can make me feel actually contaminated.

- Simply remembering a contamination experience can make me feel actually contaminated.
- I definitely avoid movies that contain foul language and explicit sex scenes.
- I have a hard time getting rid of the feeling that I am unclean.
- People will reject me if they find out about my nasty thoughts.
- When I feel bad about myself, having a shower makes me feel better.
- If a nasty, immoral person touched me I would have to wash myself thoroughly.
- If I do not overcome my feelings of dirtiness, I will become sick.
- If I did something immoral it would make me feel unclean.
- People who use disgusting language make me feel dirty, tainted.

Self-contamination

The cognitive–behavioural treatment of obsessions provides a bridge for the treatment of self-contamination and the treatment of mental pollution. It is worth noticing that scores on the scale for measuring mental contamination correlate 0.51 with scores on the obsessions sub-scale of the Vancouver Obsessive Compulsive Inventory (see Appendix).

In many cases of *self-contamination* the feelings of contamination and pollution are stirred up by unwanted, intrusive, and repugnant thoughts and urges. If a patient suffering from *obsessions* shows signs of avoiding contaminants, it is worth assessing the presence or absence of mental contamination, using the combination of special interviewing, psychometrics, and behaviour tests. If the feelings of contamination are being provoked and/or sustained by obsessions then a course of cognitive treatment for the intrusions should be considered. In these cases, as in other instances of mental contamination, manifestations of contact contamination are also evident and need to be tackled.

The technique for treating obsessions is based on the cognitive theory that obsessions are caused by a catastrophic misinterpretation of the personal significance of one's unwanted intrusive thoughts (Rachman 2003; see also Freeston *et al.* 1997). The aim of the treatment is to help the patient replace the unadaptive interpretations of their thoughts by more appropriate and adaptive construals. To the extent that the patient succeeds in this task, the frequency and duration of the obsessions should diminish and even disappear.

Didactic component of treatment

It is explained that in addition to the familiar form of contact contamination, people can develop feelings of contamination even without physically touching a contaminant. Sometimes it happens after having certain thoughts or images, and can cause such intense feelings of contamination that the person has to wash it away. Most patients have trouble comprehending that feelings of contamination can be aroused by thoughts, their own thoughts. (The exceptions include those patients who consciously try to remove their self-instigated feelings of pollution by repeated washing.) Like most of us they think of contamination as the result of touching a nasty tangible substance. The educational part of the treatment of the contamination therefore includes an explanation of the evocation of such feelings, with or without actual physical contact. The information can be reinforced by simple demonstrations in which the patient is asked to observe the effects of forming vivid images of the contaminating people or cues, and by the deliberate recall of significant episodes of contamination.

The next part of the didactic component is an explanation of the nature of unwanted, intrusive thoughts and how they are transformed into persistent obsessions. Patients are told that virtually everyone experiences unwanted intrusions and for the most part, simply dismiss them. However, if the intrusions are interpreted as being highly significant and even revealing of the person's fundamental personality, trouble can arise. The mis-appraisals of the significance of the intrusions tend to be so upsetting that the person feels compelled to block or suppress the unwelcome, tormenting thoughts. Sadly, this rarely helps and often increases the frequency of the obsessions, leaving the person polluted and wretched.

Certain obsessions are prone to induce feelings of mental pollution/contamination. A prime example is seen in repugnant sexual obsessions, such as incestuous images. If the images, or dreams, are misappraised as expressions of incestuous intent, the person may feel polluted, and interpret the obsessions as revealing a lurking, vile part of their true character. The feelings of internal dirtiness and pollution prompt attempts at physical and/or mental cleansing. This process of self-contamination is distressing, seemingly uncontrollable. As the source of the contamination, the self, is always present, the threat of recontamination is present at all times. There is no period of safety.

If the self-contamination is linked to obsessions (usually sexual in content), the treatment is an amalgam of CBT for obsessions and for contamination. The patient's cognitions pertaining to the obsessions and to the feelings of contamination are analysed and a compilation is made of the evidence for and against the person's interpretations. The planning of treatment, and the assessment of progress, is facilitated by the use of the scale for measuring the personal significance which the patient places on the main obsessions (Personal Significance Scale—see Appendix). The patient completes the scale at the start of each session. Where necessary, and they often are, behavioural experiments are constructed in order to collect direct, personal evidence (see Rachman 2003). As progress is made in unravelling the patient's unadaptive/ erroneous interpretations of the significance of the obsessions and contamination fears, behavioural exercises including ERP are carried out.

The treatment of self-contamination can be illustrated by the case of the young man mentioned on p.43 who believed that he was a latent paedophile. He was extremely anxious that he might, against his wishes, sexually molest a child and therefore took great care to avoid being alone with children or even walking past places where children congregate. When he encountered children (only when other adults were present) he was tormented by doubts about whether he had looked at the children inappropriately, and whether he had touched them or spoken to them inappropriately. As a result he was tensely vigilant in their presence, and confused and troubled by his bodily sensations. He was unsure whether his sweaty hands and thumping heart meant that he was sexually aroused or anxious. These confusing sensations set off the frightening possibility that one day he might lose control and actually molest a child. His belief that he was a latent paedophile led him to avoid long-term relationships because he had decided that under no circumstance would he risk having children of his own. His emotional and sexual relationships were in other respects satisfactory.

The occurrence of the intrusive and repugnant thoughts on the subject of paedophilia made him feel uneasy, dirty, untrustworthy, and distressed. He tried to block or suppress the intrusions but found that this merely increased their frequency. Washing his hands vigorously provided short-term relief, but at times he felt obliged to shower repeatedly (e.g. after a disturbing dream in which children featured). At its worst he was washing 10–20 times per day, and having repeat showers 3 or 4 times per week.

He described how at the age of 8–9, he had been sexually abused for approximately 18 months by the father of his friend, and when he defied the abuser by disclosing what was taking place, the perpetrator was prosecuted. The patient gradually provided details of these events and by session six related that the abuser had told him on several occasions that 'We are alike, we both enjoy these games, and when you grow up, you will be like me and enjoy playing our games with children. We are the same.' The patient had accepted this assertion, and only started to search for information about paedophilia at age 13 after he saw a television programme in which the subject was mentioned. In his secret untutored search he found references to the 'cycle of abuse' and these confirmed his fear that he was a paedophile, and caught in an inescapable cycle.

After completion of the didactic phase of treatment, in which the nature and frequency of unwanted intrusive thoughts were explained, an analysis of his confusing reactions to children was carried out. A comparison was made between his fear of heights and his feelings and reactions in the presence of children, and they appeared to be similar—sweaty hands, racing heart, uneasiness. A description of his feelings during sexual events with his partner/s was mainly different—positive desire and anticipation, nil avoidance, increased heart rate, nil sweaty palms, satisfaction, and no fear. Some behavioural experiments were designed in order to collect direct personal evidence pertaining to the analysis, and also to compare the time course of his sexual feelings with his partner and the time course of his reactions to heights and to children. The uneasy anticipation and bodily reactions to walking across a city bridge were charted, with particular interest in the onset and offset of the unpleasant bodily sensations. The sensations and uneasiness were evoked well before reaching the bridge, and ceased once the walk was completed. This fear was predominantly anticipatory, and disappeared after completion of the exposure. A similar pattern was then recorded on a planned contact with a child; intense uneasiness and unpleasant bodily sensations for hours before the event, followed by a quick disappearance of both forms of tense discomfort directly the task was over. The time course of his feelings towards his sexual partner was different, with a gradual build-up that intensified to a climax, followed by a slow fading of pleasure. In the hours before the event he had thoughts about the anticipated intimacy but had few bodily sensations; these were evoked in the sexual situation itself. Additionally, the feelings in the sexual event were utterly different from the trips to the bridge and to the children. The patient was enabled to discriminate efficiently between his thoughts/reactions in the sexual and the other circumstances. After completing the cognitive analysis and the behavioural experiments he no longer felt confused about the meaning of his thoughts and bodily sensations in the presence of children. It was fear arousal not sexual arousal, he concluded.

The deep belief that he was a potential paedophiliac, a belief insinuated by the abuser, was approached by tackling the concept of a cycle of abuse. The patient was encouraged to carry out research into the revelations about the sexual abuses perpetrated by some priests in the Boston area. He learned that the many of the people who had helped to uncover and expose the abuses, seek justice for the victims and terminate the scandals, were themselves victims of childhood sexual abuse. In these instances, and in many other similar circumstances, so far from being drawn into an inescapable cycle of abuse, the victims actively opposed such abuse and successfully ended it. This information changed his views about the nature and consequences of childhood sexual abuse and he no longer felt destined to turn into a child molester. For a short period he continued to have occasional unwanted intrusive thoughts about children but was able easily to dismiss them. His cognitions and beliefs were substantially modified and newly adaptive, and the obsessions and mental contamination faded away. His thoughts no longer made him feel dirty, and the compulsive washing came to an end.

The problems of an introverted 21-year-old student were more complex. In addition to her aggressive and sexual obsessions, she experienced episodes of panic, had an impoverished social life, and was moderately depressed. As the distressing obsessions occurred every day and were her primary problem, they were selected as the focus of treatment. Her sexual obsessions consisted of inappropriate images, and impulses to make explicit suggestions to members of her family, friends, and occasionally, strangers. The thoughts and impulses, which involved ugly, rough, and crude language, were completely alien to her. A proportion of the sexual obsessions were also aggressive. She avoided a variety of situations and people and engaged in strenuous and protracted washing for 1–4 hours per day. Her hands and arms, up to the elbows, were abraded and sore. The urges to wash were provoked by her 'bad thoughts' which horrified her. She felt ashamed, guilty, and polluted. Sexual/aggressive dreams upset her and she was obliged to have an extended hot shower to rid herself of the dirtiness before starting her day. The compulsive washing gave some temporary relief but did nothing to ease her shame and self-denigration. Test probes, in which she formed some of her obsessional images, reliably produced feelings of pollution and an urge to wash.

After a course of CBT that was directed at her obsessions and feelings of self-contamination, she progressively reinterpreted her obsessions as non-significant intrusive thoughts. The self-denigration and interpretation of the obsessions as revealing that she was wicked and that she had a permanent flaw in her character gradually evaporated, and the compulsive washing then declined into non-significance. No ERP exercises were required. Construing the problem as one of self-contamination and treating it accordingly, was successful. Despite these useful gains her social life did not improve appreciably and she had patches of low mood that lasted for a few days at a time.

In view of recent progress in understanding and treating obsessions, the treatment of cases of self-contamination should advance smoothly. With our improved understanding of mental contamination, and self-contamination in particular, a basis for treatment is now available.

Beliefs and appraisals about self-contamination

These 'personalized' beliefs and appraisals drawn from the list on p.93, can be helpful during assessment and treatment. In addition it can be helpful to track the patient's interpretations of their uninvited thoughts by administering the

Personal Significance Scale at the beginning of each session. The responses indicate which misinterpretations are changing; those which are not changing require extra attention.

- It is very important for me to be clean in body and in mind.
- It is extremely difficult for me to block my unacceptable nasty thoughts.
- Unacceptable aggressive thoughts are always unworthy and unkind.
- The best way for me to deal with unwanted and unacceptable sexual thoughts is to have a good wash.
- It is wrong for me to have unwanted unacceptable thoughts or impulses.
- An unwanted objectionable thought is as bad as an objectionable deed.
- I feel tainted or dirty if I have a disgusting dream.
- My unwanted unacceptable thoughts mean that there is something badly wrong with my character.
- It is important for me to control my thoughts better.
- I must always keep my mind clean.
- Unacceptable sexual thoughts or impulses make me feel dirty.
- Having a good wash helps me to get rid of nasty unwanted thoughts.
- Having unwanted unacceptable thoughts or impulses means that I might lose control of myself one day.
- If I have a really disgusting thought it makes me feel dirty and tainted.
- It is important for me to keep my repugnant thoughts secret from other people.

Discussion

The fundamental questions about the nature of the processes involved in the reduction of fear by exposure will not be reopened here because it would be a digression from the main topic, but the gradual and progressive changes that take place during ERP treatment, plus the differences between intra- and inter-session changes in fear, are suggestive of a process of steadily increasing habituation. There are problems with this construal however, including an unfortunate circularity (Rachman 1990). The occurrence of habituation is assessed by a decline in responsiveness to a repetitive stimulus; however, as there is no independent measure of habituation, the theory that fears are reduced by a process of habituation cannot be tested. A competing explanation, which invites investigation, is that the therapeutic exposures produce changes because of the repeated disconfirmations of the person's expectation of harm. In cases of contamination fear however, especially those pertaining to threats of infection, the threat is not regarded as imminent and hence the repeated exposures cannot provide convincing disconfirmation of expected harm (say falling ill in 3 year's time). 'The fact that I have not fallen ill despite omitting my compulsive cleaning does not convince me that the long-term danger to my health has diminished.' Perhaps the treatment operates by disconfirming other key cognitions, such as the following: 'This contaminated item is not as dangerous as I thought it was'; 'Despite touching the contaminant repeatedly and not washing, I still feel OK and have not gone out of control'; 'The effects of touching the contaminant are not permanent'; 'Despite touching the contaminant repeatedly and refraining from washing, people are not avoiding me'.

Drawing a lesson from the positive results achieved by cognitive behaviour therapy in managing other anxiety problems, such as panic, and also from clinical experiences in treating obsessions with cognitive behaviour therapy, it is preferable to precede the taxing exposure exercises with therapeutic sessions devoted to the provision of important information about the fear and then proceed to cognitive analysis and therapy. In difficult cases the initial use of cognitive therapy can modify the maladaptive beliefs and cognitions sufficiently to smooth the way for behavioural experiments and cognitively structured ERP exercises. The behavioural experiments, and the cognitively shaped ERP exercises, not only modify the unadaptive cognitions but also have a way of unearthing previously unidentified cognitions. When the cognitive therapy begins to reduce the fear of contamination it becomes a little easier to introduce the ERP exercises which formerly were blocked by the presence of overriding fear. Behavioural experiments are a valuable tactic for gaining new information about the fear while simultaneously engineering successive disconfirmations of over-predicted fear. Patients with an overriding fear of contamination are better able to approach and then touch a contaminant if the task is presented as a limited behavioural experiment designed to collect information rather than as a first exercise that commits them to touching a lengthy list of very disturbing contaminants.

If and when the patient's maladaptive beliefs and misinterpretations are substantially reduced, the ERP exercises can proceed at a good pace, and the fear and avoidance decline accordingly. In the absence of a clear cognitive analysis, progress in ERP can be slow. For example, the progress of ERP in treating a patient with strong fears of contamination and severe compulsive cleaning was indeed slow, erratic, and puzzling until it emerged that she had feelings of mental contamination (brought on by serious but unjustified accusations of repugnant immoral conduct). It turned out that these feelings were responsible for the puzzling jumps and shifts in her fear hierarchy. When the mental contamination was reduced, her progress in ERP accelerated and her fears declined to an insignificant level.

If the pattern of contamination seems changeable, unusual, and puzzling and/or therapeutic progress is erratic, it is worth considering the possible presence of mental contamination and pollution, especially if the fears and cognitions have a moral element (e.g. 'Whenever a contaminated person comes near me I feel frightened and guilty, as if I've done something really awful, even though I know that I haven't'). The patient who developed a fear of being contaminated by some items of her own clothing found it so perplexing that she wondered if she was losing her mind. Another puzzled patient developed a fear of certain items of her jewellery and clothing. It transpired that she had worn most of the contaminated items to church services at one time or another and if she had experienced repulsive and blasphemous sexual images during prayers, the jewellery and clothes became contaminated. She was tormented by repugnant, uncontrollable thoughts and concluded that she was a hypocrite and secretly subservient to the devil. When her feelings of religious contamination were tackled she made gratifying progress in overcoming her fears of contamination. In view of the evidence that many victims of sexual assault experience mental pollution (Fairbrother and Rachman 2004) clinicians may wish to be alert to this possibility when attempting to assist such victims.

As mentioned, Rozin and Fallon (1987) presciently anticipated that 'conceptual reorientation' might be an effective way to modify feelings of disgust. Disgust can be reversed by simple reorientations, as in the examples given earlier (the rotten milk was actually yogurt, the forbidden pork that you inadvertently ate was actually lamb, the brown spot on your hand is chocolate not fecal matter, etc.). As mentioned in the case of the disgusting package, interpersonal factors can be central; 'The dry-cleaned sweater that you refused to wear because it would pollute you does not belong to your despised enemy, but to a close friend'. It remains to be seen whether conceptual reorientations that reverse ordinary feelings of disgust can be made equally effective in dealing with abnormal feelings of disgust and ultimately, whether such reorientations can be deployed to overcome mental contamination. At this early stage, our clinical experiences in dealing with mental contamination and pollution give some grounds for optimism about the potential therapeutic power of cognitive reorientations.

Some of the abnormal beliefs that underpin contamination fears are strongly held and so impervious to contradictory evidence that no change seems possible. In these circumstances some of the methods developed for treating obsessions can be helpful, particularly the collection of personal, direct information by means of behavioural experiments. The planned collection of 'survey' information in which the patient gathers the views and experiences of friends and relations can be helpful, especially in weakening the abnormal belief that one is specially, even uniquely, vulnerable to contracting diseases by contamination. At a tactical level it sometimes is more effective to tackle the patient's anxiety and fear before addressing the abnormal beliefs, because of the operation of the *ex-consequentia* bias. This sequence has proved successful in helping some patients suffering from health anxiety—first reduce their fears and then tackle their stubbornly abnormal beliefs.

Do fears of contamination ever disappear permanently? The evidence from randomized control trials of therapy for OCD (Abramovitz 1997; Barlow 2002; Clark 2004) shows that in many cases the answer is affirmative, in the limited sense that no recurrence had occurred during the follow-up period. On the other hand we are able to affirm that the return-of-fear phenomenon (Rachman 1990; Craske 1999) certainly occurs in some cases after the initially successful treatment of OCD. Recurrences can emerge after minimal re-contacts and in the absence of major stressors, and worryingly, the fear that returns can be intense, even exceeding the original level of fear. This raises the possibility that some fears of contamination never disappear. The fear can be suppressed by treatment for a period at least, but continues to lurk. It is exceedingly difficult to find a satisfactory answer, for how can one prove that a fear, in this instance of contamination, has disappeared permanently? How much time must elapse before the absence of the fear qualifies as a disappearance? The fact that many patients with OCD, including those with a fear of contamination, do benefit from treatment, lastingly, can not be ignored.

Reappearing fears (of contamination) sometimes exceed the intensity of the original fear; if it is a permanent fear, it is one of a changed intensity. Furthermore, the returned fear is not always an exact replica of the original fear; sometimes the fears have new features, even new contaminants. This fascinating phenomenon, in which a 'dormant' fear acquires new tentacles, is thought-provoking. Using a conditioning model, the initially successful treatment and the subsequent return of fear, can be construed as extinction followed by spontaneous recovery. However, if the returning fear is not a replica of the original fear, we need to ask how it is possible for a fear to *evolve during a period of 'dormancy'*?

In the present instance how does a fear of *contamination* evolve during a period of dormancy? Is it worthwhile construing the changes during 'dormancy' as a form of latent learning? This construal can be combined with the law of similarity. The fear of contamination has been suppressed (treated), but during this period of dormancy, associations are formed between the original contaminants and similar but previously neutral stimuli. When the fear returns it comprises the main features of the original fear of contamination plus some new features. In one case, the original fear of blood returned some years after treatment but had spread to a new range of objects, anything that contained brown spots, even though the patient asserted that she knew full well that the spots were not blood. In other instances, a sort of mental generalization takes place. For example, a patient's fear of being contaminated by her former husband was successfully treated but when she experienced a return of the fear a few years later, she was surprised to discover that it had spread to all of his family and friends.

Reappraising response prevention

The tactic of response prevention is an intrinsic component of the psychological treatment of OCD, and for good reasons. The development of the treatment in 1966–1979 was much influenced by experiments on animals which demonstrated that fears can be reduced by exposing the animal to the fear stimuli for prolonged periods during which escape from the experimental chamber is prevented—response prevention. Additionally, the concept of response prevention was justified by the plausible belief that compulsive actions are self-reinforcing, and hence should be reduced or even eliminated. Consistent with the belief that compulsive actions are self-reinforcing because they relieve some anxiety, it was demonstrated in a set of experiments on OCD patients that compulsive actions, especially compulsive washing, do indeed dependably reduce anxiety (Rachman and Hodgson 1980), and presumably reinforce the compulsions. It was argued that the compulsions maintain the neurotic patterns in a circular fashion—the famous 'neurotic paradox'. Contact with a contaminant produces anxiety—washing reduces the anxiety—the washing habit is thereby reinforced because it succeeds in reducing the anxiety. Accordingly, it was argued that the cycle should be broken, and prevention of the compulsive behaviour became an essential component of behavioural treatment.

The research also showed that if the compulsive behaviour is prevented, or at least delayed, the feelings of anxiety decay spontaneously—very slowly at first, but with repetition, they decay within minutes. The intention was to break the link between the contamination anxiety and compulsive washing by repeatedly promoting the spontaneous decay of the anxiety.

As described in Chapter 1 the research findings on patients and animals were incorporated into the rationale for the first versions of behaviour therapy, as exemplified by Meyer's (1966) case studies. With the infusion of cognitive concepts into behaviour therapy the response prevention method was retained but the arguments justifying its use were expanded. It was proposed that response prevention (RP) facilitates the disconfirmation of the patient's maladaptive cognitions about the need to wash in order to avert the feared catastrophes.

Response prevention was now construed as an essential tactic for reducing the unadaptive resort to 'safety behaviour', including compulsive washing.

It may be however, that an unqualified belief that it is essential to prevent all 'safety behaviour', and at all stages of the treatment, should be reappraised. Firstly, there are cases in which the compulsive washing is undermined, and in some instances eliminated, by cognitive means. Once the abnormal cognitions are replaced by more adaptive, benign interpretations, the hand washing can be ended without direct behavioural tactics, even without response prevention. It is broadly similar to the cognitive treatment of panic in which the catastrophic cognitions ('I can't breathe, I am in danger of dying') are replaced by realistic adaptive interpretations of the cognitions. When the current threat is removed, there is no need for exercises to improve one's breathing, or resorting to the use of brown bags, or training in relaxation, or other behavioural tactics. They are redundant and deleted from the protocol for treating panic. The cognitive treatment of some cases of mental contamination and associated compulsive washing have proceeded to a successful conclusion without any exercises in response prevention. For example, a patient whose feelings of contamination and the associated compulsive washing were driven by repugnant sexual intrusions that produced feelings of pollution. Her obsessions were successfully treated by modifying the catastrophic interpretations she had placed on her unwanted intrusive thoughts, and the feelings of contamination and compulsive washing collapsed. The removal of the feelings of mental pollution undercut the need to wash compulsively, and a simple discussion of the redundancy of the washing was sufficient to bring the habitual urges to wash under control within a few days. In a second illustration, a patient whose chronic, uncontrolled, intensive daily washing was charged by her feelings of mental pollution, was able to gain control of her compulsions after completing a major reappraisal of her mistaken belief that she had behaved immorally; it turned out that she had in fact been manipulated by two members of her family who had misled her for a substantial financial gain. Her sense of mental pollution and guilt was replaced by anger towards the relatives who had betrayed her. The steep decline in her feelings of pollution/contamination so weakened the compulsive urge repeatedly to wash herself that two or three sessions of exposure and response prevention were sufficient to overcome 10 years of uncontrolled washing.

Successful cognitive treatment of mental contamination reduces the need for repeated and prolonged exposures to contaminated stimuli. The emphasis of treatment shifts away from behavioural exposure exercises to cognitive analyses and reappraisals. Essentially cognitive problems are well-suited to cognitive solutions.

Even though RP is not always needed in the treatment of mental contamination, it is likely to remain an important component in the treatment of contact contamination. However, an unqualified insistence that RP is the essence of treatment and should be adhered to throughout treatment should be reconsidered.

Interestingly, at certain points in the exposure treatment of contact contamination, especially in the early stages, safety behaviour, even washing, can be turned to advantage. It is likely to reduce the refusal rate, and also ensure lengthy therapeutic exposures to the contaminants in place of brief, nervous touching. It has been shown that the treatment of participants with a circumscribed fear is expedited by the provision of safety apparel and tactics in the early exposure exercises (Rachman *et al.* 2003). Specifically, participants with an intense fear of snakes were encouraged to select any of the safety gear that they felt might be of use to them (e.g. thick gloves) during exposures to the caged snake. These 'safety' participants made significant improvements in overcoming their fears—equal in magnitude to the participants who carried out the exposure exercises without safety gear. Furthermore, the safety participants spent longer periods in close contact with the snake than did the comparison partcipants; it appears that they were able to endure longer and closer exposures because of the safety gear. Most interesting, they reported significant cognitive changes—the snake was no longer believed/perceived to be as dangerous as originally appraised ('It looked interesting, had complex markings on its body, not too dangerous.'). Our conclusion was that the judicious, early use of safety gear, or tactics, facilitated the reduction of fear. Given the intense fear manifested by patients with contact contamination, and the high refusal rates, the judicious early use of safety gear and behaviour may be equally facilitative. It can enable very frightened patients to participate in exposure exercises because they are assured that the ensuing contamination will be controlled and they will be free to remove the contamination at the end of the session if they wish to do so. Some patients decline treatment because they fear the consequences of transferring the contamination from the clinic to their cars, homes, or families. The early use of safety procedures can overcome their reluctance to start treatment, and they feel free to return home without carrying the contamination with them. The availability of a safety procedure also enables patients to remain in close contact with the contaminants for lengthy periods—enhanced exposure.

In summary, the judicious use of safety gear and tactics during early exercises of exposure can be facilitative, and in some cases of mental contamination the treatment is entirely cognitive.

Increasing the tolerance of contamination and anxiety

Patients who decline to participate in exposure treatments, the 'refusers', give two overlapping reasons for their decision. They fear that the treatment might harm them by increasing the severity of the problem and they dread the anticipated intensity of the fear and anxiety which they will experience during treatment. Combined, it is expressed in this way—'I cannot endure the fear and the treatment may harm me'. In principle, this manifestation of the common phenomenon of over predicting one's fear reactions, can be managed by engineering repeated disconfirmations of the fear predictions. In practice, one of the simple methods for reducing the overpredictions is the touch–wipe sequence repeated over and over again. With frequent, controlled, safe repetitions the fear reactions to touching the contaminant diminish. This decline in fear is then followed by a decline in the prediction of fear.

In a broad sense the controlled safe repetitions increase the person's tolerance of the feelings of discomfort that are produced by touching the contaminant; they get used to the feelings. The growing tolerance is also promoted by the steady accumulation of contact time as the use of the controlled safety contacts enables the person to spend an increasing amount of time actually touching the contaminants, just as the snake-phobic participants were able to build up exposure time to the snake by wearing safety gear. In the snakephobia experiment, a welcome consequence of the extended exposure time was the participants positively changing perceptions and cognitions about snakes. The safety procedures enabled them to 'study' the snake calmly and for lengthening periods. A similar sequence can be anticipated when patients are enabled to extend their contacts with contaminants by using safety procedures in the early stages of treatment. Our exploratory work on the simple touch–wipe method also suggests that the patient's estimation of the dangerousness of the contaminant gradually declines, and, of course, one is better able to tolerate contact with an item that is not too dangerous.

Compulsive behaviour can be generated and maintained by cognitions

The theory that compulsive behaviour, such as compulsive washing, is reinforced precisely because it is successful in reducing anxiety, was and is plausible. Moreover, it provided a rationale for the development of reasonably effective treatment. However, it is time to consider, as a minimum, *that compulsive behaviour can be generated and maintained by cognitions. This mechanism can operate regardless of any fluctuations in anxiety.*

Particularly clear and persuasive evidence of the cognitive generation and maintenance of compulsive behaviour is provided by the phenomenon of self-contamination. In these instances the person's unwanted, intrusive, and re-pugnant thoughts (e.g. about incest) produce feelings of mental contamination that usually include mental pollution—a strong sense of internal dirtiness. These feelings of mental contamination and pollution generate a need to remove the dirtiness and frequently this takes the form of intensive and repeated washing. The abhorrent thoughts/images generate compulsive washing. The recurrence of the thoughts/images produces recurring feelings of pollution and a recurring need to wash. The compulsive behaviour is main-tained by the recurrency of the repugnant thoughts/images. Cognitions drive compulsive behaviour and the particular form of the compulsion—cleaning, checking, neutralizing—is determined by the specific content of the cognition.

The cognitive generation and maintenance of compulsive washing is also encountered in some cases of *physical* contamination. A young man errone-ously believed that he had inadequate control of his bladder and felt that he invariably urinated on himself whenever he took a shower. The faulty cognition generated strong feelings of pollution and repeated but unsuccessful showers, a process that commonly lasted 2 hours. The compulsive washing rarely brought relief and, in fact, often left him more anxious than he had been before starting the washing (see Appendix for the details). His compulsive washing was driven and maintained by recurring cognitions, not by reductions in anxiety.

Cognitively-driven compulsions oblige us to reappraise the role of exposure and response prevention exercises. As described earlier, the ERP method was introduced as a means of reducing anxiety, and often is successful, but in cases of cognitively-driven compulsions, anxiety might be of little relevance. In cases of self-contamination for example, preventing the response (say, wash-ing) can be beside the point. The compulsive washing is driven and main-tained by intrusive and repugnant cognitions, and it is these cognitions that are the focus of the treatment. If they remain active, no amount of response prevention will be successful.

Recognition that all forms of compulsive behaviour can be generated and maintained by cognitions is overdue. It opens the way for a more compre-hensive explanation of compulsive behaviour and that brings the probability of significantly more effective treatments.

Three threats

The point of departure for a cognitive analysis and treatment is the premise that the fear of contamination comes down to three broad threats—a threat of physical harm, of mental harm, and of social harm. These threatening cognitions are associated with abnormal beliefs about contamination and its dangers. The details of a cognitive treatment, flowing from this point of departure, embrace assessment, the modification of the abnormal cognitions and beliefs, some exposure work, behavioural experiments, and with the exceptions described, the discouragement of safety behaviour.

At this stage in the development of methods for treating the fear of contamination, some observations and suggestions are worth mentioning. Early progress in tackling complex cases of mental contamination was made by adapting and modifying existing techniques for treating anxiety disorders. Two of the manifestations of mental contamination, self-contamination and cases arising from physical violations, have important similarities to specific types of anxiety disorder and hence, it was easier to borrow techniques from existing knowledge in order to deal with the newly recognized problems. Given the connections between self-contamination and obsessions, the techniques used for treating obsessions were modified to make them suitable for treating self-contamination. The connections, and overlaps, between contamination after physical violations and PTSD, also made a transfer of techniques possible. Methods for treating PTSD are now being applied in the management of some post-violation cases of contamination. Some progress has been reported in shaping methods for treating a fear of morphing even though there is no guide to be found in the literature on anxiety disorders. Specific treatments for contamination that arises from prolonged psychological violation must await advances in the delineation and explanation of this large topic, but in the interim, treatment based on the general principles of cognitive behaviour therapy should be helpful.

In concluding, it is necessary fully to investigate mental contamination, and to refine and disseminate the methods for recognizing its presence and effects. Progress will make it possible for clinicians to provide help for those many patients whose fears of contamination are perplexing and intractable.

It will not pass unnoticed that the present analysis of the fear of contamination has significant implications for the concept of OCD.

Appendix

VOCI contamination subscale

1. I feel very dirty after touching money
2. I use an excessive amount of disinfectants to keep my home and myself safe from germs
3. I spend far too much time washing my hands
4. Touching the bottom of my shoes makes me very anxious
5. I find it very difficult to touch garbage or garbage bins
6. I am excessively concerned about germs and disease
7. I avoid using public telephones because of possible contamination
8. I feel very contaminated if I touch an animal
9. I am afraid of having even slight contact with bodily secretions (blood, urine, sweat etc.)
10. One of my major problems is that I am excessively concerned about cleanliness
11. I often experience upsetting and unwanted thoughts about illness
12. I am afraid to use even well kept public toilets because I am so concerned about germs

(Each item is rated as *not at all* (0), *a little* (1), *some* (2), *much* (3), or *very much* (4). The total score for this contamination subscale is the sum of the scores of all of the items.)

Reproduced from The Vancouver Obsessional Compulsive Inventory (VOCI) by Thordarson *et al.* (2004) with the kind permission of the authors and the publishers, Elsevier Press.

Information about the VOCI

Derived from Thordarson *et al.* (2004).

The complete VOCI consists of 55 items, scored on a scale from 0 (not at all) to 4 (very much). It comprises 6 subscales: contamination (12 items), checking (6), obsessions (12), hoarding (7), just right (12) and indecisiveness (6).

	Contamination subscale	Total VOCI score	Checking scale
Retest reliability	0.97	0.96	0.96
Internal consistency	0.92	0.94	0.96
Mean scores	19.41	86.26	12.32

Means of known-groups:

Cleaners group	25.26
Checkers group	15.60
Other OCD patients	11.72
Anxiety controls	7.10
Adult non-clinical	1.74

Correlation of contamination scale with:

Padua Test contamination scale	=	0.90
Padua Test checking scale	=	0.10 (n.s.)

Maudsley Obsessional Compulsive Inventor (MOCI) washing scale = 0.83
Maudsley checking scale = 0.19 (n.s.)
Maudsley doubting scale = 0.13 (n.s.)
Beck Depression correlation 0.22 (n.s.)
Beck Anxiety 0.12 (n.s.)
EPI Neuroticism 0.21 (n.s.)

VOCI Total score with YBOCS Self-report 0.67

The mean scores and standard deviations of the Contamination subscale recorded by patients with OCD, patients with anxiety/depression, non-clinical community adults, and students.

Groups
OCD (n=88) Mean 19.41 (12.51)
Anxiety/depression(n=60) Mean 7.10 (8.96)
Non-clinicals(n=39) Mean 1.74 (2.94)
Students (n=200) Mean 7.31 (6.82)

VOCI mental contamination subscale

Do you *agree* or *disagree* with the following statements?	Not at all	A little	Some	Much	Very much
1. Often I look clean but feel dirty.	0	1	2	3	4
2. Having an unpleasant image or memory can make me feel dirty inside.	0	1	2	3	4
3. Often I cannot get clean no matter how thoroughly I wash myself.	0	1	2	3	4
4. If someone says something nasty to me it can make me feel dirty.	0	1	2	3	4
5. Certain people make me feel dirty or contaminated even without any direct contact.	0	1	2	3	4
6. I often feel dirty under my skin.	0	1	2	3	4
7. Some people look clean, but feel dirty.	0	1	2	3	4
8. I often feel dirty or contaminated even though I haven't touched anything dirty.	0	1	2	3	4
9. Often when I feel dirty or contaminated, I also feel guilty or ashamed.	0	1	2	3	4
10. I often experience unwanted and upsetting thoughts about dirtiness.	0	1	2	3	4
11. Some objects look clean, but feel dirty.	0	1	2	3	4
12. I often feel dirty or contaminated without knowing why.	0	1	2	3	4
13. Often when I feel dirty or contaminated, I also feel angry.	0	1	2	3	4
14. Unwanted and repugnant thoughts often make me feel contaminated or dirty.	0	1	2	3	4
15. Standing close to certain people makes me feel dirty and/or contaminated.	0	1	2	3	4

(contd.)

VOCI mental contamination subscale (*contd.*)

Do you *agree* or *disagree* with the following statements?	Not at all	A little	Some	Much	Very much
16. I often feel dirty inside my body.	0	1	2	3	4
17. If I experience certain unwanted repugnant thoughts, I need to wash myself.	0	1	2	3	4
18. Certain people or places that make me feel dirty or contaminated leave everyone else completely unaffected.	0	1	2	3	4
19. The possibility that my head will be filled with worries about contamination makes me very anxious.	0	1	2	3	4
20. I often feel the need to cleanse my mind.	0	1	2	3	4

Note: The three new scales to measure aspects of mental contamination—the Mental Contamination Scale, the Contamination Sensitivity Scale and the Contamination Thought-action fusion Scale—are under investigation, and the results of the initial psychometric studies are encouraging (Radomsky *et al.* 2005). The scales were administered to two groups of students (n=113) and a group of respondents with anxiety disorders (n=44) that included 19 with OCD. All three scales showed high internal consistency (0.92–0.95), correlated with each other (0.48–0.63), and were highly correlated with the VOCI Scale for measuring OCD (0.62–0.75), even after partialling out scores on the Beck Depression Inventory. The Contamination Sensitivity Scale correlated 0.58 with the Anxiety Sensitivity Scale and 0.35 with the Disgust Sensitivity Scale.

The results from the new Scales were factor analysed and yielded two factors—Contamination and Mental Contamination- that accounted for 56.4% of the variance.

The results will be updated as the research proceeds and made available on the Internet (Adam.Radomsky@concordia.ca).

Standardized interview schedule—contamination

(Note: Please use the Schedule flexibly. Always try for *details* wherever possible.)
1. Are there any objects or places or substances that upset or scare you if you touch them—such as public washrooms, garbage bins, public telephones,

insecticides, money, doorhandles, used bandages, blood or blood stains, greasy objects? Any others?

2. Do you attempt to avoid these items, places?
3. Please describe what happens if you do touch them?
4. After a contact of this sort, do you feel contaminated?
5. Do you get really bothered, or even scared, if your hands feel sticky?
6. Do you spend a lot of time washing and/or cleaning each day?
7. Are there times when you can't seem to wash clean no matter how hard you try?
8. Do you ever feel dirty or contaminated even though you haven't touched anything dirty or germy?
9. Do some things look clean but *feel* dirty?
10. Do *you* ever look clean but feel dirty?
12. Have you ever had strong feelings of contamination that faded away for a long time, say for longer than 6 months, and then returned?
13. If yes, were the feelings that returned very similar to the original feelings of contamination, or were they different?
14. Do you ever feel contaminated without knowing why? Do you ever feel contaminated even though you *know* that you have not touched anything dirty or dangerous?
15. Can other people sense when you feel contaminated?
16. Are there any items, people, or places in your own home or in the outside world, that have been contaminated for a very long time (more than a year at least)?
17. In your home and outside, does the contamination spread from one object or person or place to another?
18. Do you try to keep your outdoor and indoor clothing strictly separate?
19. Are your feelings of contamination ever set off even without touching a contaminated object?
20. Are the feelings of contamination ever set off by memories?
21. Are the feelings of contamination ever set off by an upsetting remark or criticism of you?
22. Are the feelings of contamination associated with any particular person?
23. Are there any people whom you try to avoid touching, or being touched by, because of concerns about contamination?
24. Do you ever get feelings of dirtiness or contamination that are set off by having an unwanted, nasty, or repugnant thought?
25. Do you ever feel dirty *under* your skin?
26. When you feel contaminated, does it ever feel as if you are contaminated outside and *inside* your body?

27. If a weird, or shabby, or mentally unstable person comes close to you, does it make you feel dirty or contaminated?
28. Does standing close to a person whom you feel can contaminate you, ever make you feel dirty, even if there is no physical contact?
29. If you touch the clothing of someone whom you strongly dislike does it make you feel dirty or contaminated?
30. If you feel very contaminated do you get nervous that you might become crazy?
31. When you feel contaminated do you ever try to overcome the feelings by doing things in your head, such as counting, or praying, or trying to push away thoughts associated with the contamination? If yes, is it ever helpful?
32. Are your feelings of contamination ever accompanied by feelings of shame, or guilt, or anger?
33. Have you ever been contaminated by objects, places, substances that did NOT contaminate other people?
34. Do you feel that you pick up contagious illnesses more easily than do other people?
35. When you are feeling contaminated do you try your very best to ensure that you don't pass the contamination on to other people?
36. For you, is the thought of passing contamination on to someone else much more frightening than yourself being contaminated?
37. If you have a thought about getting contaminated, does it increase the risk that you will actually become contaminated?
38. Do you ever wake up in the morning feeling contaminated?
39. After a really upsetting dream do you ever feel contaminated?
40. Do you ever worry that if you stare at, or come too close to people who seem weird or mentally unstable that you might begin to resemble them?
41. Some people feel that mental instability can be contagious, and avoid contact with people who appear to be weird or mentally unstable. What do you think about that?
42. If you do something that you feel was bad or sinful, do you ever feel a strong urge to wash yourself thoroughly, all over?
43. If so, does the washing and/or showering make you feel a bit better about yourself?
44. Do some things look safe, but *feel* dangerous?

Finally, therapist and patient combined—*What is the current threat?*

Contamination sensitivity scale

Do you *disagree* or *agree* with the following statements?	Strongly Disagree	Disagree	Neutral	Agree	Strongly Agree
1. It scares me when my hands feel sticky.	0	1	2	3	4
2. When there is something wrong with my stomach, I worry that I might be seriously ill.	0	1	2	3	4
3. It scares me when I feel dirty *inside* my body.	0	1	2	3	4
4. I can always smell if there is something rotting.	0	1	2	3	4
5. It is always important for me to wash myself absolutely clean.	0	1	2	3	4
11. If I cannot get rid of worries about contamination, I am nervous that I might be going crazy.	0	1	2	3	4
12. Touching clothing that belongs to someone I strongly dislike would make me feel nervous.	0	1	2	3	4
13. Eating fruit or vegetables that are not organic makes me feel tense and nervous.	0	1	2	3	4
14. I keep well away from people who look ill.	0	1	2	3	4
15. For me, unpleasant smells are extremely nauseating.	0	1	2	3	4
16. It scares me if I feel dirty *under* my skin.	0	1	2	3	4

(contd.)

Contamination sensitivity scale (*contd.*)

Do you *disagree* or *agree* with the following statements?	Strongly Disagree	Disagree	Neutral	Agree	Strongly Agree
17. It is important for me to keep well away from weird or mentally unstable people.	0	1	2	3	4
18. It embarrasses me when my stomach is upset.	0	1	2	3	4
19. It scares me when my skins feels all prickly.	0	1	2	3	4
20. If I feel very contaminated, I get nervous that I might become mentally unstable.	0	1	2	3	4
21. For me it is much safer to eat fruit that has a removable skin.	0	1	2	3	4
22. I pick up illnesses far more easily that do other people.	0	1	2	3	4
23. Other people can tell if I feel contaminated.	0	1	2	3	4
24. If a weird or mentally unstable person comes close to me, I get very nervous.	0	1	2	3	4
25. If food is not completely fresh, I can tell right away.	0	1	2	3	4
26. When I get sick, I get really sick.	0	1	2	3	4
27. I am extremely sensitive to tastes.	0	1	2	3	4
28. It scares me if I feel contaminated.	0	1	2	3	4
29. I am extremely sensitive to air pollution.	0	1	2	3	4

Contamination sensitivity scale (*contd.*)

Do you *disagree* or *agree* with the following statements?	Strongly Disagree	Disagree	Neutral	Agree	Strongly Agree
30. I worry about picking up some illness whenever I visit a hospital.	0	1	2	3	4
31. Unusual sensations on my skin make me very nervous.	0	1	2	3	4
32. I am extremely sensitive to smells.	0	1	2	3	4

CONTAMINATION–Thought–action fusion (TAF) Scale

Do you *disagree* or *agree* with the following statements?	Strongly Disagree	Disagree	Neutral	Agree	Strongly Agree
1. If I have a thought about a friend/relative getting ill, it increases the risk that he/she will actually get ill.	0	1	2	3	4
2. If I get an image of myself being contaminated, it will make me feel contaminated.	0	1	2	3	4
3. If I have a thought of a friend/relative becoming contaminated, it increases the risk of them getting contaminated.	0	1	2	3	4
4. If I have a thought about myself getting ill, it increases the risk that I will get ill.	0	1	2	3	4

(contd.)

CONTAMINATION–Thought–action fusion (TAF) Scale (*contd.*)

Do you *disagree* or *agree* with the following statements?	Strongly Disagree	Disagree	Neutral	Agree	Strongly Agree
5. If I have a thought about getting contaminated, it increases the risk of actually becoming contaminated.	0	1	2	3	4
6. If I have a thought that I might pass on contamination to a child, it increases the risk that the child will become contaminated.	0	1	2	3	4
7. Having a thought that I might pass contamination on to someone else is almost as bad as actually doing it.	0	1	2	3	4
8. If I get a clear memory of having been contaminated in the past, it will make me feel contaminated now.	0	1	2	3	4
9. If I get an image of a friend/relative being contaminated, it will increase the risk that he/she will actually become contaminated.	0	1	2	3	4
10. If I have a thought that I might pass on contamination to a child, that is almost as bad as actually passing it on.	0	1	2	3	4

Personal Significance of Intrusive Thoughts Scale

Please read the following statements carefully and make a mark anywhere on the line provided to show the extent to which you agree with each statement.

1. How important are these thoughts in your life?

not at all important   somewhat important   extremely important

2. Do these thoughts reveal something important about you?

not at all important   somewhat important   extremely important

3. Is it important for you to keep these thoughts secret from most or all of the people you know?

not at all important   somewhat important   extremely important

4. Do these thoughts mean that you might lose control and do something awful?

not at all   possibly   definitely

5. Do these thoughts mean that you are an imaginative person?

not at all imaginative   somewhat imaginative   extremely imaginative

6. Do these thoughts mean that you might go crazy one day?

not at all likely   somewhat likely   very likely

7. Are these thoughts a sign that you are original?

not at all   somewhat   very original

8. Do these thoughts mean that you are a dangerous person?

not at all dangerous   somewhat dangerous   definitely dangerous

9. Do these thoughts mean that you can not be trusted?

completely trustworthy   somewhat trustworthy   not at all trustworthy

10. Would other people condemn or criticize you if they knew about your thoughts?

not at all   somewhat   definitely

11. Do these thoughts mean that you are really a hypocrite?

    not at all   somewhat   definitely

12. Do these thoughts mean that you have an artistic talent?

    not at all   somewhat   definitely

13. Would other people think that you are crazy or mentally unstable if they knew about your thoughts?

    not at all   somewhat   definitely

14. Do these thoughts mean that one day you may actually carry out some actions related to the thoughts?

    not at all likely   somewhat likely   very likely

15. Do these thoughts mean that you enjoy company?

    not at all   somewhat   definitely

16. Do you feel that it is important for you to cancel out or block the thoughts?

    not at all important   somewhat important   extremely important

17. Would other people think that you are a bad, wicked person if they knew about your thoughts?

    not at all   somewhat   definitely

18. Do you think that you should avoid certain peolple or places because of these thoughts?

    not at all   somewhat   definitely

19. Do these thoughts mean that you are weird?

    not at all   somewhat   definitely

20. Do these thoughts mean something else? (Details:_____)

    not at all   somewhat   definitely

This scale is designed to assess important interpretations of the intrusive thoughts, and how they change during treatment. It is a self-correcting scale and if little or no positive changes are taking place during therapy, the need for a reanalysis of the problem and the treatment plan is recommended. Once the main misinterpretations have been identified, each is analysed in depth. This includes the patient's spontaneous interpretations, strength of belief, evidence and reasons for the interpretation, contrary evidence and reasons, spontaneous methods of resisting the thoughts and their efficacy, effects of formal treatment, and so forth.

After completing this detailed appraisal of the significance, proceed to an analysis of the evidence for and against the significance, and the reasons for and against the significance. As an aid, this work sheet can promote an initial evaluation of the foundations and scaffolding that support the catastrophic interpretations.

This is primarily a qualitative scale, but in some circumstances, mainly research, it is useful to score it. It is a 0–10 scale, ranging from 'not at all' to 'definitely', 'important' or 'dangerous'. In this version the respondents mark their replies on a 10cm scale. In order to discourage response sets, 4 buffer items are included, such as 'Do these thoughts mean that you enjoy company'. These items should be deleted form any qualitative analysis—Items 5, 7, 12, and 15.

Additional case illustrations

Case 1

This account of the treatment of a fear of morphing was provided by Dr. R. Shafran.

A rather perfectionist 28-year-old mature student had been forced to leave her studies due to the fear that she would lose her intellectual capacity ('become stupid') by coming into contact with people who were less intelligent than herself. She determined people's intelligence by their ability to use grammar correctly and avoided people whom she feared could 'turn her stupid'. She had repeated intrusive images of particular people she regarded as unintelligent, and believed that these images could contaminate the quality of her work in two ways. First, she feared that she would be so preoccupied with the images (and countering them in her head) that she would be unable to concentrate and would do poorly. This was not an unrealistic fear. Second, she feared that the images would magically influence her degree result although she accepted this was unlikely to be the case. The patient also avoided touching any objects (e.g. a stapler) that may have been used by 'stupid' people. If forced to touch these objects, she would not wash her hands but instead would engage in repeated tests of her intelligence e.g. making sure she 'fully' understood a passage she was reading. Such tests were in fact repeated mental rituals involving visualizing and 'working through' words. The repeated testing of her intellectual capacity was so time-consuming that she had no time for relationships or hobbies, and instead worked most of the day and night. She also avoided people who were homeless or whom she regarded as 'thuggish' lest they attack her and cause a head injury that would mean she could not study. One year prior to the start of her particular concerns about her intellectual capacity, this patient had received a diagnosis of a mild learning difficulty in which it had been suggested that she visualize words to help ensure she fully understood them. She did not connect the diagnosis with her obsessional behaviour prior to treatment.

She received 15 sessions of treatment which encouraged her to take the default position that she understood what she was reading or hearing without having to test herself. A distinction was drawn between 'emotional under-standing' and 'intellectual understanding'. She was encouraged to allow the images to enter her head and then to continue to work without engaging in neutralizing behaviour. The patient agreed to come into contact with people and objects that she regarded as 'stupid' and was able to do this relatively easily. She was able to conclude from this, and other behavioural tests and surveys, that her unwanted images of people and contact with them could not affect her intellectual performance. She was much improved after treatment.

Case 2

The cognitive-behavioural treatment of a case of self-contamination.

A 22-year-old man was admitted to hospital in a state of agitated desper-ation because of his intense anxiety and out of control compulsive behaviour. He felt overwhelmed and unable to function. He had lost his job because his prolonged washing and checking compulsions interfered with his perform-ance, and was unable to afford his rent. His psychological problems made social activities virtually impossible, and, worst of all, he felt that his life was blighted and that he would never be free of his severe OCD. At the age of 11 he began washing so intensively that his hands were cracked and bleeding, and he also developed extensive worries and subsequent checking behaviour. Over the next 11 years he received a good deal of treatment, psychological and pharmacological, but with little lasting improvement.

His childhood was turbulent as he grew up in a disturbed family that barely functioned. His father was on long-term disability as a result of multiple medical problems and spent most of his time grumbling in bed, incessantly criticising his wife and children. The patient's mother had been treated for depression and was withdrawn and inaccessible. In the circumstances the patient had been landed with great responsibility for running the house and ensuring that his parents attended their many medical appointments, received and used their medications, and so forth. All the while his father criticised and humiliated him, and his mother complained that he did not keep himself sufficiently clean and repeatedly sent him back to the bathroom to re-wash and re-shower. The patient developed an intense and unrelenting fear of being contaminated by bodily secretions, especially urine. At the time of his admission to hospital he was washing approximately 30 times each day and taking multiple showers that lasted for 2 hours or more, but left him feeling dirty. The main problem was (physical) self-contamination. He was also checking the stove, doors, and windows for up to 30 minutes daily.

Shortly after he was discharged from hospital a course of CBT was arranged. After an extensive cognitive analysis it was decided to start working on the checking compulsions because they were comparatively straightforward and amenable to progessive modification. Useful improvements were achieved within 3 weeks and attention was then turned to the more complex feelings of contamination and compulsive washing. It emerged that in addition to the common fears of possibly picking up a disease by contact, he was tormented by thoughts/sensations that he was involuntarily urinating on himself, mainly during showering. For this reason he had to shower over and over again to clean the urine off his body. But it was a 'trap' because when he re-showered he felt that he was re-contaminating himself all over again, and he was unable to convince himself that the moisture on his lower body was purely water and not a confusion of water and urine. He rarely succeeded in convincing himself that he was properly clean and hence re-washed and re-washed until he ran out of time or energy; it was extremely difficult to terminate his washing.

On analysis we agreed that he had had the thoughts and sensations thousands of times and never once definitely urinated on himself. It was defined as a problem of his thoughts not his behaviour. The feeling of urine was strong and convincing during his attempts at cleaning himself, and his belief that he was contaminating himself was not modifiable by discussions. It appeared to be a delusional perception, and it was decided that he needed to collect evidence which would enable him finally to decide whether or not he was actually contaminating himself. Accordingly we considered what evidence might have evidential value for him and settled on a visual marker that would tell him whether the water in the shower contained urine. He was to eat beetroots every day, which famously reddens one's urine, and check whether the water in his shower was reddened, by drying himself with a fresh clean white towel after every shower. During the next 3 weeks he conscientiously carried out the behavioural tests and the white towels never showed any traces of red. He began to report a gradual weakening of the sensations/thoughts about the presence of urine, and observed that the showers were reducing in frequency and duration—but grumbled that he never wished to eat another beetroot for the rest of his life. Instead we substituted vitamin B tablets which turn urine distinctively yellowish, and within 3 weeks the senstions/thoughts virtually disappeared. He was showering only once per day, for no longer than 15 minutes, and found it easy to terminate the shower. He observed that, 'I feel clean for the first time in years'. He also made progress socially and was working fulltime at a new and preferred job.

Case 3

This account of the treatment of a fear of morphing was provided by Dr. A. Radomsky.

A 36-year-old single heterosexual male had unwanted intrusive repugnant thoughts and images of a homosexual nature. The images typically involved him engaged in sexual acts with some of his male friends. He began to wonder if these images meant that he was homosexual. He began to avoid spending time with his male friends if any sports were involved, as this usually involved changing; following any sporting activities with his friends, the patient reported being plagued by images of them showering which he said was very distressing. He began to wonder if the anxiety he experienced following these images was actually a sign of sexual arousal and this exacerbated his fears.

Initially, there was no washing behaviour associated with these thoughts or images and early attempts at thought suppression were reportedly successful. However, as these grew less successful, the patient decided that one way to correct this problem was to masturbate while imagining, as vividly as possible, sexual acts with girlfriends and other women. If any thoughts or images of other men intruded during this act, he would engage in compulsive washing, primarily of his hands and genitalia, often lasting for 30–45 minutes. If he was 'successful' at not having any images of men, no compulsive washing would follow. Over time, the washing could be provoked simply by the intrusive thoughts and images, regardless of whether or not he was masturbating or suppressing. When asked about this, he said that he was trying to wash away his thoughts and images.

Treatment began with psychoeducation and was followed by behavioural experiments and cognitive exercises designed to provide and test alternate interpretations of his images and thoughts. This included discussion of the function of his washing behaviour as well as the differences between feeling dirty and being dirty. The treatment included some, but not much exposure and response prevention and over a period of approximately 12 sessions, his thoughts, images, and washing behaviour were all dramatically reduced. He now reports the occasional intrusive thought or image, but no associated distress or compulsive washing.

References

Abramovitz, J. (1997). Effectiveness of psychological and pharmacological treatments for OCD: A quantitative review. *Journal of Consulting and Clinical Psychology* **65**, 44–52.

Abramovitz, J., Franklin, M., Schwartz, S., and Furr, J. (2003). Symptom presentation and outcome of CBT for OCD. *Journal of Consulting and Clinical Psychology* **71**, 1049–57.

Anand, M. (1940). *Untouchable.* London: Penguin Books.

Antony, M., Downie, F., and Swinson, R. (1998). Diagnostic issues and epidemiology in OCD, in R. Swinson, M. Antony, S. Rachman, and M. Richter (eds) *OCD: Theory, Research and Treatment.* New York: Guilford Press.

Applebaum, A. (2003). *Gulag: A History.* New York: Doubleday.

Arkes, H. (1981). Impediments to accurate clinical judgement and possible ways to minimize their impact. *Journal of Consulting and Clinical Psychology* **49**, 323–30.

Arntz, A., Rauner, M., and van den Hout, M. (1995). 'If I feel anxious, there must be danger': ex-consequential reasoning in inferring danger in anxiety disorders. *Behaviour Research and Therapy* **33**, 917–25.

Ayto, J. (1990). *Dictionary of word origins.* New York: Arcade Publishing.

Bandura, A. (1969). *The Principles of Behavior Modification.* New York: Holt.

Barlow, D. (2002). *Anxiety and its Disorders,* Second Edition. New York: Guilford Press.

Baum, M. (1970). Extinction of avoidance responding through response prevention (flooding). *Psychological Bulletin* **74**, 276–93.

Booth, R. and Rachman, S. (1992). The reduction of claustrophobia. *Behaviour Research and Therapy* **30**, 207–21.

Bunyan, J. (1947). *An Anthology.* A. Stanley (ed). London: Eyre and Spottiswoode.

Bunyan, J. (1998 Oxford Edition). *Grace Abounding To The Chief Of Sinners (1666).* Oxford: Oxford Univesity Press.

Chadwick, P. and Lowe, C. (1990). The measurement and modification of delusional beliefs. *Journal of Consulting and Clinical Psychology* **58**, 225–32.

Clark, D.A. (2004). *Cognitive-behavior therapy for OCD.* New York: Guilford.

Clark, D.M. (1986). A cognitive approach to panic. *Behaviour Research and Therapy* **24**, 461–70.

Clark, D.M. and Fairburn, C. (Eds) (1997). *Science and Practice of Cognitive Behaviour Therapy.* Oxford: Oxford University Press.

Clark, D.M. and Wells, A. (1995). A cognitive model of social phobia, in R.G. Heimberg, M.R. Liebowitz, D.A. Hope, and F.R. Schneier (eds) *Social Phobia: Diagnosis, Assessment, Treatment.* New York: Guilford Press.

Craske, M. (1999). *Anxiety Disorders.* Boulder: Westview Press.

Craske, M. (2003). *Origin of Phobias and Anxiety Disorders: Why more women than men?* Oxford: Elsevier Press.

de Jong, P., Andrea, H., and Muris, P. (1997). Spider phobia in children: disgust and fear before and after treatment. *Behaviour Research and Therapy* 35, 559–62.

de Jong, P., Vorage, I., and van den Hout, M. (2000). Counterconditioning in the treatment of spider phobia: Effects on disgust, fear and valence. *Behaviour Research and Therapy* 38, 1055–69.

de Silva, P. and Marks, M. (1999). The role of traumatic experiences in the genesis of OCD. *Behaviour Research and Therapy* 37, 941–51.

Di Nardo, P., Guzy, L., and Bak, R. (1988). Anxiety response patterns and etiological factors in dog-fearful and nonfearful subjects. *Behaviour Research and Therapy* 21, 245–52.

Douglas, M. (1966). *Purity and Danger.* London: Routledge and Kegan Paul.

Eddy, K., Dutra, L., Bradley, R., and Westen, D. (2004). A multi-dimensional meta-analysis of psychotherapy and pharmacotherapy for OCD. *Clinical Psychology Review* 24, 1011–30.

Edwards, S. and Salkovskis, P. (2005). An experimental demonstration that fear, but not disgust, is associated with a return of fear in phobias. *Journal of Anxiety Disorders,* 20, 58–71.

Ehlers, A. and Clark, D.M. (2000). A cognitive model of PTSD. *Behaviour Research and Therapy* 115, 319–45.

Ehlers, A., Clark, D., Hackmann, A., McManus, F., and Fennell, M. (2005). Cognitive therapy for PTSD: development and evaluation. *Behaviour Research and Therapy* 43, 413–32.

Eysenck, H.J. (Ed) (1960). *Behaviour Therapy and the Neuroses.* Oxford: Pergamon Press.

Eysenck, H.J. and Rachman, S. (1965). *Causes and Cures of Neurosis.* London: Routledge and Kegan Paul.

Fairbrother, N. and Rachman, S. (2004). Feelings of mental pollution subsequent to sexual assault. *Behaviour Research and Therapy* 42, 173–90.

Fairbrother, N., Newth, S., and Rachman, S. (2005). Mental pollution: Feelings of dirtiness without physical contact. *Behaviour Research and Therapy* 43, 121–30.

Foa, E., Steketee, G., Grayson, J., and Doppelt, H. (1983). Treatment of obsessive-compulsives: when do we fail? In E. Foa and P. Emmelkamp (eds), *Failures in Behavior Therapy.* New York: Wiley.

Foa, E., Kozak, M., Salkovskis, P., Coles, M., and Amir, N. (1998). The validation of a new OCD scale: The Obsessive-Compusive Scale. *Psychological Assessment* 10, 206–14.

Foa, E., Liebowitz, M., Kozak, M., Davies, S.I., Campeas, R., and Franklin, M.E. (2005). Randomized, placebo-controlled trial of exposure and ritual prevention, clomipramine and their combination in the treatment of OCD. *American Journal of Psychiatry* 162, 151–61.

Frazer, J.G. (1922). *The Golden Bough.* New York: Criterion Press. (Present references from 1999 Edition, New York: Touchstone Press.)

Freeston, M., Ladouceur, R., Gagnon, F., Thibodiau, N., Rheaume, J., Letarte, H., *et al.* (1997). Cognitive behavioral treatment of obsessive thoughts: a controlled study. *Journal of Consulting and Clinical Psychology* 65, 405–13.

Frost, R. and Steketee, G. (Eds) (2002). *Cognitive Approaches to Obsessions and Compulsions.* Oxford: Elsevier Press.

Garety, P. Kuipers, L., Fowler, D., Chamberlain, F., and Dunn, G. (1994). Cognitive behavioral therapy for drug-resistant psychosis. *British Journal of Medical Psychology* 67, 259–71.

Gershuny, B., Baer, L., Radomsky, A., Wilson, K. and Jenike, M. (2003). Connections among symptoms of OCD and PTSD: A case series. *Behaviour Research and Therapy* 41, 1029–42.

Gilbert, M. (1986). *The Holocaust.* London: Collins.

Haidt, J., McCauley, C., and Rozin, P. (1994). Individual differences in sensitivity to disgust. *Personality and Individual Differences* 16, 701–13.

Herba, J. (2005). Individual differences in psychological feelings of contamination. M.A. Dissert., University of British Columbia.

Hodgson, R. and Rachman, S. (1977). Obsessional compulsive complaints. *Behaviour Research and Therapy* 15, 389–95.

Huizinga, J. (1957 edn). *Erasmus and the Age of Reformation.* New York: Harper and Row.

Human Rights Watch Report (1999). *Broken People: Caste violence against India's 'Untouchables'.* New York: Human Rights Watch Publication.

Inhorn, M. (1994). Kabsa (aka mushahara) and threatened fertility in Egypt. *Social Science and Medicine* 39, 487–505.

Jacobi, D., Herba, J., and Rachman, S. (2005) Vancouver University Hospital: Anxiety Disorders Clinic, unpublished data.

Janet, P. (1903). *Obsession et la Psychasthenie.* Paris: Alcan.

Janet, P. (1925 edn). *Psychological Healing.* London: Unwin Brothers.

Kafka, F. (1983 edn). The metamorphosis (1912), in *The Penguin Complete Stories of Franz Kafka.* London: Penguin Books.

Koch, M., O'Neill, K., Sawchuk, C., and Connolly, K. (2002). Domain-specific and generalized disgust sensitivity in blood–injection–injury phobia. *Journal of Anxiety Disorders* 16, 511–27.

Kroeber, A. (1948). *Anthropology.* New York: Harcourt Brace.

Lang, P. (1985). The cognitive psychophysiology of emotion, in A. Tuma and J. Maser (eds) *Anxiety and the Anxiety Disorders.* Hillsdale: Erlbaum Associates.

Mackintosh, N. (1983). *Conditioning and associative learning.* New York: Oxford University Press.

McKay, D. (Ed) (2002). The role of disgust in anxiety disorders. *Journal of Anxiety Disorders* 16, 475–566.

Merckelbach, H., de Jong, P., Arntz, A., and Schouten, E. (1993). The role of evaluative learning and disgust sensitivity in the etiology and treatment of spider phobia. *Advances in Behaviour Research and Therapy* 15, 243–55.

Meyer, V. (1966). Modification of expectations in cases with obsessional rituals. *Behaviour Research and Therapy* 4, 273–80.

Mowrer, O.H. (1960). *Learning Theory and Behaviour.* New York: Wiley.

Newth, S. and Rachman, S. (2001). The concealment of obsessions. *Behaviour Research and Therapy* 39, 457–64.

Obsessive Compulsive Cognitions Working Group (2003). Psychometric validation of the Obsessive Beliefs Questionnaire and the Interpretation of Intrusions Inventory: Part 1. *Behaviour Research and Therapy* 41, 863–78.

Olatunji, B., Sawchuk, C.N., Lohr, J.M., and de Jong, P.J. (2004). Disgust domains in the prediction of contamination fear. *Behaviour Research and Therapy* 42, 93–104.

Orwell, G. (2001 edn) *The Road to Wigan Pier.* London: Penguin Books.

O'Sullivan, G. and Marks, I. (1991). Follow-up studies of behavioral treatment of phobic and obsessive-compulsive neuroses. *Psychiatric Annals* 21, 368–73.

Poulton, R. and Menzies, R. (2002). Non-associative fear acquisition: A review of the retrospective and longitudinal research. *Behaviour Research and Therapy* 40, 127–50.

Rachman, S. (1978). *Fear and Courage.* San Francisco: W.H. Freeman.

Rachman, S. (1990). *Fear and Courage,* Second Edition. New York: W.H. Freeman.

Rachman, S. (1983). Obstacles to the successful treatment of obsessions. In E. Foa and P. Emmelkamp (eds), *Failures in Behaviour Therapy.* New York, Wiley, pp. 35–57.

Rachman, S. (1991). A psychological approach to the study of co-morbidity. *Clinical Psychology Review* 11, 461–65.

Rachman, S. (1994). Pollution of the mind. *Behaviour Research and Therapy* 32, 311–14.

Rachman, S. (1997). The evolution of cognitive behaviour therapy. In D.M. Clark and C. Fairburn (eds), *The Science and Practice of Cognitive Behaviour Therapy.* Oxford: Oxford University Press.

Rachman, S. (2003). *The Treatment of Obsessions.* Oxford: Oxford University Press.

Rachman, S. (2004). *Anxiety,* Second Edition. East Sussex: Psychology Press.

Rachman, S. and Hodgson, R. (1980). *Obsessions and Compulsions.* Englewood, New Jersey: Prentice Hall.

Rachman, S. and Lopatka, C. (1986). Do fears summate? *Behaviour Research and Therapy* 24, 653–60.

Rachman, S. and Shafran, R. (1998). Cognitive and behavioural features of OCD. In R. Swinson, M. Antony, S. Rachman, and M. Richter (eds), *Obsessive-Compulsive Disorder.* New York: Guilford Press.

Rachman, S., Cobb. C., Grey, S., McDonald, B., and Sartory, G. (1979). Behavioural treatment of obsessional compulsive disorder, with and without clomipramine. *Behaviour Research and Therapy* 17, 467–78.

Rachman, S., Radomsky, A., and Hammond, D. (2003). The judicious use of safety gear in overcoming a fear of snakes. University of British Columbia: unpublished ms.

Radomsky, A. and Rachman, S. (1999). Memory bias in OCD. *Behaviour Research and Therapy* 37, 605–18.

Radomsky, A. and Rachman, S. (2004). Symmetry, ordering and arranging compulsive behaviour. *Behaviour Research and Therapy* 42, 893–913.

Radomsky, A., Rachman, S., Shafran, R., Herba, J., and Milosevic, I. (2005). Fear of contamination: A psychometric analysis. Conference of European Cognitive Behaviour Therapy Association, Thessaloniki, Greece, September 2005.

Rasmussen, S. and Eisen, J. (1992). The epidemiology and clinical features of OCD. *Psychiatric Clinics of North America* 15, 743–58.

Rassin, E. (2005). *Thought Suppression.* Oxford: Elsevier Press.

Ricciardi, J. and McNally, R. (1995). Depressed mood is related to obsessions, but not to compulsions in OCD. *Journal of Anxiety Disorders* 9, 249–56.

Rozin, P. and Fallon, A. (1987). A perspective on disgust. *Psychological Review* 94, 23–41.

Rozin, P., Haidt, J., and McCauley, C. (1993). Disgust. In M. Lewis and J. Haviland (eds), *Handbook of Emotions.* New York: Guilford Press, pp. 574–594

Salkovskis, P. (1985). Obsessional compulsive problems: A cognitive behavioural analysis. *Behaviour Research and Therapy* 23, 571–83.

Salkovskis, P. and Warwick, H. (1986). Morbid preoccupations, health anxiety and reassurance: A cognitive behavioural approach to approach to hypochondriasis. *Behaviour Research and Therapy* 24, 597–602.

Sanavio, E. (1988). Obsessions and compulsions: the Padua Inventory. *Behaviour Research and Therapy* 27, 169–177

Sawchuk, C., Lohr, J., Tolin, D., Lee, T., and Kleinknecht, R. (2000). Disgust sensitivity and contamination fears in spider and blood–injection–injury phobias. *Behaviour Research and Therapy* 38, 753–762.

Seligman, M. (1988). Competing theories of panic. In S. Rachman and J. Maser (eds), *Panic: Psychological Perspectives*. Hillsdale, New Jersey: Erlbaum Publishers.

Shafran, R. and Rachman, S. (2004). Thought–action fusion: A Review. *Journal of Behavior Therapy and Experimental Psychiatry* 35, 87–108.

Tallis, F. (1997). The neuropsychology of OCD. *British Journal of Clinical Psychology* 36, 3–20.

Tarrier, N., Beckett, R., Harwood, S., Baker, A., Yusupoff, L., and Ugarteburu, I. (1993). A trial of two cognitive-behavioral methods of treating drug–resistant residual psychotic symptoms in schizophrenic patients. *British Journal of Psychiatry* 162, 524–32.

Taylor, S. (1998). Assessment of OCD. In R. Swinson, M. Antony, S. Rachman and M. Richter (eds), *OCD: Theory, Research and Treatment*. New York: Guilford Press, pp. 229–35.

Taylor, S. (Ed) (1999). *Anxiety Sensitivity*. Mahwah, New Jersey: Erlbaum.

Taylor, S.E. (1989). *Positive Illusions*. New York: Basic Books.

Thordarson, D., Radomsky, A.S., Rachman, S., Shafran, R., Sawchuk, C.N., and Hakstian, A. (2004). The Vancouver Obsessional Compulsive Inventory (VOCI). *Behaviour Research and Therapy* 42, 1289–1314.

Tolin, D., Worhunsky, P., and Maltby, N. (2004). Sympathetic magic in contamination-related OCD. *Journal of Behavior Therapy and Exp. Psychiatry* 35, 193–205.

Ware, J., Jain, K., Burgess, I., and Davey, G. (1994). Disease-avoidance model: Factor analysis of common animal fears. *Behaviour Research and Therapy* 32, 57–63.

Wolpe, J. (1958). *Psychotherapy by Reciprocal Inhibition*. Stanford: Stanford University Press.

Woody, S. and Teachman, B. (2000). Intersection of disgust and fear: Normative and pathological views. *Clinical Psychology: Science and Practice* 7, 291–311.

Woody, S and Tolin, D. (2002). The relationship between disgust sensitivity and avoidant behavior. *Journal of Anxiety Disorders* 16, 542–59.

Zucker, B.G. (2004). Early intervention for sub-clinical OCD. Ph.D. Thesis, University of California at Los Angeles.

Index

Date Due
